THE
RUSSIA TRAP

How Our Shadow War with Russia Could Spiral
into Nuclear Catastrophe

GEORGE S. BEEBE

THOMAS DUNNE
BOOKS

NEW YORK

First published in the United States by Thomas Dunne Books, an imprint of St. Martin's Publishing Group

THE RUSSIA TRAP. Copyright © 2019 by George S. Beebe. All rights reserved. Printed in Canada. For information, address St. Martin's Press, 120 Broadway, New York, NY 10271.

www.thomasdunnebooks.com

Designed by Omar Chapa

The Library of Congress Cataloging-in-Publication Data is available upon request.

ISBN 978-1-250-31662-2 (hardcover)
ISBN 978-1-250-31663-9 (ebook)

Our books may be purchased in bulk for promotional, educational, or business use. Please contact your local bookseller or the Macmillan Corporate and Premium Sales Department at 1-800-221-7945, extension 5442, or by email at MacmillanSpecialMarkets@macmillan.com.

First Edition: August 2019

10 9 8 7 6 5 4 3 2 1

For Sarah, Sophia, Nora, Grant, and Nathan

CONTENTS

Preface   *ix*

Introduction   *xi*

PART I

Analysis: Understanding the Problem

   1. War by Other Means   3

   2. Deadly Perceptions   26

   3. Brake Failure   72

   4. Triggers   100

PART II

Synthesis: Managing the Problem

   5. Escaping the Simplicity Trap   127

   6. Absorbing Shocks   150

   7. Working the System   166

Conclusion   180

Acknowledgments   *185*

Notes   *187*

Index   *209*

PREFACE

How could this have happened? We often ask this question in the aftermath of unforeseen fiascoes, whether on a small or grand scale. We wonder how we could have made what in retrospect look like dumb mistakes, failed to anticipate unintended consequences that appear obvious upon reflection, or ignored pivotal interconnections between factors that seem as clear in hindsight as they were obscure before things went bad.

Unforeseen developments have figured prominently in the course of my career. I began work as an analyst of the Soviet Union in 1986, not long after Mikhail Gorbachev began his tenure in the Kremlin. Much of the next three decades was filled with events that surprised many of us in the foreign affairs profession: the fall of the Berlin Wall; the collapse of the Soviet Union; the failure of liberal reforms in Russia under Yeltsin; the terrorist attacks of September 11, 2001; the futile search for weapons of mass destruction in Iraq; the so-called Color Revolutions in several former Soviet republics in the early 2000s; and the Maidan uprising in Ukraine, followed by Russia's annexation of Crimea and the estrangement and growing hostility in the US-Russian relationship over the next several years.

These developments impressed upon me how difficult it is to anticipate significant discontinuities from prevailing trends, how often experts can be wrong about facts and forecasts, and how important it is to approach the challenges of understanding and navigating the realm of foreign affairs from the basis of humility. They have made me sensitive to the tendency we all share to see news and information through the prism of our expectations, and how critical it is to expose and examine our key assumptions. They have shown me that avoiding surprise and defending our own national interests require trying to see things through the eyes of adversaries and competitors, without endorsing their perceptions as necessarily valid. Most of all, they have taught me the importance of wrestling with this question—*How could this have happened?*—before disasters strike, if we are to have any hope of averting them. This book is born of that wrestling.

INTRODUCTION

This book is a premortem: an examination of a failure that has not yet happened. It focuses on one of the most difficult problems that statesmen face: how to anticipate and avoid a war that no one wants and that few believe is likely or even possible but nonetheless arises because of a combustive mixture of clashing ambitions, new technologies, misplaced fears, entangled alliances and commitments, domestic political pressures, and mistaken assumptions about how adversaries might react. In other words, it is about diagnosing and defusing a nascent "World War I problem" with Russia.

What was then called *the Great War* produced what was arguably the greatest man-made catastrophe in human history. It ended a century of a relatively peaceful balance of power among Europe's leading states. It destroyed the Ottoman Empire and laid the basis for a century of war and terrorism in the Middle East. It hastened the demise of the British Empire and led to Hitler's rise, the destruction of World War II, the tragedy of the Holocaust, and the development of nuclear weapons. It paved the way to Soviet Communism and decades of Cold War that spanned the globe. It decimated a generation of Europeans and left in its wake a nihilistic philosophical legacy that has had devastating consequences for societies across the Western world. And almost no one saw it coming.[1]

World War I resulted more from miscalculation and ineptitude than from design. Historians have long debated which of the combatants bore the most responsibility for the conflict, but few dispute that "each of the major powers contributed its quota of shortsightedness and irresponsibility" to the disaster.[2] Germany feared encirclement by France, Russia, and Britain, but ham-handedly threatened each in ways that encouraged them to unite in an unprecedented alliance against Berlin. That alliance, in turn, cemented Germany's dependence on Austria-Hungary and ultimately made it a hostage to its southern neighbor's actions. Britain believed the alliance would contain Germany's growing military and economic might, not lock London into a set of rigid commitments that made diplomatic resolution of a localized conflict all but impossible. Austria-Hungary's fear that nationalism could tear its empire apart from within blinded it to the dangers that a limited war in the Balkans could spin quickly into a catastrophic European conflagration. Tsar Nicholas II assumed that a limited mobilization against Austria-Hungary could deter aggression against Russia's friend, Serbia, only to learn that his general staff's war plans mandated a full mobilization against both Austria-Hungary and Germany. The spread of railway technology, in turn, meant that any state that did not mobilize its army quickly in response faced the near-certain prospect of a rapid military defeat. The result was a potent mix of volatile ingredients that fueled what Henry Kissinger called "a political doomsday machine," susceptible to any number of potential triggers.[3]

Few people in Washington today believe that our tense relations with Russia pose this type of challenge. Rather, the dominant paradigm for understanding and responding to the Russian threat is the "World War II problem." American editorials and op-ed columns about Russia abound with disparaging references to Munich, where British prime minister Neville Chamberlain made his tragic bid to appease Hitler's territorial ambitions in 1938 and achieved his ill-fated "peace in our time." During the 2016 US presidential campaign, Democratic Party candidate Hillary Clinton explicitly warned that Moscow's claims that it must protect Russian minorities in Ukraine echoed Nazi Germany's arguments that it "had to protect German minorities in Poland and Czechoslovakia."[4] Similarly, Senator Lindsey Graham and many other Republicans have likened Russian president Putin to Adolf Hitler,[5] while newspaper columnists refer to him as "Putler."[6] Like Hitler, Putin is perceived as an authoritarian leader harboring deep resentments over lost territory and unfair treatment. Like Hitler, Putin is believed to regard calls for diplomatic compromise as signs of weakness that he can exploit. Like Hitler, Putin is thought to harbor expansionist designs that will be curbed only by pushing back now before he grows too strong.

For those who see the Russian threat through this prism, the chief danger is the Kremlin's aggressive intentions, and the imperative is to deter aggression through strength. Wars often happen because those who start them think they can win. Disabusing an aggressor of that belief, therefore, is critical to preserving peace. For intelligence analysts, this translates into a focus on studying Russian war plans and weapons systems while looking for signs of impending attack. US and NATO military experts analyzing Russia's preparations for its large Zapad ("West") military exercise in 2017, for example, issued warnings that the event could be "a Russian Trojan horse" masking preparations for occupying Belarus or invading one of the Baltic states.[7] British intelligence officials caution that Russian cyberoperators have acquired the ability to shut down power plants, hijack air traffic control, and even turn off air-conditioning systems.[8] US Intelligence Community leaders sound alarms about Moscow's desire to undermine Western democracies and destroy the "post–World War II international order."[9] Hollywood actor Morgan Freeman, sponsored by a committee that includes former director of national intelligence James Clapper, solemnly warns Americans in a viral social media video that "we are at war" already with Russia and must fight back or suffer defeat.[10]

For policymakers, these warnings lead to a focus on demonstrating the will to fight and the ability to triumph. Diplomacy plays a minor role in dealing with World War II–type aggression. One does not strike deals with aggressor states—one punishes and isolates them.[11] Failure to resist Russia's aggression in Georgia, Ukraine, Syria, and the cybersphere only invites more aggression. Strength and resolve, on the other hand, prompt the would-be aggressor to back down and look elsewhere for easier conquests. The Trump administration's National Security Strategy largely reflects this broad consensus: "Experience suggests that the willingness of rivals to abandon or forgo aggression depends on their perception of US strength and the vitality of our alliances." To paraphrase the old Roman aphorism, if we want peace, we must show ourselves ready and willing to fight a war.

Not everyone views Russia as offensive-minded, however. A smaller and less popular school of thought sees Russia under Putin as a weak and declining power fighting a defensive battle against NATO's eastward expansion and Washington's efforts to transform Russia's internal politics. "Putin has been primarily reactive," according to New York University professor emeritus Stephen Cohen.[12] Realist scholar John Mearsheimer puts it even more bluntly: Russia's actions, including its annexation of Crimea and proxy war in eastern Ukraine, "have been defensive, not offensive . . . motivated by legitimate security concerns."[13] Adherents of this school are wont to quote George Kennan, the father of America's Cold War containment strategy, on the likely consequences of NATO expansion some twenty years ago: "There is going to be a bad reaction from Russia, and then [the NATO expanders] will say that we always told you that is how the Russians are—but this is just wrong." Russia is not, he said, "a country dying to attack Western Europe."[14] Russia is not Nazi Germany, nor is Putin comparable to Hitler. For these analysts, such analogies not only produce more emotional heat than analytic light, but they also lead to policy responses that are dangerous.

Those in the "defensive Russia" school point out that when a country's hostile actions are rooted in fear and vulnerability, the unwavering resolve and military readiness that are so vital to dealing with a Hitler-type threat can be counterproductive.[15] Rather than averting aggression by demonstrating the will to fight back, coercive steps against a state that already sees itself as threatened can magnify perceptions of vulnerability and kick off a dangerous escalatory reaction. The United States experienced this phenomenon in the former Soviet republic of Georgia in 2008. Convinced that Russia harbored aggressive designs on its southern neighbor, Washington policymakers accelerated US military training of Georgia, openly advocated bringing Tbilisi into the NATO alliance, and issued multiple warnings to Moscow against military action, assuming this firm support would deter Russian aggression.[16] In fact, it had the opposite effect. Russia grew increasingly alarmed by the prospect of Georgian membership in NATO, while Tbilisi felt emboldened by American support to launch a military operation in the breakaway Georgian region of South Ossetia, which produced an immediate and massive Russian military response that included a coordinated set of cyberattacks.[17] The result was a readily foreseeable war that the United States failed to avert, leaving the White House with an unpalatable choice between ineffectually protesting Russia's conquest of Georgia's breakaway regions, or threatening nuclear war in response to Russia's local conventional superiority.[18]

For those who perceive Moscow to be playing defense, the preferred policy response is largely Hippocratic and diplomatic: stop doing harm by threatening the threatened state, and start talking about compromise and conflict resolution. Cohen argues against reintroducing intermediate-range missiles in Europe and selling weapons to Ukraine, for example, and calls instead for co-operating against shared threats and reaching agreement on new rules to govern the relationship.[19] Mearsheimer proposes ending what he calls the "triple package of policies"—NATO expansion, EU enlargement, and democracy promotion. The goal for Ukraine, and presumably for other states in the "gray zone" between Russia and the NATO alliance, he avers, should be to "abandon [the] plan to westernize Ukraine and instead aim to make it a neutral buffer between NATO and Russia, akin to Austria's position during the Cold War."[20] If we want peace with Russia, they reason, we need to stress common ground and compromise, not weapons and sanctions.

Neither of these contrasting schools for explaining and deal-ing with Russian behaviors is entirely wrong. There is little doubt that Russia sees itself as on the defensive in the face of NATO expansion and Washington's extensive involvement in Russia's domestic affairs in the 1990s. Moscow harbors deep resentments, misperceptions, and mistrust of American intentions, and its views of the United States have changed from partner to adversary over the course of the past twenty-five years, in part due to American actions that it perceives as threatening. At least some of the Russian behavior that appears to Americans as unprovoked aggression— such as interference in the 2016 presidential election—appears to Russians as a natural reaction to years of Western meddling in Russia and its neighbors.

But Russia's behavior is not driven solely by defensive motives. It also sees itself as rightfully a great power, albeit one that
was down on its luck in the 1990s, that should play a key role in
international affairs along with the United States, Europe, and
China, and that should dominate its neighboring states as it believes all great powers do. It is difficult to argue that Moscow's
military involvement in South America, a region far from Russia's
borders with only the most tenuous of connections to any vital
Russian interest, is motivated by anything other than a desire to
show Washington that Russia is a great power capable of stirring
up trouble in regions dominated by the United States.[21] Part of the
resentment of the United States that has grown within Moscow's
political class over the past two decades stems from the belief that
Washington treats Russia as a subordinate and has stood in the
way of its return to great-power glory. Russia's desire to dominate neighboring states has been a key factor driving their efforts
to join NATO and seek American help, which in turn has fueled
Moscow's insecurities in a spiral of escalating hostility. This mix
of offensive and defensive motivations is, in fact, an old theme in
Russian foreign policy. Commenting on tsarist Russia's behavior
in the period leading to World War I, Henry Kissinger observed,
"Partly defensive, partly offensive, Russian expansion was always
ambiguous, and this ambiguity generated Western debates over
Russia's intentions that lasted through the Soviet period."[22]

Further clouding this picture is the fact that Russia, unlike
the Ottoman Empire in 1914 or China today, defies categorization
as either a declining or rising power. The Soviet Union was jok-
ingly described as a first world military perched atop a third world
economy, an "Upper Volta with nuclear weapons." Its collapse left
Moscow with neither a capable military nor a functioning economy,
and the subsequent plunge in Russia's birth rate and surge in its
death rate convinced many in the West that the country was on

a long-term path toward decline and irrelevance. Russia's birth rate and life expectancy have been rising since the early Putin era, however, and by 2013, the country experienced overall population growth for the first time since the Soviet period.[23] Despite setbacks posed by Western economic sanctions and the decline in world oil prices, Russia's economy has grown by an average of almost 4 percent annually since 2000. Russia's confident intervention in the Syrian civil war in 2015, its first projection of military power outside the confines of Soviet borders since the 1979 Afghan War, demonstrated that its military reform program has made impressive progress.

Whether this recovery will continue is an open question. Russia remains plagued by corruption and heavily dependent on energy sales, but despite this, it has managed its energy earnings wisely, modeling its successful rainy-day investment fund on that of Norway, and it has risen steadily in world "ease of doing business" rankings.[24] It has struggled to diversify its economy and compete in international commercial markets, but it has developed sophisticated cybercapabilities and advanced weaponry. Russia may never overcome the tension between its political preference for centralized control and its economic need to unleash the creativity and innovation of its people. But its history, geography, resources, and scientific talent suggest that Russia will nevertheless remain an important player on the international stage, punching above the weight class that its economic weakness might suggest.

The theme of this book is that the chief danger in the increasingly hostile US-Russian relationship is not primarily a function of the capabilities or intentions of either party, however. Rather, it is what scientists describe as a *complex systems* danger. Unsettled questions about Europe's post–Cold War security architecture are fueling antagonisms. Starkly differing perceptions of the other side's intentions have garbled the signals that each believes it is sending and reinforced mistaken assumptions about how the other will react to events. New and still poorly understood cybertechnologies, coupled with the development of advanced strategic weapons delivery systems, are providing enormous advantages to the attacker over the defender, reinforcing perceptions of vulnerability and incentivizing aggression. Changes in the global geopolitical order have simultaneously threatened US preeminence and provided tempting opportunities for Russia and other rival powers to advance their influence. Each side has increasingly tethered itself to unreliable proxies whose interests overlap with—but do not coincide with—those of their sponsors. And each side is struggling to cope with domestic political challenges that magnify its feelings of vulnerability and complicate its ability to formulate and implement effective foreign policies. Meanwhile, the old rules that governed the Cold War competition between Washington and Moscow have withered away, and new understandings that could contain and stabilize the renewed rivalry have not replaced them. All these factors are reinforcing each other in a vicious cycle of dynamic interactions.

The good news is that although Russia has few warm feelings for Washington, it is not trying to destroy American democracy and send the international order hurtling into chaos. The bad news is that "systems problems," in which multiple factors interact and reinforce or diminish one another, are much more difficult to resolve than single-factor issues. Our various disputes with Russia represent not an aggregation of discrete problems but rather what management guru Russell Ackoff has called a "mess"—that is, "a system of problems. This means that the problems interact. Therefore, if we do the usual thing and break up a mess into its component problems and then try to solve each one separately, we will not solve the mess."[25] Focusing on either deterring or accommodating Russia, as suggested by the "offensive Russia" and "defensive Russia" schools of thought, will not solve the problem and could make it worse. Moreover, the interconnection between component parts of the US-Russia system means there is a high potential that accidents and incremental actions will produce unintended knock-on effects. Just as in Sarajevo in 1914, small events can cause ripples in this complex set of problems that produce large, catastrophic outcomes.

This book does not aspire to be an analysis of how the US-Russian relationship descended from nascent partnership to alarming hostility over the course of the past decade and a half; others have covered that ground in impressive depth.[26] Neither does it grapple with the full range of costs and implications of the deteriorating relationship between Washington and Moscow, which include increased Russian-Chinese cooperation against American interests, as well as reduced opportunities to work together against such common threats as weapons proliferation, terrorism, and contagious disease. Its focus is narrower: to show how easily the US-Russian relationship could spiral unexpectedly from animosity to war and to consider what must be done to reduce the chances of that disaster.

This book is not, as Ebenezer Scrooge famously sought to confirm with the Ghost of Christmas Yet-to-Come, a glimpse of things that will be, as opposed to things that may be. No one undertakes construction of a premortem study without some faith that the anticipated bad outcome is avoidable. Unlike the cascade of events that led to World War I, the combustive mix of dangers in our relations with Russia need not become a political doomsday machine that will inevitably lead to nuclear war. Understanding the dangers posed by the system in which Washington and Moscow are operating, and examining the individual elements that it comprises, are important prerequisites for defusing the threat.

The first part of this book focuses on analysis of that threat. It looks at each element of the "wicked problem" between the United States and Russia in turn, with a view toward identifying the interactions that can amplify their effects and produce unintended consequences.[27] Chapter 1 focuses on the ways our shadow war with Russia is playing out in the areas of cyberespionage, cybersabotage, and influence operations. Chapter 2 looks at the perceptual side of this war, examining the views that each country holds of the other's intentions. Chapter 3 examines our disappearing rules of the game and the absence of mechanisms that could serve as brakes on dangerous escalation spirals. Chapter 4 looks at the roles that economic warfare, military gamesmanship, and proxy warfare might play in triggering an unexpected US-Russian crisis.

The second part of the book focuses on how to defuse the threat. It begins in chapter 5 with an examination of how Washington and Moscow might apply a "systems approach" to avoid missteps that might produce unintended escalation. Chapter 6 looks at ways to build shock absorbers into our system to lessen the impact of radical disruptions and new technologies. Chapter 7 looks at the ways we can use systems dynamics to our advantage to manage the competition between the United States, Russia, China, and other great powers and minimize the risks we face.

As a premortem, this book serves as a warning of impending Russian danger, but it is a call to mental—not military—arms. Had the protagonists who stumbled into World War I realized the consequences of their actions and the ways that events could spin disastrously out of their control, they undoubtedly would have handled their decisions differently. Today, mindful of the potential for producing unintended consequences, we should approach the Russia threat with the caution that we wish in retrospect those European leaders had demonstrated.

Avoiding their fate requires subjecting several popular conceptions that Russia and the United States hold about each other to deeper scrutiny. Americans who view Russia through the perceptual lens of Nazi Germany are prone to misunderstanding Russia's governance and its intentions, with potentially tragic consequences. Similarly, Russians have misperceived US support for democratization in Russia and neighboring regions as an effort to encircle and ultimately overthrow the Russian government. Reluctance in both countries to think more deeply about these perceptions, and the rapidity with which those who question them are labeled apologists, constitute a cognitive trap—a Russia trap—that heightens the chances we will stumble unawares into catastrophe.

After years of unsuccessful post–Cold War efforts to forge a cooperative relationship, it is now clear that the United States and Russia have entered a period in which we will be competitors, not partners. But we need not become enemies. Amid the swirl of emotions and domestic political pressures in both Washington and Moscow, our approach to Russia needs dispassionately to balance firmness with accommodation, and military readiness with diplomatic outreach, without skewing too far toward either concession or confrontation. Failure to discern the nature of the danger looming before us is perhaps the biggest threat we face. The following pages are a humble attempt to bring that danger into focus.

PART I

Analysis: Understanding the Problem

In war, events of importance are the result of trivial causes.

—William Shakespeare, *Julius Caesar*

The combination of causes of phenomena is beyond the grasp of the human intellect. But the impulse to seek causes is innate in the soul of man. And the human intellect, with no inkling of the immense variety and complexity of circumstances conditioning a phenomenon, any one of which may be separately conceived of as the cause of it, snatches at the first and most easily understood approximation, and says here is the cause.

—Leo Tolstoy, *War and Peace*

1

War by Other Means

The United States and Russia are fighting an undeclared virtual war. It is not a hot war, as between Japan and the United States in World War II. And it is not a cold war, driven by two ideologically incompatible world powers, as between the United States and Soviet Union from the late 1940s through the 1980s. Rather, it is something in between, a shadow war, wherein the combatants attempt to achieve goals that, for much of human history, would have required the direct use of military force or other physical action, but today can be accomplished through less kinetic means. The United States, with its vast "soft power" capabilities and unparalleled technological prowess, has pioneered the use of these new approaches. Moscow, however, has been a diligent student, and it has turned these techniques back on America in Russianized, asymmetric form, attempting to exploit US weaknesses while maximizing the few areas in which Russia has advantage. Unlike the Cold War at its peak, this is a war being waged largely without rules, and it is driven by a different logic. Moreover, in contrast to the shared appreciation of risks and dangers that characterized the US-Soviet relationship after the Cuban missile crisis, neither side recognizes how easily this shadow war could spiral out of control. Understanding the various fronts on which this war is being waged is a critical step toward coping with its dangers.

CYBERSABOTAGE

In September 2017, analysts at the internet security firm Symantec got a firsthand glimpse into the US-Russian shadow war. According to *Wired* magazine, the analysts were investigating malware infections in the computer networks of American electricity generation facilities when they discovered that hackers had taken screenshots of the system's human-machine interface, the control panels governing the regional power grid. They were stunned. Dealing with attempted network intrusions was a daily occurrence for cybersecurity analysts, something so routine that it was like clicking through their email in-boxes. But never before had they seen network intruders reach the point where they could send remote commands to circuit breakers, valves, and other power company controls in the United States, allowing them to cut the flow of electricity to homes and businesses. Few things could send a modern society more quickly into panic and chaos than an extended loss of electrical power. The screenshots suggested that the only thing preventing the hackers from flipping a switch that would send the region into darkness was their decision to hold back—for now.[1]

The analysts could not be sure that the hackers were Russian, but the circumstantial evidence looked damning. Russian hackers had created blackouts in Ukraine in 2015 and 2016 during Moscow's undeclared war there, timed to take place in winter, when they would cause maximum damage to the nation's psyche. Each of the Ukrainian blackouts had lasted only for a few hours and had affected only hundreds of thousands, not millions, of people. They were only one part, however, of a massive sustained cyberassault on "practically every sector of Ukraine: media, finance, transportation, military, politics, energy."[2] The United States was much more dependent on digital networks than was Ukraine. The flow of planes, trains, and automobiles increasingly relied on automated transportation networks and satellite-based Global Positioning System (GPS) technology. Public water systems and chemical plants and Wall Street trading and basic business inventory controls were linked to the internet. Even such common household appliances as refrigerators and microwave ovens "talked" over the internet using smart technology embedded inside them. All this technology had made the operations of the modern world faster and more efficient than anything achieved in the past, but it had also made these systems more vulnerable to penetration and disruption by hackers. As a small preview of what cybersabotage could do if directed at the United States, the attacks in Ukraine had sent an ominous message.

There were also more recent reports that the Russians had penetrated the business systems, though not the control panels, of US nuclear power generation facilities—an intrusion dubbed *Palmetto Fusion* by US government investigators.[3] Clearly, the business systems were not the Russians' ultimate goal; they were obviously attempting to gain control not just of conventional electrical power generation but nuclear power plants as well. The scale and sophistication of the intrusions, coupled with the targets themselves, made clear that these were not mere novices or "patriotic hackers," harassing perceived enemies of the Russian state without direction from the government. Nor were they simply knocking on any cyberdoor they encountered, trying to gain entry to all the systems they could willy-nilly. These were professionals, working against specific targets for specific reasons. One other aspect of the intrusion stood out: the Russians were among the world's best at concealing their cyberoperations when they wanted to, but whoever it was that had penetrated the power grid was not trying very hard to avoid detection.[4] It seemed the hackers were sending a not-so-subtle message that they were able to sabotage the power grid whenever they chose.

If that message was meant to prompt Americans to think twice before intruding into Russia's critical infrastructure, however, it backfired. In fact, reports about Russian cyberintrusions of varying types and severity produced increasing calls in the United States for retaliation in the form of offensive cyberoperations. Convinced that America's cyberadversaries had not paid a sufficient price for their hacking, the Trump administration announced in its 2018 National Cyber Strategy changes that improved the ability of US Cyber Command to undertake offensive operations.[5] Many US experts began to argue that cyberdeterrence based on imposing greater costs on hackers while trying to deny them the benefits of intrusions was not enough. "The United States should be pursuing a more active cyberpolicy, one aimed not at deterring enemies but at disrupting their capabilities. In cyberwarfare, Washington should recognize that the best defense is a good offense," argued a former Obama administration cyberpolicy official.[6] Unlike in the Cold War, the specter of mutually assured destruction did not seem to be inducing mutual restraint in the new era of cyberconflict.

What might be called *cybersabotage*—the use of computers to destroy, disrupt, or disable a machine or a system—represents a high-technology twist on an old tactic. The term derives from the French word for a peasant's wooden shoe, a *sabot*, and evokes the act of throwing a shoe in the gears of a machine to interfere in its functions. States have employed sabotage of various sorts throughout history. The Office of Strategic Services (OSS), the American progenitor of the CIA, conducted numerous secret sabotage operations behind enemy lines during World War II. Its classified *Simple Sabotage Field Manual*, published years after the war, highlighted the value of "slashing tires, draining fuel tanks, starting fires, starting arguments, acting stupidly, short-circuiting electric systems, [and] abrading machine parts" for disrupting and demoralizing the enemy.[7] The Soviet Union's intelligence services were enthusiastic saboteurs, both during and after World War II. In *Special Tasks: The Memoirs of an Unwanted Witness*, Pavel Sudoplatov describes running networks of illegal agents charged with sabotaging American and NATO installations in the event that the Cold War turned hot.[8]

But this new twist on an old practice has potentially devastating implications. Sabotage has traditionally been a tactical measure. It could help one's fortunes in a military skirmish or provide an important advantage in a battle, but it could not win wars or force national-level leaders to negotiate a settlement. In a networked world, by contrast, cybersabotage is potentially strategic. The Stuxnet worm, which damaged or destroyed systems that Iran was using to enrich uranium to weapons-grade specifications, demonstrated that twenty-first-century sabotage could have profound effects on a nation's most significant strategic military capabilities. In a special report on the cyberthreat, the Defense Science Board, a group not generally given to hyperbole, compared the implications of cybersabotage to nuclear weapons:

> The benefits to an attacker using cyber exploits are potentially spectacular. Should the United States find itself in a full-scale conflict with a peer adversary, attacks would be expected to include denial of service, data corruption, supply chain corruption, traitorous insiders, kinetic and related non-kinetic attacks at all altitudes from underwater to space. US guns, missiles, and bombs may not fire, or may be

directed against our own troops. Resupply, including food, water, ammunition, and fuel may not arrive when or where needed. Military Commanders may rapidly lose trust in the information and ability to control US systems and forces. Once lost, that trust is very difficult to regain.

Based upon the societal dependence on these systems, and the interdependence of the various services and capabilities, the Task Force believes that the integrated impact of a cyber attack has the potential of existential consequence. While the manifestations of a nuclear and cyber attack are very different, in the end, the existential impact to the United States is the same.[9]

The board was equally pessimistic about prospects for defending against such cybersabotage: "Today, much of DoD's money and effort are spent trying to defend against just the inherent vulnerabilities which exist in all complex systems. Defense-only is a failed strategy."

The reason for this pessimism is that cybertechnology has tilted the age-old competition between offensive and defensive measures starkly in favor of the offense.[10] It is far easier to penetrate a network than it is to prevent a would-be intruder from gaining access. Software code inevitably includes mistakes that clever hackers can exploit. No matter how much training they receive, some percentage of system users will click on links that they should not, use passwords that are maddeningly simple to determine, or fail to update software in a timely manner, offering easy ways for attackers to steal credentials and enter networks. Intrusion-detection systems can be circumvented or fooled. Antivirus software is designed to spot hacking code that has already been used in past intrusions; it cannot detect new exploits that take advantage of what hackers call *zero-day vulnerabilities*—coding flaws previously undiscovered and unpatched.[11] In a very real sense, antivirus software defends against yesterday's attacks, not tomorrow's. Defenders can complicate the tasks of cyberattackers, and they are getting better at discovering and identifying intruders, but rarely can they stop them prior to an intrusion.

Awareness of these realities fuels a pervasive sense of vulnerability among those charged with securing computers and networks and among national security professionals more broadly.[12]

This vulnerability, together with the advantages enjoyed by intruders, has created a vicious circle of aggression and counteraggression in the cyberarena, where the real or imagined compromise of systems on one side prompts the other side to redouble efforts to compromise its rival's systems. Just as American experts have questioned the effectiveness of cyberdefense in the face of sophisticated intrusions, the Russians have equal reason to believe cyberoffense is their most effective form of defense. Devoting countless hours to scouring millions of lines of code to uncover malware is often a fruitless approach when dealing with sophisticated attackers. The Russian cybersecurity firm Kaspersky has alleged, for example, that highly sophisticated American malware was operating undetected in Russian networks for more than a decade before being discovered.[13] Even when searches come up empty, defenders cannot be certain that a malware bomb is not lying undiscovered somewhere in their vast web of infrastructure. Nor can they be certain that what they do discover is not a false flag operation—malware planted by a third country in disguise, hoping to benefit by stoking Russian-American tensions. These vexing problems argue for a different response to the problem of cybersabotage: to penetrate an opponent's networks even more deeply to learn what exactly it might be doing—and to plant a few more cyberweapons of one's own to deter the adversary from any detonation. Cybertechnology has, in many ways, created a new form of existential threat for the world that is reminiscent of the impact of nuclear technology on the Cold War, but it operates according to a different logic. Largely invisible, these weapons can quickly become ineffective if they are not implanted and constantly updated, even if not detonated. And their very invisibility encourages states to assume and plan for the worst.

CYBERESPIONAGE

The perverse dynamics of cybersabotage, where acts meant to deter can wind up incentivizing aggression, and where inherent uncertainties in the attribution of intrusions serve as perpetual temptations to take risks that few would undertake in the bricks-and-mortar world, are only one part of the undeclared virtual war going on between Russia and the United States. Another is in the world of espionage.

This world was undergoing a little-noticed revolution in the wee hours of a Sunday in 1998. It began when a technician at a materials company happened to notice that someone was connecting from the company's network to Wright-Patterson Air Force Base in Ohio at three o'clock in the morning. This was unusual, to say the least. He reached out to the owner of the account to ask about the connection, but the employee denied that he was even online at that time, let alone surfing around on Wright-Patterson sites. The technician's curiosity quickly turned into suspicion. He alerted several Computer Emergency Response Teams, including that of the US Air Force, which determined that the technician had stumbled upon an ongoing cyberintrusion.

Delving into the case, Air Force investigators learned that the connection from the materials company was only one of many suspicious connections. The same user had also connected to Wright-Patterson from the University of South Carolina, Bryn Mawr, Duke, Auburn, and other universities, and he was pilfering sensitive, albeit unclassified, files on such things as cockpit design and microchip schematics.[14] Moreover, he was not just targeting Wright-Patterson; he used computers in various university research labs to gain continuing access to a wide range of military sites and networks in search of specific information. He was also technically advanced, rewriting network logs after leaving sites so that no one would discover evidence that he had ever been there. Struck by the unprecedented scale and sophistication of the hacks, the FBI opened an official investigation and brought in officials from law enforcement, the military, and other parts of government to form a forty-person working group on the intrusion set. And they gave it a code name: Moonlight Maze.

The first task in the investigation was to determine the attacker's origins and intentions. The intrusions all seemed to take place during the same nine-hour span, one that coincided with business hours in Moscow, and they did not occur on Russian Orthodox holidays. But was Moscow really the attack's point of origin, or was it simply one of many other transit points in the pathway, like the universities the attacker was using to mask his location? The working group decided to pursue answers by using a "honey pot," a fake set of digital files on a topic that would interest the attacker. Once he ventured into those files, investigators would be able to follow his moves in real time and track him down. To aid their efforts, the investigators also implanted within the honey pot files a digital beacon, a few lines of code that automatically attached to the attacker and sent back a signal to investigators as he hopscotched from point to point along the internet back to his home origin. The approach worked; the attacker took the bait, and the beacon traced him back to an IP address at the Russian Academy of Sciences in Moscow.[15] Further research indicated that the attacker's programming code, prior to encryption, had been written in Cyrillic characters. All the indicators pointed in the same direction: American military networks had been victimized by a massive, ongoing, state-directed cyberespionage operation—what cybersecurity professionals later came to call an *advanced persistent threat*—originating in Russia.

As investigators learned more and more about the intrusion set, they were stunned by its scale. It had been going on for years before being discovered, since at least 1996, a year when the United States was using its economic might and electoral expertise to help Boris Yeltsin win a second term as president of Russia. And it had produced a haul of information comparable in size to the holdings of a municipal library: some 5.5 gigabytes of data, the equivalent of nearly three million pages, on such topics as helmet design, hydrodynamics, oceanography, satellites, aerodynamics, and various surveillance technologies. It was the kind of thing that once would have required a large network of agents, clandestine photographs, dead drops, and secret communications, with information delivered through painfully slow and risky channels, using individuals whom Russia had convinced to betray their country. By contrast, Russian cyberoperators could exploit the ever-occurring imperfections in software coding and boundless gullibility of system users to gain access to virtually any network they wanted and grab mind-boggling amounts of information. Large support organizations were not required. If done well, in fact, no one in the target organization would even know their information had been compromised. It represented a quantum leap in espionage capabilities.

Some twenty years since the revelations of Moonlight Maze, cyberespionage has become commonplace in the intelligence world and widely known outside it, featured in numerous Hollywood films and covered frequently in media reports. But beyond remarking on the new capabilities afforded by gee-whiz technology, few observers have grappled with the broader implications of this phenomenon for international stability. Cyberespionage is not merely facilitating the collection of information by both government intelligence organizations and non-state actors; it is, by its nature, blurring the lines between spies, warriors, diplomats, criminals, and private citizens—and between acts of espionage and acts of warfare—in ways that have major implications for international stability.

First, cybertechnology is not only changing the way states collect sensitive information; it has also changed the targets of that collection. In the Cold War, the United States and Soviet Union each focused collection efforts on the other's national security apparatus, a restricted world of senior political leaders, militaries, intelligence organizations, defense industry, weapons systems, and high-technology laboratories. Private citizens could get occasional glimpses into this espionage through media reports about the spying going on behind closed doors, and they could marvel at the glamorized Hollywood versions of the spy game at the cinema, but seldom would the worlds of espionage and civilian society intersect. In cyberespionage, these worlds not only overlap to a much greater degree, but there is increasingly little distinction between national security targets and civilian targets. Internet "packets" conveying a public Facebook post about a family vacation speed through privately owned telecommunications networks side by side with encrypted national security information meant for select, cleared audiences. Critical infrastructure, such as power utilities or water treatment plants, is often privately owned, but could cause national damage if its systems crashed. Many advances in artificial intelligence, machine learning, and other aspects of information technology—indeed, in most technological areas—depend not on government-funded laboratories or large private companies but on local start-ups and private or university-based accelerators, making these entities attractive targets for intelligence collection. The laptops of private citizens can be remotely commandeered and assembled into botnets for use in penetrating national security networks. And collecting information on individual citizens—their habits and histories, likes and dislikes, friends and associates—can help hackers gather valuable insights into the private lives of targeted officials and create convincing "spear-phishing" operations that aid other efforts to penetrate national security networks. Unlike in the Cold War, there are no "stand-alone entities anymore—everything is part of a network," according to one cybersecurity expert.[16] To keep pace with these advancements, and to gain access to such sensitive information, cyberspies inevitably target and tread on what was once considered civilian territory. The shadow war is an unavoidably public-private venture, and managing public involvement in it is a formidable challenge.

One reason increased public involvement in cyberespionage is challenging is that the public typically sees only a small slice of the game of spy versus spy. Western media, for example, frequently report on Chinese and Russian cyberactivities directed against the United States, and it is not uncommon for American private cybersecurity professionals to encounter a Chinese or Russian intrusion directly. But rarely does one encounter American media reports about US intrusions into Russian or Chinese systems. The Russians certainly believe the United States is actively engaging in advanced cyberespionage; the Russian cybersecurity company Kaspersky Labs issued a report in 2015 on highly sophisticated operations by what it called the Equation Group that it all but explicitly said was run by the National Security Agency.[17] Former director of national intelligence Michael McConnell's claim in 2013 that "at least 75 percent" of President Obama's daily intelligence brief came from cyberspying is one of the few public comments on American cyberespionage.[18] For the public, it is a bit like having front-row seats to a boxing match in which viewers can see the torso of one of the boxers, but not his arms or gloves. The audience can see him getting hit by his opponent but cannot see whether he is punching. And because it cannot, its natural response is to want him to hit back. This public sentiment adds to incentives for offensive cyberoperations.

Cybertechnology is also changing the risk-reward balance in intelligence operations. In the old days, the risks of any given espionage operation—to the personnel involved and to the broader interests of the government—were often significant and had to be balanced against the potential rewards of success when considering whether to authorize it. In cyberespionage, however, the risks often seem small compared to the potential benefits, which incentivizes greater aggression and a higher pace of operations compared to the past. As cybersecurity pioneer Cliff Stoll pointed out some three decades ago, "Espionage over networks can be cost efficient, offer immediate results, and target specific locations . . . insulated from the risks of internationally embarrassing incidents."[19]

The incentives fueling offensive cyberespionage are being reinforced by new surveillance technologies in the bricks-and-mortar world that are making traditional cloak-and-dagger espionage more difficult than ever. Not long ago, intelligence organizations could create viable cover stories for covert case officers, send them overseas under aliases, and have them meet, recruit, and communicate with foreign agents in secret. In a world where nearly everyone has social media or other forms of online histories, however, cover stories become problematic.[20] The increased use of biometric surveillance systems in airports and train stations around the world makes traveling under aliases a greater challenge. Many world capitals are blanketed by video surveillance systems that track movements on every square foot of cityscape. Facial recognition software makes disappearing into obscurity a challenge. Carrying a cell phone provides counterintelligence organizations with a handy geolocational tracker; not carrying one is anomalous behavior that draws their unwelcome attention. As a result, the traditional recruitment of what intelligence agencies call *human assets* has grown more difficult. This has further incentivized aggressive cyberespionage, and it has fueled feelings of vulnerability; with fewer human agents to explain the motivations behind various cyberpenetrations, governments tend to assume worst-case intentions on the part of their adversaries.[21]

These worst-case assumptions become particularly important because, for those on the receiving end of such cyberintrusions, it can be difficult to distinguish between operations meant to grab sensitive information and those intended to prepare for cyber-sabotage. Once inside a computer, a hacker can explore the entire network connected to it and download enormous quantities of data. He can also, however, alter, corrupt, or destroy that data, or he can distort, disable, or destroy the operations of systems controlled by the network.[22] To cybersecurity operators, an intrusion penetrating the system in order to steal sensitive information or learn about an adversary's plans looks just like an intrusion mapping the network's passageways and weak points in order to "prepare the battlefield" for a damaging attack.[23] A hacker's intentions are often not apparent until sometime well after the operation has begun, and this has a profound impact on perceptions. "From a psychological perspective, the difference between penetration and manipulation may not matter much," according to cyberexpert Martin Libicki of the US Naval Academy.[24] In other words, in the cyberage, the business of espionage is increasingly indistinguishable from the business of warfare.

CYBERINFLUENCE

The third front of the shadow war is another new twist on an old activity. In the West, it has gone by a variety of names throughout history, including *propaganda, strategic communications, informa-tion operations,* and *PSYOP,* or *psychological operations.* In Russian, it is also known in various forms as *dezinformatsiya, maskirovka, kompromat,* and *aktivniye meropriyatiya*—active measures. It can be produced openly or covertly, and it can aim to inform, to inspire, or—in its darker varieties—to deceive or to subvert. But regard-less of its name or form, its target is the same: the human mind.

The Kremlin School for Bloggers was an early salvo in a US-Russian information war that only one side recognized it was fighting. It was born in fear, launched by the Russian government in 2009 not long after events in the former Soviet republic of Mol-dova that were billed as one of the first "Twitter revolutions."[25] Parliamentary elections there had produced a clear victory by the Communist Party, and in its aftermath, two obscure youth groups had posted a notice online that called for people to gather the next day on the Moldovan capital's central square at an event they called "I Am Not a Communist." One of the gathering's or-ganizers described it on her blog as little more than "six people, 10 minutes of brainstorming and decision-making, several hours of disseminating information through networks, Facebook, blogs, SMSs and emails."[26] Surprisingly, more than fifteen thousand protestors showed up, and within another day, peaceful demon-strations had turned into mass riots, arson, and vandalism.[27] The protests caused significant material damage and resulted in several deaths, but they eventually petered out following a harsh govern-ment crackdown, and they did little to produce meaningful political change in Moldova.

Moscow, however, was concerned. For those playing defense, internet campaigns were more difficult to contain than old-fashioned propaganda vehicles or traditional subversion efforts, which needed leaders, organizations, and money. Social media could deliver infor-mation directly to specifically targeted audiences without having to go through such gatekeepers as newspaper editors or television or radio producers, and they allowed users to plan and publicize actions quickly in response to news and events, creating so-called flash mobs. There were few formal organizations, recognized leaders, or significant money flows that government authorities could monitor and counter. The Moldova protests had materialized practically overnight, with almost no planning or organization, and their scale and ferocity had surprised even those who had proposed them.

It was not hard to envision similar social media–fueled instability erupting in Russia. Kremlin officials saw Twitter revolutions as a genuine threat. Gleb Pavlovsky, a Kremlin consultant and one of Russia's leading information warriors at the time, explained that "Moscow views world affairs as a system of special operations, and very sincerely believes that it itself is an object of Western special operations."[28] Information technology made this Western targeting doubly dangerous. According to Russian journalist Andrei Soldatov, "You can now mobilize people to get them to the streets without traditional means, and even without a youth movement. You can use technology; you can use social media. . . . The thing that was important for the Kremlin [was] that they saw these things as a part of a bigger plot, all arranged by the West, and namely by the US State Department. That was why they really believed that they're under real attack, and the threat is real."[29] Moscow's concerns were later captured officially in its National Security Strategy, which bemoaned the "intensifying confrontation in the global information arena caused by some countries' aspiration to utilize informational and communication technologies to achieve their geopolitical objectives, including by manipulating public awareness and falsifying history."[30]

By contrast, the developments in Moldova and in the sub-

sequent Green Revolution in Iran set Washington abuzz with
internet optimism. Social media, it seemed, were the ultimate
democratizers. They allowed everyone across the world to have
access to information unfiltered by government censors, and they
helped like-minded strangers to connect and organize despite being separated, in many cases, by vast physical distances.[31] Brimming with hope for a more liberal global future, the United States
government, Facebook, Google, and several other prominent
American-based businesses and organizations had launched the
Alliance for Youth Movements to fund and organize social media
movements in Latin America, Africa, the Middle East, Europe,
and Asia that would "change the world," holding annual sum-
mits of international youth leaders and prominent technologists
in New York and Mexico City.[32] The new digital tools created "a
greater chance for civil society organizations' coming to fruition
regardless of how challenging the [political] environment," as the
State Department's point man for cyberdiplomacy, Jared Cohen,
proclaimed in 2009.

To further the cause of free expression and hasten liberalization within Russia, the US government had also helped Russia's
Glasnost Defense Foundation, an NGO launched in the Gorbachev period, to create what it called the School for Bloggers,
aimed at enabling independent Russian voices to gain internet
platforms to deliver their views on key social and political issues.
In this effort, Americans did not see themselves as fighting an
information war or seeking regime change in Russia; they were
simply promoting cherished Enlightenment principles, freedom of
expression and freedom of assembly, through the vehicle of new
technology. The invisible hand of liberal progress would then do
its work. US diplomats and businessmen needed to do little more
than facilitate the spread of internet access, and good things would
follow. As one American columnist put it, "As new media spreads

its Web worldwide, authoritarians . . . will have a difficult time maintaining absolute control in the face of the technology's chaotic democracy."[33]

Russian officials scrambled to counter this seeming momentum. It was no accident that Moscow named its new venture the *Kremlin School for Bloggers*—it was a direct response to the Glasnost Defense Foundation's own similarly named media initiative.[34] The school comprised some eighty people working with two or three bloggers each across Russia to mount information campaigns online.[35] Whereas the Glasnost Defense Foundation focused on bloggers critical of the Russian government, the Kremlin sought to train and promote such personalities as Maria Sergeyeva, an attractive twentysomething blonde who combined posts extoling Catherine the Great with occasional photos from hip parties around town.[36] Sergeyeva, in turn, promoted training sessions for loyalist bloggers under the acronym *KGB—Kursy Gosudarstvennykh Bloggerov*, or Courses for State Bloggers—which, among other things, taught pro-Kremlin cyberwarriors how to hack into opposition blogs and find the addresses and telephone numbers of those behind them.[37] The Kremlin also worked to co-opt Rustem Adagamov, known by the pseudonym *Drugoi* (Different), a graphic designer and photographer and author of the most popular blog on the social media site LiveJournal.[38] Moscow's aim was not to block or censor information critical of the government, however, but rather to defeat it—to co-opt youth groups from the inside and make it seem cool to be patriotic, and to show Russian audiences that the ideas of the government's opponents were mistaken, ineffectual, or tainted by foreign sponsorship.

This approach marked an important shift from Soviet-era media control, which had relied on banning non-regime publications and censoring expression. As Russian internet guru and State Duma deputy Konstantin Rykov observed, blocking information was in many ways impractical in the cyberage, but more importantly, internet censorship would alienate the very audience—Russian youth—that the Kremlin most wanted to attract and persuade.[39] Under the new approach, those who challenged the Kremlin's policy line could express their views online, but they often found themselves subjected to an onslaught of orchestrated counterarguments and online harassment from an army of paid internet trolls. The Kremlin aimed to create the appearance of a marketplace of ideas in Russia's digital domain, while ensuring that the market was tilted heavily in favor of the state's preferred outcomes. Unlike in the Cold War, this information war was not fought over access to news and opinions, pitting an open society against a closed one.[40] Rather, it was a battle for hearts and minds, and it would be won, in Moscow's view, not by building walls against information and ideas but by enlisting the help of influencers who could argue and convince, as well as harass and intimidate, in the trenches of a blogosphere that transcended geographic borders.

Like cybersabotage and cyberespionage, cyberinfluence activities have added a troublesome new dimension to old-fashioned propaganda and subversion that has created new fears and uncertainties in international relations. The fears flow in part from the daunting speed and scale of modern cyberinfluence campaigns, which can put messaging content directly in front of hundreds of millions of eyes with unprecedented rapidity, and in part from our poor understanding of the degree to which online content actually shapes perceptions and motivates behaviors.

The potential impact of cyberinfluence operations seems vast. More than two and a half billion people worldwide were using social media in 2017, including more than 80 percent of the US population, and their online activity has created an enormous repository of data about who they are, what they like, what they think, and what they do.[41] Platforms such as Facebook and Twitter are designed to allow advertisers to track user engagement with ads, page likes, search results, and news feeds. This provides advertisers and political campaigns with the potential to microsegment audiences according to their interests, views, demographic attributes, and behaviors to provide them with content customized to resonate with target segments and to employ machine-learning algorithms to improve the effectiveness of proffered content over time. But by default, it also offers the same possibilities to foreign intelligence services keen to understand and affect grassroots dynamics in the societies of their adversaries. Cyberinfluence campaigns can zero in, for example, on mothers in their thirties living in Pennsylvania who are interested in preschool education, and then push content and advertising tailored to their concerns directly into their social media feeds. In turn, social media "listening" software allows content providers to optimize the timing of these placements and gauge the impact of their content on audience response.

When used to sell products and fuel economic growth, or to support causes that help society, these innovations can potentially be of benefit, but customized influence campaigns can be built to deceive as well as to inform. Twitter bots can mimic the appearance of actual human users to disseminate tweets to audiences and distort impressions about the impact of news and events. New algorithms assisted by artificial intelligence make it easy to create "deep fakes," bogus video or audio segments that depict public figures doing and saying things that they never did or said but that are so realistic that it is practically impossible for audiences to detect the deception. The speed with which these deep fakes can be delivered vastly outpaces the time it takes to detect them and disseminate warnings and corrections, which means their impact could be disproportionately great in the context of a fast-moving election campaign. This technology has put old-fashioned disinformation—the deliberate publication of false information to deceive audiences—on steroids.

There is no doubt that new information technology makes it easier than ever before to engage in grassroots political influence activities, whether constructive or destructive. But engagement and effectiveness are not the same thing. Are these new cyber-influence tools effective in shaping grassroots political behavior? Election campaign professionals generally believe that altering the views of voters is exceedingly difficult, and modern election campaigns rarely attempt it, even with an array of new digital tools and data with which to work. Rather, they use digital data to identify people who are already inclined to agree with a candidate's positions on key issues, and they employ cybertools to rally them to turn out at the polls.[42] Do they help to bolster turnout? And can cyberinfluence campaigns also motivate people to act in other ways on their preexisting beliefs, such as to protest or even to engage in violence? The truth is that no one yet knows. Vanishingly few studies have examined the link between online content, audience perceptions, and political behaviors. But the seeming potential held by new cybertools to mobilize, inflame, or deceive audiences, coupled with their ability to target customized messages at specific groups or individuals, is causing great worry in both Russia and the United States.

Layered on top of these fears is the difficulty of discerning the intent of those behind cyberinfluence efforts. Sometimes, influence efforts can aim at little more than reinforcing a state's diplomatic messaging. The Voice of America has long broadcast news and opinions into countries dominated by state-controlled media, hoping to provide these audiences with alternative perspectives on events. More recently, Moscow launched Russia Today, later renamed RT, to broadcast Russian perspectives into the United States, Europe, and other parts of the world. Other influence activities are intended not to persuade but to subvert—to rend the political fabric of an adversary nation in a way that undermines its governing authority.

But the broader goal behind subversive activity is not always clear. In his book *Cyber War Will Not Take Place*, Johns Hopkins University professor Thomas Rid explains that the goal of subversion may either be to overthrow an established economic or governmental order or to force those in power to do things they would rather not do. "The first objective is revolutionary and existential; the second objective is evolutionary and pragmatic."[43] Discerning the difference, however, is maddeningly difficult. Through American eyes, US support for independent Russian blogging was intended to push Moscow to accept principles—free expression and assembly—that the Russian government did not fully embrace. Through Russian officials' eyes, those same US efforts represented an existential threat. When hackers helped to publish embarrassing emails from within Hillary Clinton's presidential campaign in 2016, that information clearly subverted Clinton's reputation to some degree. But was it ultimately meant to torpedo Clinton's election prospects and "destroy American democracy" as claimed by many, or did it aim to force what most Russians regarded as an inevitable Clinton presidency to do things it would rather not do, such as back off evangelical democratization efforts in and around Russia and recognize the potential societal instability that an ungoverned internet might bring? Such ambiguities in assessing intentions are inherent to cyberinfluence activities and can magnify fears and destabilize state-to-state relations.

For the sake of clarity, this chapter has presented cybersabotage, cyberespionage, and cyberinfluence as separate and distinct activities. In reality, they are interwoven and mutually reinforcing. Together, they breed a pervasive sense of vulnerability and encourage aggressive responses rooted in fear. As the United States has long argued, it is quite difficult to control the flow of information in the World Wide Web. Yet for Russia, that information can pose threats to societal stability by fueling sabotage and subversion. This combination incentivizes offensive cyberinfluence operations. When one cannot block news and opinions, the best alternative is to defeat them. Similarly, software flaws, human imperfections, and the insecure nature of the internet mean that cyberdefenders have enormous difficulty stopping network intrusions. When one cannot play effective defense, there is a strong temptation to go on offense to penetrate the adversary's networks to discover what the other side is doing. Once inside a network, a cyberwarrior can not only gather information but also sabotage an adversary's systems. To deter the other side from detonating such cyberbombs, states are incentivized to take cyberhostages of their own, threatening to damage the other side's systems in response. This shadow war in the cyberdomain is the essence of a vicious circle, creating escalating spirals of aggression and suspicion. It would be dangerous enough if limited strictly to the cybersphere. But in a networked, globalized world, in which digital networks and national economies and media systems and nuclear command and control systems are all linked together in some way, limiting spillover from the cybersphere is inherently problematic. Unlike in Las Vegas, what happens in the cyberworld does not stay in the cyberworld. It sooner or later spills into other domains, including economic and kinetic military operations.

2

Deadly Perceptions

Are Russia and the United States trying to destroy each other? Each side seems to think the other is. "The Plot Against America: Inside Putin's Campaign to Destroy US Democracy," which appeared as a cover story in *Newsweek* in 2017, has become emblematic of American perceptions of the Kremlin's aims. And Russians have long been convinced that Washington seeks to encircle their country with hostile puppet regimes as part of its plan to overthrow their government and break their nation into pieces. But each side also believes its intentions are badly misunderstood by the other side. In fact, there are perhaps no two countries in the world whose views of their own behavior contrast more starkly with the perceptions of the other side than the United States and Russia. Understanding the reasons for that contrast, and how the perceptions of each side are amplifying those of the other, is a critical part of grasping the dangers of inadvertent escalation.

America views itself as an exceptional nation, playing a unique and salutary role in the world. Abraham Lincoln memorably called America "the last best hope of earth" and summed up our mission as "maintaining in the world, that form and substance of government, whose leading object is to elevate the condition of all men." Through the eyes of Americans, our purpose in that outside world has been, since our country's inception, the noble advancement of self-government and liberty. Henry Kissinger observes that "America's foreign policy has reflected the conviction that its domestic principles were self-evidently universal and their application at all times salutary. The real challenge of American engagement abroad was not foreign policy in the traditional sense but a project of spreading values that it believed all other peoples aspired to replicate."[1] We believe, with utmost sincerity, that we are not pursuing our narrow self-interest but are, in Kissinger's words, "acting for all mankind." This conviction deepened with the end of the Cold War, both because Americans believed our system of government had clearly triumphed in the arena of ideological competition and because the United States faced few external constraints on its efforts to advance the cause of democracy abroad.

The view of America's international agenda looks quite different from Moscow. Russian officials have come to see "instability and destabilization" as the defining characteristic of US foreign policy.[2] American advisers brought disorder and libertinism to Russia in the 1990s, not prosperity and virtue. Rather than advancing the cause of enlightened governance, the Kosovo and Iraq wars were "the beginning of the accelerated destruction of regional and global stability, undermining the last principles of sustainable world order." The United States' support for the Arab Spring, intervention in Libya, and opposition to Syrian president Assad all appear to Russians like "destabilization that will overwhelm all, including Russia."[3] Russian president Vladimir Putin bitterly summed up this view in a national address in 2014. The United States and its allies, he charged, "prefer not to be guided by international law but by the rule of the gun. They act as they please," believing that "they can decide the destinies of the world, that only they can ever be right." Washington may think it is spreading peace, prosperity, and democracy, but according to Putin, it is producing "chaos" and swelling the ranks of "neo-fascists and Islamic radicals."[4]

Like America, Russia has traditionally seen itself as a virtuous outsider in the world, but for much different reasons. The foundation of Russia's self-image, from the time of Peter the Great through Gorbachev and Yeltsin to Putin, has been that of a great power vital to world stability. Without Russia playing this prominent role, "geopolitical turbulence will begin."[5] Yet the world has often been slow to recognize Russia's importance. Russia sees itself figuratively as an uninvited guest looking in on an elegant dinner party of the world's leading Western nations, alternately demanding a seat at their table and assuring himself that he should not deign to join them. With the notable exception of the Soviet period, Russians historically have seen their uniqueness not in new and better approaches to governance but in their ability to bridge East and West and uphold tried-and-true tradition.[6] Where America has carried aloft the banner of liberalism, embracing the trendy Silicon Valley concept of creative disruption, Russia has sounded the cautionary notes of conservatism, often viewing change more as threat than opportunity.[7] From Moscow's vantage point, Russia is a status quo power, seeking to preserve the established Westphalian order against reckless revisionists who claim an obligation to intervene in the sovereign affairs of other governments despite the instability that ensues.

To say that Washington sees Russia in a different light would be a vast understatement. Through American eyes, Russia is a revisionist power seeking to upend the international order, not preserve it. "Putin is a calculating master of geo-politics with a master plan to divide Europe, destroy NATO, reestablish Russian influence in the world, and, most of all, marginalize the US and the West," according to a veteran Democratic political consultant.[8] Former vice president Joe Biden lamented that America had extended the hand of friendship throughout the 1990s and early 2000s, but Russia "has chosen a different path," combining repression at home with disdain for the interests and sovereignty of Russia's neighbors. Echoing this theme, the Trump administration has accused Moscow of a "pattern of behavior in which Russia disregards the international rules-based order, undermines the sovereignty and security of countries worldwide, and attempts to subvert and discredit Western democratic institutions and processes."[9]

The tendency to view oneself as virtuous, attributing any ethical lapses or bad outcomes to one's circumstances, but discounting the good intentions of others—something psychologists call the *fundamental attribution error*—is more the norm than the exception in international relations and, indeed, in human affairs more broadly. Russia and the United States have begun to exhibit an extreme form of this tendency, however. Each side is not simply convinced that what it is doing is legitimate, defensive, and benign, while the actions of the other are illegitimate, aggressive, and dangerous. More alarmingly, each side is increasingly persuaded that the other is actually intent on its demise. These perceptions of existential threat are ominously raising the stakes in the US-Russian relationship well beyond the limited geopolitical competition that should flow from the objective mix of conflicting and compatible American and Russian interests. They have created a self-reinforcing loop of suspicions and mistrust that is impeding steps that could manage risks in the relationship and removing important brakes on escalatory spirals. Ironically, these perceptions are helping to create the very existential peril that each side fears yet neither country actually intends.

"THEY'RE IN TO DO US IN"

This was the pithy sound bite that James Clapper, the recently retired director of national intelligence, employed in the spring of 2017 to sum up Russian intentions toward the United States. And Clapper is far from alone in this assessment. The late Republican senator John McCain charged that Russia is attempting to "destroy democracy" in the United States.[10] Conservative columnist George Will avers that "Russia hopes to fatally undermine a distracted West."[11] Liberal pundit Paul Waldman argues that Putin's fundamental goal is "undermining American democracy."[12] Democratic senator Ben Cardin warns that Russia is trying to "bring down our way of government."[13] Yale University historian Timothy Snyder accuses Russia of using "cyber warfare to destroy the United States of America."[14] Americans may not be able to agree on much in our increasingly polarized society, but we all seem to concur that Russia has deadly things in mind for the United States. This perception has spanned American political parties, institutions of government, media outlets, geographic regions, and demographic groups, quickly becoming so widespread that the burden of proof is now assumed to lie on those who think otherwise. Chicago Council on Global Affairs surveys taken in 2017 showed that nearly three-quarters of Americans believed Russia was working actively to undermine US influence and power, and more than 80 percent believed Russian influence in American elections posed a critical or important threat.[15] The near unanimous passage in 2017 of the Countering America's Adversaries Through Sanctions Act, a law imposing new sanctions on Russia that not only formally defined it as an American adversary but lumped it together with notorious "rogue states" Iran and North Korea, testified to the depth and breadth of the perception that Moscow poses a fundamental threat to American security. Russia may not aspire to the physical incineration of American territory, according to this view, but it certainly hopes to undermine our democratic institutions and to set Americans against each other, subduing our nation by exacerbating divisions and dysfunction.

The belief that Moscow poses an existential threat is relatively recent for post–Cold War America, despite the fact that Russia is the one country whose strategic nuclear capabilities rival those of the United States. Less than thirty years ago, in 1992, US president George H. W. Bush and Russian president Yeltsin formally declared an end to the Cold War, signing a joint statement avowing that "Russia and the United States do not regard each other as potential adversaries. From now on, the relationship will be characterized by friendship and partnership founded on mutual trust and respect and a common commitment to democracy and economic freedom." Gallup surveys from that period showed that two-thirds of Americans had favorable views of Russia, while vanishingly few saw Moscow as an enemy. Almost no one thought that nuclear war posed any realistic danger, according to another Chicago Council on Global Affairs survey.[16] Reflecting this view, the Clinton presidency drew heavily on what it called "the peace dividend" to enact large cuts in defense spending and other national security outlays. Optimism abounded that the United States could midwife democracy in Russia and integrate it into the Western world. But the euphoria fueled by visions of a peaceful, prosperous, and democratic new world order was short-lived.

American suspicions of Moscow's intentions in the world, and particularly toward Russia's neighbors, started to rekindle fairly early in the post-Soviet relationship as conflicts flared in several newly independent former Soviet republics, Russian peacekeeping forces began playing more prominent roles beyond Russia's borders, and Moscow seemed to drag its feet over returning Soviet-era military forces to Russia from their old bases in the Baltic states, Moldova, Georgia, and elsewhere. These developments played on lingering American concerns that some in Moscow might harbor residual hopes of rebuilding the Soviet empire and reconstituting a geopolitical threat to Europe and the United States. Zbigniew Brzezinski summed up these concerns in an article he published in *Foreign Affairs* in 1994:

> Regrettably, the imperial impulse remains strong and even appears to be strengthening. This is not only a matter of political rhetoric. Particularly troubling is the growing assertiveness of the Russian military in the effort to retain or regain control over the old Soviet empire. Initially, these efforts may have been the spontaneous acts of rogue military commanders in the field. However, military self-assertion in such places as Moldova, Crimea, Ossetia, Abkhazia, Georgia and Tajikistan, as well as military opposition to any territorial concessions in the Kuriles and to the reduction of Russian forces in the Kaliningrad region and to a prompt withdrawal from all the Baltic republics, perpetuates imperial enclaves on the outer edges of the former empire.
>
> In addition, the last two years have seen a concerted effort by Moscow to rebuild some of the institutional links that used to bind the old Soviet Union together. Much energy has been invested in promoting a host of new agreements and ties, including the CIS charter, a collective security treaty (which in several cases also gives Russia control over the external frontiers of the former Soviet Union), a collective peacekeeping agreement (used to justify intervention in Tajikistan), a new ruble zone (meant to give the Russian central bank the decisive role in monetary matters), and a formal economic union (transferring key economic decision-making to Moscow), to a common CIS parliamentary institution.[17]

As indecisive hot wars in Georgia, Moldova, and Nagorno-Karabakh turned into long-term "frozen conflicts" in the mid-1990s, and Russia began staking out positions in the Balkans that were at odds with American preferences, Washington increasingly worried that Russia was becoming more spoiler than partner in resolving regional conflicts. Deputy Secretary of State Strobe Talbott acknowledged these concerns in a speech in 1997: "Will [Russia] play by the rules? There is still a lot of skepticism on this point that resonates in our national debate about Russia and US policy. Many experts and commentators start from a presumption of guilt about Russia's strategic intentions. They nurture a suspicion that Russians are predisposed genetically, or at least historically, to aggression and imperialism."[18]

Despite this suspicion, Russia's hostile reaction to the Kosovo war in early 1999 shocked many in Washington. Seen through Western eyes, NATO had launched the military operation in response to clear crimes by Yugoslav forces against ethnic Albanians in Kosovo. At the time, Russian and NATO forces had been serving together cooperatively in Bosnia, having undertaken a similar mission there to prevent ethnic cleansing. But in contrast to the Bosnia effort, Moscow called the NATO bombing against Yugoslavia the worst aggression in Europe since World War II. Russia's State Duma voted symbolically to form a new Slavic nation by uniting Yugoslavia with Russia and Belarus, and Russian peacekeeping forces attempted preemptively to seize and control a sector of Kosovo by making a mad dash to the Pristina airport without first coordinating with NATO commanders. American officials wondered, "How could a country aspiring to join the West be against stopping genocide?"[19] A Clinton National Security Council staffer recalled, "The Kosovo War provoked this moment of incredible rupture that I don't think any of us knew was coming."[20] There were now real questions in Washington about whether Russian leaders shared the values espoused by the Western community.[21]

American suspicions deepened in the new millennium after President Yeltsin resigned, Vladimir Putin was elected as his successor, and a disillusioned and disoriented Russia struggled to pick up the pieces following the political, economic, and societal collapse it endured in the 1990s. Some concerns flowed from circumstances and our interpretations of specific Russian actions. Talbott worried in early 2000, for example, that "the privatization of power" in Russia during the 1990s had "given a bad name to democracy, reform, the free market, even liberty itself," putting Russia's Westernization at risk. Moreover, renewed fighting in Chechnya had "generated fears, resentments, and frustrations" in Russia that magnified a "more general sense of grievance and vulnerability after a decade of other difficulties and setbacks, real and imagined, most conspicuously the enlargement of NATO and the Kosovo war."[22] Other concerns reflected personal impressions of Putin himself. Most US officials were skeptical of Putin's KGB background, and what it might mean for his intentions toward the West, right from the start of his presidency, according to Talbott.[23]

The terrorist attacks of September 11, 2001, marked another turning point in US perceptions of Russia. Putin had telephoned President Bush two days before the attacks to warn that Russian intelligence had detected signs of an incipient terrorist campaign, "something long in preparation," coming out of Afghanistan. Then on September 11, Putin was the first foreign leader to call the White House to express sympathy and support following al-Qaeda's attacks on New York City and Washington. His message was clear: "I want you to know that in this struggle, we will stand together."[24] It was at that moment, according to National Security Advisor Condoleezza Rice, that she "realized that the Cold War was really over."[25] Within weeks, Russia was providing the

United States with intelligence and facilitating America's establishment and use of military bases in Central Asia to support the war in Afghanistan. Rice enthusiastically praised Moscow's assistance: "Russia has been one of our best allies in terms of intelligence sharing, in terms of support for American operations that have taken place out of Central Asia—this has been an extremely important relationship to us."[26]

But American perceptions of Moscow's intentions in the outside world, and of the potential for bilateral conflict or cooperation, were also tied inextricably to the course of liberal reforms inside Russia. Many American officials had embraced Immanuel Kant's concept of democratic peace, believing that democracies tend not fight one another, and that by extension, the course of Russia's democratic transformation was a critical variable affecting the chances it would revert to an aggressive foreign policy.[27] Putin's outreach to the United States following the attack of September 11 was "widely interpreted as Putin's embrace of the West, a new course for Russia that put an end to equivocation between the East and the West."[28] The United States expected this embrace to include Russia's liberalization domestically, in addition to its cooperation in foreign affairs. For a time, its expectations seemed justified. Putin's advancement of land, tax, and judicial reforms early in his first term helped the Bush administration feel comfortable about a strategic partnership with Russia aimed at countering terrorism and advancing common bilateral interests. These reforms facilitated a "measured, collected response" from the White House when Russia sided with Germany and France in opposing the Iraq War in early 2003.[29] A senior State Department official from that time observed:

> It almost seemed like the Russians did not want to be separate
> from the West on Iraq. But on Iraq, the Western countries

themselves divided. The United States and Britain were for using military force; France and Germany were opposed. And in the end, Russia sided with France and Germany, but I didn't have the feeling that the Russians were wholly comfortable with that situation. I think they would have preferred actually a more unified stance that they could have aligned with.[30]

But Putin's growing restrictions on press freedoms and his crackdown on prominent political opponents in late 2003 and 2004 compounded the impact of US-Russian policy differences over Iraq, Georgia, and Ukraine in shaping American perceptions of Russian intentions. A senior Bush aide recalled a conversation between Bush and Blair in October 2003 in which they were saying to each other, "You know, I'm not sure he's the guy we thought he was. I'm worried about this throttling of the independent media. This is not good. This is not the guy we were signing up to help and bring into our inner circle of world leadership."[31] By 2005, President Bush had privately concluded, "We've lost him," meaning that he believed Putin was no longer pursuing democracy. And when it became clear that Putin was not moving toward democracy, "then it's very difficult for us to justify why we are still cooperating with the Russians."[32] As Russia grew increasingly authoritarian, Washington grew increasingly convinced that, as Bush put it, "in terms of whether or not it's possible to reprogram the kind of basic Russian DNA, which is centralized authority, that's hard to do."[33]

These deepening American concerns about Russia's course were reinforced by two withering blows late in the Bush administration's second term. First, in 2007, Putin delivered a venomous indictment of US foreign policy in a speech at the annual Munich Security Conference, creating the impression within the Bush administration that Moscow was no longer interested in integration with the West and had opted for an aggressive, anti-Western foreign policy.[34] Then, in August 2008, Russia went to war with Georgia. The conflict had started when Georgian military forces attempted to seize control of the separatist territory of South Ossetia, killing several Russian peacekeepers, who had long been stationed there, in the course of the attack.[35] Russia responded almost immediately with a massive counterinvasion of both South Ossetia and Abkhazia, another breakaway Georgian region, quickly defeating the Georgians and later recognizing the independence of both regions. Many US officials were convinced that Moscow had laid a trap for Georgian president Saakashvili, baiting him into war.[36] This was "a game changer," according to then US ambassador to Russia John Beyrle. "That was really the first time that territory belonging to a sovereign neighbor of Russia, which had been recognized as part of that sovereign neighbor by Russia up to that point, suddenly changed [hands]. There were other disputed areas in [the region], but the two in Georgia and the unilateral recognition of their independence by Russia made it clear that Russia would go to some lengths to [show] that it still needed to control what happened in those countries."[37] This marked an important evolution in American perceptions. Russia had become more than just an increasingly authoritarian state lamenting its lost superpower status and wielding a long list of grievances toward Washington. It was now actively using force to bolster its influence in neighboring states and oppose NATO enlargement and US involvement around its borders.

Obama's first term in office featured a reset of bilateral relations and renewed optimism about Russia's course, after Putin had orchestrated the transfer of the presidency to Dmitry Medvedev and moved to the post of prime minister. American concerns came roaring back, however, after Putin announced in late 2011 that he would run for the presidency in the 2012 election and cracked down hard on pre- and postelection protests, political opposition, and civil society in general. Putin had run much of his campaign on crude anti-American themes. "On good days, Putin saw the United States as a competitor. On bad days, the United States was his enemy," according to Michael McFaul, who had moved from a senior position on Obama's National Security Council staff to become US ambassador to Russia just a few months prior to Putin's election victory.[38] Putin's return to presidency was a key moment, according to former *Washington Post* Moscow bureau chief Susan Glasser, in understanding his real intentions. His second inauguration, she observes, was very different from his first. "His speech is different. He never mentions the word 'democracy' in his second inaugural address. He did in the first. He walks in by himself into this gilded hall in the Kremlin, down this endless red carpet in a way that suggests the crowning of the old kings and that no one else can put the crown on their head."[39] If Putin envisioned himself as tsar, would he not also be longing for an empire to rule beyond Russian borders?

As the Obama team attempted to make progress in bilateral cooperation following Putin's return to the presidency, it increasingly saw a gap between Moscow's words and its actions. "Both sides were saying, 'Yes, we want to be partners,'" recalls an Obama Pentagon official, "but we started to see, in the Pentagon, well perhaps [the Russians] are not so fully engaged in being our partner. It took some time before we got to the [realization that] they're actually an adversary. That happened, though, relatively quickly in my office, once we started really doing a deep dive, after Putin came [back] into office."[40] Moscow's decision in the summer of 2013 to offer political asylum to Edward Snowden, an American intelligence contractor who had illegally provided over a million classified documents to WikiLeaks and was charged under the

US Espionage Act, enraged many Washington officials. American media reacted harshly to a Russian law passed in June that criminalized the distribution to minors of materials promoting what Russia called *nontraditional sexual relationships*. Increasingly frustrated, President Obama canceled his planned summit with Putin in the fall of 2013 and "took Russia off his desk," delegating management of the vexing relationship to his secretaries of defense and state. In explaining his decision, Obama accused the Russians of slipping "back into Cold War thinking and Cold War mentality."[41]

Russia forced its way back onto Obama's desk quickly, however. Its annexation of Crimea and launch of a separatist war in eastern Ukraine in 2014 created a crisis in relations with the West and produced another quantum leap in American perceptions of Russian aims, persuading Obama officials that Moscow sought to undo the Helsinki Rules that had been codified in 1975 by the Conference on Security and Cooperation in Europe (CSCE) stipulating, among other things, that borders could be changed only by peaceful means. The Ukraine operation showed that Putin "was not only speaking out against the international order and international institutions and the status quo, but that he was going to act against it." According to a senior State Department official, Putin's aggression in Ukraine "made clear the challenge Russia was posing. One of the fundamental tenets of any international order is that big countries don't get to swallow up parts of small countries just because they can."[42] But Russia was done with "trying to be a normal nation. [It] wants to be a nation that makes its own rules and is surrounded by satellites."[43] It "no longer worried about what the West or the rest of the world said or thought about it."[44]

Still, while American officials had come to view Russia as an aggressive revisionist power, they believed its ambitions were much more regional than global, even after Moscow launched a military intervention in support of Syrian leader Bashar al-Assad in 2015. A Pentagon official cautioned in the wake of the Ukraine crisis that Americans needed to keep the Russian threat in perspective: "Russia doesn't make anything. Immigrants aren't rushing to Moscow in search of opportunity. The life expectancy of the Russian male is around sixty years old. The population is shrinking. And so, we have to respond with resolve in what are effectively regional challenges that Russia presents." President Obama was even blunter: "Russia is a regional power that is threatening some of its immediate neighbors—not out of strength but out of weakness," Obama said in response to a reporter's question about whether his 2012 election opponent, Mitt Romney, had been right to characterize Russia as America's biggest geopolitical foe. "[The Russians] don't pose the number one national security threat to the United States. I continue to be much more concerned when it comes to our security with the prospect of a nuclear weapon going off in Manhattan."[45]

Russian interference in the 2016 US presidential election catapulted these perceptions of Russia across an important threshold, transforming concerns about Russia's authoritarian governance and regional aggression into an alarming new belief that Moscow poses an existential threat to the United States, not through nuclear attack but by undermining the very foundations of our democratic political system and our society. It was one thing to oppose key US foreign policy objectives in the Middle East or to seize and annex neighboring territories. But interfering with an American presidential election was another thing altogether, an act striking at the heart of our nation. "The Russians violated our sovereignty over one of the most sacred things we do," explains McFaul. "We choose our leaders. That's the most sacred thing you do as a democracy. And they meddled in that." Through McFaul's eyes, it was an act of aggression comparable to Japan's attack on Pearl Harbor and al-Qaeda's terrorist campaign. "Thankfully, people didn't die as they did in 1941 or September 11, but it was a violation of our sovereignty."[46]

Russian hackers had allegedly penetrated the computer servers of the Democratic National Committee and helped to publish embarrassing emails revealing corrupt favoritism toward Hillary Clinton's election campaign. Russia had also launched a propaganda campaign on social media, websites, and television. All this had been directed, according to the US Intelligence Community, by Putin himself, with the explicit purposes of damaging Clinton and "undermining our democracy and the liberal international order."[47] It was, in the words of *The Washington Post*, the "Crime of the Century." Former CIA director Michael Hayden dubbed it the "most successful covert operation in the history of intelligence."[48]

What could motivate such aggression? In a word, ideology. "Putin wants to make the world safe for Russian autocracy, which means compromising every democratic center of power he can find, and crushing democracy closer to home, like Ukraine,"[49] explained one senior American official. Clapper agreed: "I think fundamentally there is an aversion to our whole system, an aversion to democracy. [Putin] doesn't believe in it and views it as threatening to him, personally. That is what it all boils down to in Russia. I just think that's almost in his genes, in the Russian genes, to do what they did [in meddling in the US election], and they'll continue to do it."[50] Tony Blinken, who served in the Obama administration as National Security Advisor to Vice President Biden, explained Russian motivations in similar terms:

> For Putin, when Western democracy is successful, it's the most profound indictment of the system that he's built in Russia, a country that started to embrace democracy and capitalism after the end of the Cold War, but now it's turned into this kleptocracy, this illiberal democracy, and, indeed,

self-recognized illiberal democracy. Putin, I think, came
to the conclusion that the more he could do to undermine
the Western democratic model, to foment trouble, to create
tension, difficulties within the West, between the United
States and Europe, within Western European countries,
within the United States, the better [off] he would be.[51]

In sum, by 2018, America's natural optimism about the arc of
history bending toward progress had turned to deep pessimism
that this perceived Russian objective—to torpedo democracy—
would change anytime soon. American officials had concluded
that under Putin, Russia's leadership had come to view democracy
itself as a mortal threat to be countered not only inside Russia and
its neighboring regions but in the United States. Russian hostility toward America was not seen as a function of what we do but
rather as a reaction to the essence of what we are, and it flowed
from the very nature of the regime that Putin had constructed.
That hostility would continue, therefore, until Russia's political
system changed fundamentally.[52] American officials had spent
much of the past decade denying Russian accusations that they
sought regime change in Moscow. In the aftermath of the 2016
election, many were telling themselves that relations with Russia
could not improve without it.

AMERICA, A CLEAR AND PRESENT DANGER

If by 2017 Americans were convinced that Moscow was seeking
their country's demise, then they were only making up conceptual
ground that Russians had already covered years before in their
perceptions of US intentions. Russian president Putin had come
into office at the turn of the millennium hoping that a strategic
partnership with the world's foremost power would help to accelerate Russia's recovery from the collapse of the 1990s, address

terrorist threats to Russia's security, and hasten its return to great-power status. He began studying the English language, and he even mooted the possibility of Russia's membership in NATO. In May 2002, he and President Bush signed a strategic framework agreement that announced that the "era in which the United States and Russia saw each other as an enemy or strategic threat has ended" and that they would work as partners to counter global challenges and resolve regional conflicts.[53] But by early 2004, he had concluded that Washington wanted to lock Russia into permanent subordinate standing or worse.

Putin is not an outlier in such perceptions, which are widely shared among Russia's most knowledgeable elites. Chief of the General Staff Valery Gerasimov argues the US "goal is to liquidate the statehood of undesirable countries, to undermine their sovereignty and replace their legally elected governments. . . . The Pentagon has started developing a completely new strategy of military action, which has already been called 'Trojan Horse.' It's based on the active use of the 'fifth column protest potential' to destabilize the situation along with precision strikes on the most important targets."[54] Security Council Secretary Nikolai Patrushev alleges that "Americans are trying to involve the Russian Federation in an interstate military conflict, cause regime change and ultimately dismember our country."[55] Foreign Minister Sergey Lavrov claims that America "does not merely seek to change Russian policy . . . but it seeks to change the regime—and practically nobody denies this."[56] Sergey Glazyev, an economist who has served in the Gorbachev, Yeltsin, and Putin administrations, argues that the United States is using "depopulation techniques" to prevent "reunification of the Russian people" and provoke "further dismemberment of Russia."[57] Andrei Kostin, head of Russia's External Trade Bank (VTB), calls US economic sanctions "a full-scale attack on Russia . . . so that Russia changes its government and its president to someone more suitable."[58] State Duma deputy Vyacheslav Nikonov, a well-educated, fluent English-speaker who has traveled widely in the West, avers that America's aim is for Russia "to cease to exist as a state."[59] Even former Soviet leader Mikhail Gorbachev, still revered in the West as the author of glasnost and perestroika and partner of US president Ronald Reagan in ending the Cold War, has charged that Americans have sought to create "a new empire headed by themselves." They "patted us on the shoulder, they kept saying, 'Well done, well done.' But all the while they were tearing us down, looting us, tearing us apart."[60]

Like American perceptions of Russia, Russia's belief that Washington poses an existential threat evolved over time, though it advanced more quickly. Russia's unhappy experience with American advice on domestic reforms during the 1990s laid the basis for many contemporary Russian perceptions of Washington's intent, with many Russians suspecting that the United States wanted Russia to collapse rather than recover. But there is little evidence that Putin had anti-American views when he first entered public life in the early 1990s as deputy mayor of Saint Petersburg, which had a reputation as Russia's most European metropolis. Unlike some hard-line Russians and most KGB veterans, he did not blame the United States for destroying the Soviet Union, which he attributed to mistakes made by Soviet leaders. His interactions with US officials and businessmen while in the Saint Petersburg government were reportedly pragmatic and helpful, and he was perceived as pro-business. According to Russian journalist Irina Borogan, generally a Putin skeptic, "Putin [at that time] was not furious about the West. He worked with a prominent democrat, and he didn't leave him. . . . His career was dependent on [Saint Petersburg mayor] Anatoly Sobchak, who was a really big friend of the West."[61] But Putin received a lesson in American power politics after he had been promoted to head Russia's Federal Security Service (FSB) in 1998.

That lesson revolved around NATO. Russian officials, almost to a man, opposed NATO's possible expansion when it was first being discussed in the early 1990s. Russian hard-liners regarded the alliance as a genuine military threat. Russian liberals, aware of lingering popular perceptions of NATO as a Cold War foe, feared that expansion would fatally compromise their political position relative to the hard-liners.[62] Ex-Soviet officials such as Mikhail Gorbachev averred (despite American denials) that Washington had orally pledged not to move NATO eastward in return for Moscow's agreement that a united Germany could be part of the alliance.

Clinton administration officials sought to assuage Russian concerns by creating the NATO-Russia Permanent Joint Council, which would give Moscow "a voice but not a veto" in NATO affairs, and by arguing that it was much better for Russia to have prosperous democratic neighbors within NATO than to have those countries untethered, nationalistic, and unstable. Few Russians were persuaded. President Yeltsin made his anger plain over the prospect of NATO expansion in a speech at the Budapest summit meeting of the CSCE in 1994. "We hear explanations to the effect that this is allegedly the expansion of stability, just in case there are undesirable developments in Russia," he said, but "history demonstrates that it is a dangerous delusion to suppose that the destinies of continents and of the world community in general can somehow be managed from one single capital." He warned that the plan to expand NATO threatened to plunge Europe "into a cold peace."[63]

Russian skeptics did not have to wait long for events to justify their fears. America's assurances that NATO posed no military threat and that it would operate in consultation with Moscow were almost immediately proved wrong, in Russia's eyes, when NATO unilaterally launched bombing operations against Yugoslavia—Russia's "Slavic brother"—only two weeks after Hungary, Poland, and the Czech Republic were admitted as new members in early 1999. Many in Russia were "stunned that NATO took the unprecedented step of bypassing the UN Security Council to attack Yugoslavia not for actions it took against another sovereign state" but rather for actions against ethnic Albanians inside the country.[64] Russian hard-liners felt vindicated in their suspicions; Russian liberals felt betrayed. Yeltsin lamented that all international "rules of the game" had been thrown out the window. Opinion polls indicated that some 90 percent of Russians viewed NATO's bombing as a mistake, and nearly two-thirds regarded NATO as the aggressor.[65]

Russian officials strongly objected to NATO's actions but felt powerless to prevent them. Prime Minister Primakov, in a plane en route to Washington to negotiate debt relief with the International Monetary Fund when the bombing started, dramatically reversed course in protest and returned to Moscow. Russia "interpreted the intervention as a means of expanding NATO's influence in the Balkans, not as an effort to deal with a humanitarian crisis" in Kosovo.[66] Years later, State Duma vice speaker Pyotr Tolstoy asked the Serbs to forgive Russia's inability to protect them. "We were both taught a lesson," he said, "that we will never forget."[67] To many Russians, that lesson was an affirmation of the infamous Athenian counsel to the Melians recorded by Thucydides in his history of the Peloponnesian War centuries ago: "The strong do what they will, and the weak suffer what they must." Absent Russian strength, Kremlin officials fretted, nothing would prevent NATO from carrying out a similar operation against Moscow.

Russia could not regain its strength, however, without first taming the centrifugal forces inside Russia exemplified by the conflict in Chechnya. Chechen separatism had long roots in Russian and Soviet history, but it intensified in the early 1990s as the central government weakened and power devolved from Moscow to the country's constituent regions, and it erupted into full-scale war in 1994. Following a cease-fire and an inconclusive peace accord signed in 1996, the republic had become a hotbed for organized crime and Islamic extremism that posed significant challenges to Russia beyond the confines of Chechnya itself. Then, in the summer of 1999, a notorious Chechen warlord launched several armed raids into neighboring Dagestan, which were accompanied by a series of terrorist bombings in Moscow and other Russian cities that were blamed on Chechens. Putin, whom Yeltsin had just named as prime minister, oversaw a massive air-and-ground offensive against Chechnya in response, ultimately blockading its capital, Grozny, and reducing it to near rubble.

In Putin's eyes, dealing decisively with the Chechen uprising was a critical part of halting the disintegration of the Russian state and restoring law and order in the country. The war drew widespread support in Russia, quickly boosting Putin's popularity and contributing to his successful election to the presidency. But unlike in the case of Yeltsin's unpopular use of tanks to shell his opponents in the Russian legislature in 1993, the United States strongly criticized Putin's conduct of the war. It insisted on referring to the Chechen fighters not as bandits or terrorists, as Russia preferred, but as separatists, implying a measure of political legitimacy. Secretary of State Madeleine Albright asserted that "Russia could not consider this war simply an internal affair."[68] Sensing potential American receptivity, Chechen president Maskhadov asked NATO for help in the war in October 1999, stoking Russian fears of Western intervention that were already simmering over NATO's Kosovo operation.[69] If NATO would use force to help Kosovar Albanians against the central Yugoslav government, might it not do the same to help Chechens against Moscow? Russian officials accused the United States of abetting terrorism by criticizing Russia's Chechnya policy while supporting Kosovar Albanians who were themselves employing terrorist tactics.[70] In frustration, Putin sought to help Americans understand Russia's perspective in an op-ed penned for *The New York Times* in November entitled "Why We Must Act":

> I ask you to put aside for a moment the dramatic news reports from the Caucasus and imagine something more placid: ordinary New Yorkers or Washingtonians, asleep in their homes. Then, in a flash, hundreds perish in explosions at the Watergate, or at an apartment complex on Manhattan's West Side. Thousands are injured, some horribly disfigured. Panic engulfs a neighborhood, then a nation.
>
> Russians do not have to imagine such a calamity. More than 300 of our citizens in Moscow and elsewhere suffered that fate earlier this year when bombs detonated by terrorists demolished five apartment blocks. . . .
>
> The antiterrorist campaign was forced upon us. Sadly, decisive armed intervention was the only way to prevent further casualties both within and far outside the borders of Chechnya, further suffering by so many people enslaved by terrorists. As the United States media frequently point out, we have other pressing challenges that demand our resources.
>
> But when a society's core interests are besieged by violent elements, responsible leaders must respond. That is our purpose in Chechnya, and we are determined to see it through. The understanding of our friends abroad would be helpful.[71]

The inexorable exercise of American power in Kosovo, coupled with Washington's reluctance to support Russia's war in Chechnya, prompted Putin to make an important strategic calculation: "The only way to sustain [Russia's] great power status and influence was to be inside the Western decision-making structures and with the West."[72] If the world was indeed unipolar, increasingly run out of Washington, then "to be someone, you have to be an ally or partner of the US."[73] Putin got an opportunity to press his case in September 2001, as terrorism struck the United States in the form of al-Qaeda's attacks in New York City and Washington, D.C. Surely, in the wake of this tragedy, Americans could see that the United States and Russia faced a common terrorist enemy. Despite the private objections of nearly all his senior advisers, Putin announced in a nationally televised address that Russia would provide logistical, intelligence, humanitarian, and diplomatic support in America's war against terrorists in Afghanistan.[74] Shortly afterward, he decided that Russia would close its intelligence collection site in Lourdes, Cuba, and its naval base in Cam Ranh Bay, Vietnam, sending a clear signal to Washington that Moscow had made a strategic choice to align itself with the West. "At the same time," relates Russian journalist Mikhail Zygar, "Putin asks [President] Bush and Lord George Robertson, ex-secretary general of NATO, to invite Russia to NATO. That's probably the most bold idea [sic] that any Russian leader could have. [At] that time, Putin was the most pro-Western leader of Russia."[75]

Putin undertook significant domestic political risk in his unilateral steps to support Washington, but he saw important upsides in these moves.[76] As he attempted to resurrect Russia from its political, economic, and spiritual collapse in the 1990s, Putin hoped that recasting Moscow's relationship with the United States into a partnership against terrorism could help spur Russia more quickly toward regaining its status as an acknowledged great power, with a

voice in key international issues and a privileged role in its neigh-
borhood. According to then Russian foreign minister Igor Ivanov,
"We wanted an anti-terrorist international coalition like the anti-
Nazi coalition. That would be the basis for a new world order."[77]
But Russian leaders soon came to believe that Washington had
much different goals in mind.

Several developments dashed Russian expectations. The first
came in December 2001 in the form of Washington's unilateral
announcement that it would withdraw from the Anti-Ballistic
Missile (ABM) Treaty signed in 1972. The treaty had for nearly
three decades served its intended purpose of preventing a destabilizing "defensive" arms race that might cause Washington and
Moscow to doubt the reliability of their retaliatory nuclear capability and undermine the assurances of mutually assured destruction. But the prospect of Iranian and North Korean nuclear
weapons coupled to strategic missile systems prompted Washington to rethink this approach. Fanatics in Teheran and Pyongyang
might not be deterred the way the Soviets had been. Americans
needed national missile defense as an added layer of protection in
case deterrence failed. To deploy such a system, the ABM Treaty
had to go. American officials discussed the move with the Russians
well in advance of the announcement, and together they carefully
orchestrated the public rollout and Moscow's response. Putin said
that the Bush administration had been clear about its intentions
and had not deceived him. Still, Moscow called the decision "a
mistake," and viewed the withdrawal as a sign that Washington
"had put Russia in its place" and would push ahead with its plans
irrespective of Moscow's views.[78] Privately, the Russians suspected that US missile defense was aimed more at weakening Russia's second-strike capability than countering prospective missile
launches from North Korea and Iran.[79] How could Moscow be
sure its nuclear forces would deter a Kosovo-style intervention by

NATO inside Russia if US missile defenses changed the strategic equation?

The timing of Bush's ABM announcement, coming on the heels of the first major victories over the Taliban and al-Qaeda in Afghanistan, also stoked broader Russian suspicions that Washington would exploit Russian help when it wanted but reject Moscow's input on key issues when it clashed with American preferences.[80] Foreign Minister Ivanov hinted at Russian concerns in a *New York Times* op-ed in January 2002, "Organizing the World to Fight Terror," in which he called for "constructing a system of international security adequate to address 21st-century threats." Russian-American cooperation should play a decisive role in creating that system, he said, but "such cooperation can be effective only if it is based on the principles of equality."[81]

Less than four months after the events of September 11, however, Russian doubts about whether Washington shared that vision were growing. Putin's advisers had warned him that facilitating the establishment of US bases in Central Asia would lead to a long-term American military presence in Russia's southern neighbors.[82] He had pressed for and received assurances from Washington that these bases would be temporary, tied to progress in the Afghan war. But as the Taliban's defeat was growing clearer, the American presence was looking more rather than less permanent to Moscow. Why, Russian officials asked, was America fortifying its allegedly temporary military bases in Central Asia? American officials explained that *temporary* did not necessarily mean *short-term*. The United States wanted access to the bases "for as long as we need them," which was undefined and could be for a long period.[83] Russian fears flared that US and NATO forces were starting to encircle Russia's borders.[84]

Those fears deepened further in November 2002 in response to NATO's summit meeting in Prague, where the alliance announced that it would undertake a second round of enlargement and invite Lithuania, Latvia, Estonia, Romania, Bulgaria, Slovakia, and Slovenia to join in 2004. In inviting the Baltic states, the alliance was for the first time offering membership to ex-Soviet republics. Much like its reaction to the American withdrawal from the ABM Treaty, Russia muted its public response to the announcement. But below the surface, Russian consternation was clear. Enlargement seemed to be driven by the oft-articulated American vision of "Europe whole and free," and it was not evident to Moscow where the alliance's eastward momentum would stop. Dmitry Suslov, a foreign policy expert at the Moscow State Institute of International Relations (MGIMO), observes that NATO expansion was not simply a military threat: "For Moscow, NATO expansion symbolized that the US was treating Russia as the Cold War loser rather than its second winner. Instead of building a new security order in Europe with Russia as a codesigner, the US was just institutionalizing its own 'victory.'"[85]

American power could be an asset for Russia when it could bandwagon on Washington's international clout to bolster Moscow's own prominence, and when it could exploit US military capabilities to tackle security threats that Russia could not handle alone, as in Afghanistan. But that power could pose big problems for Moscow when misdirected. For Russia, the US intervention in Iraq in the spring of 2003 was just such a misdirection, aimed at enhancing the US geopolitical position rather than at addressing a legitimate security challenge. "Putin and his intelligence officials knew that Iraqi leader Saddam Hussein was bluffing about his possession of chemical and other weapons of mass destruction (WMD). Indeed, they stated this bluntly to US officials on numerous occasions."[86] For Moscow, the Iraq War was a disturbing manifestation of what later became known as the Bush administration's Freedom Agenda—to "support the growth of democratic movements and institutions in every nation and culture, with the ultimate goal of ending tyranny in our world."[87] Through Russian eyes, this agenda appeared both destabilizing and cynical. In removing functioning, albeit authoritarian, governments, Washington risked losing any semblance of governance whatsoever and producing chaos. Russian officials warned against such a result in Iraq, only to be dismissed by their American counterparts. And tellingly, Americans only seemed to push for regime change in countries that provided geostrategic advantages against Russia, rather than in dictatorial US friends like Saudi Arabia. This suggested to Moscow that Washington's true motive was not advancing democracy but bolstering US global hegemony. The Iraq War, together with America's ABM withdrawal and the second round of NATO enlargement, convinced Russians that the United States was a difficult partner, prone to creating instability through mistaken policies and incompetent intelligence, reluctant to listen to the cautionary advice of others, and unwilling to view Moscow as a partner worthy of respect.

Russian views continued to darken as new developments unfolded. Four closely packed events in late 2003 and 2004 combined cumulatively to push Moscow's perceptions across an important threshold: the belief that Washington was not just a troublesome partner but was actively seeking to weaken Russia and overthrow its government. The first took place, oddly enough, in Moldova, one of the poorest countries in Europe, landlocked and located far from anything Europeans or Americans would consider important. The western (culturally and linguistically Romanian) and eastern (Slavic and Russian-speaking) portions of the ex-Soviet republic had been locked in a frozen conflict since 1992, when the eastern portion had declared its independence as "Transnistria." Transnistrians feared that the central Moldovan government planned to reunite with Romania, and they sought protection against this eventuality by separating from Moldova and seeking the help of Russian military forces that had been stationed in the region since Soviet times. A joint peacekeeping force comprising Russian, Moldovan, and Transnistrian units, monitored by an observer mission from the Conference on Security and Cooperation in Europe (CSCE), effectively ended the fighting.[88]

Nonetheless, little progress had been made in resolving the broader dispute until the fall of 2003, when Russia achieved a breakthrough. One of Putin's close Kremlin aides, Dmitry Kozak, succeeded in persuading Moldovan president Voronin and Transnistrian leader Smirnov to settle the conflict by reunifying Moldova as a federation under what became known as the Kozak Memorandum. The two leaders scheduled a signing ceremony for the accord, and Putin indicated that he would attend amid considerable pomp and circumstance. But when the Moldovan government notified the United States and asked for Washington's support shortly before the signing, American diplomats refused, complaining that they had not been consulted, arguing that the plan would provide Transnistria with too much leverage over Moldovan policy decisions, and objecting to an unpublished provision that allowed for a small Russian military presence in Transnistria. US objections were quickly followed by street protests against the plan. Voronin backed away on the eve of the ceremony, and a chagrined Putin called off his travel at the last minute.[89] Russian officials concluded bitterly that Washington viewed its interests as so far-reaching that "even the most distant and strategically marginal areas in the post-Soviet space" should be subject to American hegemony.[90] What did it say about American intentions that eradicating Russian influence in lowly Moldova was so important? In this context, how could Moscow trust American assurances that NATO expansion was not directed against Russia?

The second event occurred only weeks later in Georgia, a

country that bridges the oil-rich Caspian basin and Russia's vola-tile North Caucasus. Georgia's relations with Moscow had long been problematic. Ethnic separatists in Georgia's breakaway re-gions of South Ossetia and Abkhazia, persecuted under Geor-gia's first post-Soviet leader, Zviad Gamsakhurdia, had for years counted on Moscow for protection, angering Tbilisi. In turn, former Soviet foreign minister Eduard Shevardnadze, who had ruled Georgia since 1992, looked to US and European support as a counterweight to Russia, riling Moscow. In the late 1990s and early 2000s, Chechen fighters had used Georgia's Pankisi Gorge as a refuge from which to launch attacks in Russia, and Moscow accused Tbilisi of aiding and abetting their activities. In 2002, the United States began training, equipping, and modernizing the Georgian military for counterterrorism operations, in part to re-duce the likelihood that Russia would take action of its own in the Pankisi.

Against this backdrop of tension, Georgia held legislative elec-tions in early November 2003. The elections pitted government loyalists under the increasingly unpopular Shevardnadze against self-proclaimed liberals playing upon the public's growing un-happiness with bureaucratic corruption. Official results indicated that Shevardnadze's ruling party had won, but opposition groups alleged massive fraud in the vote tabulation. Citing independent exit polls conducted by US-trained and -funded nongovern-ment organizations, Mikheil Saakashvili, an American-educated former Georgian official who had gone into political exile after a falling out with Shevardnadze, claimed that his party had won the election. Rallying around Saakashvili's claims, massive anti-government demonstrations erupted in Georgia's major cities, inspired and organized by an American-backed youth movement. On November 22, when Shevardnadze attempted to open the new session of the parliament, Saakashvili and other protestors burst in holding roses in their hands. Shevardnadze fled the building and resigned the next day. A presidential election was quickly scheduled for January 2004, and Saakashvili won an overwhelming 96 percent of the vote, promising in the course of his short campaign to impose Tbilisi's writ on Georgia's separatist regions. The "Rose Revolution" had triumphed.

Moscow viewed Shevardnadze's departure with ambivalence. Russians shed few tears for a man who had nudged along the Soviet Union's collapse and who had long been a thorn in Russia's side while governing Georgia. But they looked askance as Saakashvili quickly became the darling of Washington, drawing upon his fluent English and extensive roster of high-level contacts to press Georgia's case for joining NATO and the EU. Suspicion spread in Moscow that the Rose Revolution was no accident, that behind the scenes, American democracy-builders and intelligence officers had carefully trained and funded Georgia's opposition for just such a moment. Through Russian eyes, Washington's undisguised glee over the revolution was not mere jubilation over the advance of democracy; it reflected an important strategic advance in checking Russia's influence in its former empire.

The third event took place in Beslan, a town in Russia's North Caucasus, where a small group of heavily armed Chechen and Ingush terrorists seized control of an elementary school on the first day of classes in September 2004 and held nearly 1,200 children, parents, and teachers hostage for three days. Russian forces finally stormed the school and killed the terrorists, but the assault resulted in the deaths of 332 people, including 186 children. The incident was emotionally and politically wrenching. The nation watched the tragedy unfold in real time. Putin had made anti-terrorism a central theme of his domestic and foreign policies, but it now appeared that all his efforts had fallen short. He addressed the nation mournfully, hours after the bloody rescue operation, articulating some bitter lessons.

> We have to admit that we failed to recognize the complexity and danger of the processes going on in our own country and the world as a whole. At any rate, we failed to react to them adequately. We demonstrated weakness, and the weak are beaten. Some want to tear off a big chunk of our country. Others help them to do it. They help because they think that Russia, as one of the greatest nuclear powers of the world, is still a threat, and this threat has to be eliminated. And terrorism is only an instrument to achieve these goals. In these conditions, we simply cannot, we should not, live as carelessly as before. We must create a more effective security system, and demand from our law enforcement agencies actions adequate in level and scale to the new threats.[91]

One target of that more effective security system would be the United States. Putin had all but expressly pointed his finger at Washington for abetting terrorism. Russians bristled at the fact that Chechen government-in-exile officials were living openly in the United States and that some private American organizations supported and funded the Chechen rebellion. Imagine, they asked, how Americans would feel if Moscow allowed al-Qaeda members to live and raise funds in Russia?[92] Gleb Pavlovsky, a Kremlin consultant at the time, claims that "Bush did not fully control his secret services, or he did not think he needed to fully control [them], so in the Caucasus, American intelligence services had been sometimes helping the Chechens. Putin certainly thought that this came at Bush's order, and that Bush was a hypocrite."[93] Unofficial American support for the Chechen cause, Russian intelligence allegations of US meddling in the Caucasus, and the strong emotions attending the Beslan tragedy proved to be a toxic mix for Russian perceptions of the United States.

A handful of months after the Beslan attack, Ukraine plunged into a political crisis. Moscow regarded Ukraine as its top foreign policy priority. The largest country in Europe, Ukraine had deep historical and cultural ties to Russia, and it housed pipelines that delivered some 80 percent of Russia's gas exports to Europe, accounting for almost a quarter of Russia's overall state revenues. As NATO and the EU moved eastward, however, Ukraine's geopolitical orientation was very much up in the air. Western portions of the country were largely Ukrainian-speaking, predominantly Catholic, and favorably oriented toward Europe and the United States. The country's eastern regions were dominated by Russophones, primarily Russian Orthodox, well disposed toward Moscow. The Crimean peninsula, where the Russians leased a base hosting their Black Sea Fleet, had been officially part of the USSR's Russian republic until 1954, when Soviet leader Khrushchev had gifted it to the Ukrainian republic, and it had long been a part of the Russian Empire before Soviet times. Each of Ukraine's presidential elections since post-Soviet independence in 1992 had been closely contested races pivoting on turnout in the eastern and western regions. In the fall of 2004, the election pitted a dynamic pro-European reformer from the west, Viktor Yushchenko, against Viktor Yanukovych, the lumbering hardscrabble governor of the Donetsk region in the east.

In view of the high stakes in the election, Putin opted for a hands-on approach. A flood of Russian experts and money poured into Kiev to help the Yanukovych campaign, Russian television blanketed the Ukrainian airwaves with pro-Yanukovych advertising and news coverage, and Putin himself (who at the time ranked as the most popular politician in Ukrainian opinion polls) visited

Ukraine seven times during the campaign and explicitly endorsed Yanukovych, campaigning with him on the eve of the election. On election day in November 2004, the efforts appeared to pay off in a narrow Yanukovych victory. But exit polls and parallel vote counts by American-trained and -funded nongovernmental organizations indicated that the official results had been falsified. Thousands of orange-clad protestors occupied Kiev's central square, demanding that elections be rerun. Secretary of State Colin Powell announced that the United States "cannot accept the Ukrainian election as legitimate."[94] After weeks of protest-fueled political turbulence, the Supreme Court of Ukraine declared the election null and void. A new election was held on December 26, and Yushchenko emerged as the clear winner. Washington rejoiced. Ukraine's "Orange Revolution" had triumphed, apparently setting the country on a Westward trajectory.

For Putin, the Orange Revolution could only have happened with outside orchestration. As in the Rose Revolution several months earlier, American-trained and -funded nongovernmental organizations had played a pivotal role in the outcome. Washington had been working to bolster Ukrainian independence from Russia since early in the Clinton administration, making Kiev the third-largest recipient of American foreign aid after Israel and Egypt.[95] From the Kremlin's perspective, Ukraine and Russia had essentially been one country, ruled from Moscow, for almost the entire time that the United States had been a nation. Their union had not affected America's security. What did it say about US intentions toward Russia that Washington now devoted such effort to driving a wedge between them? It could mean only one thing: the United States aimed to surround Russia with NATO-allied puppets, imperil Russia's vital trade links to the outside world, and ultimately foment regime change in Moscow itself. Russian foreign affairs expert Vladimir Frolov summed up Russia's concerns about the Orange Revolution shortly after the events in Ukraine:

> Elections in the CIS countries are turning from an instrument of the people's will into a convenient pretext for outside multilateral interference. This new environment is aimed at creating international legal conditions for changing a regime by challenging election results, claiming as illegitimate the existing constitutional procedures and provoking an acute political crisis. As a rule, the crisis either turns into a "color" revolution, that is, an unconstitutional change of power through a coup that is automatically recognized by the "international community," or else it leads to long-lasting political destabilization that is controlled from outside and which ultimately paralyzes the legally elected power.[96]

If such an approach could topple the government in Ukraine, it could do the same thing in Russia. By early 2005, Russia's belief that the United States posed an existential threat was fully formed. At the same time, rising oil prices, China's escalating power, and signs of friction within the Western alliance suggested to Moscow that the unipolar world was becoming multipolar and that Russia had broader strategic options than hitching its wagon to a duplicitous Washington. Putin changed course, using engagement with Washington not as a promising path toward great-power status but as a means of influencing America's exercise of power in areas important to Russian interests. He stepped up Russia's courtship of China and other non-Western powers. More strikingly, he battened down the hatches inside Russia, cracking down on NGOs and American democratization programs while launching new initiatives designed to thwart nascent opposition movements, hoping to reduce Russia's vulnerability to meddling.

The Kremlin decided that now the [US had] found a way how to get people to the streets without trade unions, without opposition parties, just building some youth movement very quickly out of scratch. And they thought, look, we need to do something about it. And they came up with their own ideas. They launched their own pro-Kremlin youth movements to have someone to send to the streets, to counter [the] threat of color revolutions. They turned to informal actors. They turned to some people who officially are not part of the government, but they enjoy direct access to the Kremlin, and these people [were] tasked to deal with the new threat. That was a moment when we got these trolls, troll factories, lots of people who started contaminating the space of public debate.[97]

Subsequent events over the course of the next decade only served to turn Russia's belief about hostile US intentions into an unshakable and widely held conviction: the West's recognition of Kosovo's independence over Moscow's objections in 2008, the US emergency airlift of Georgian troops serving in Iraq to fight against Russians in their war later that year, America's support for violent regime change in Libya in 2011, Washington's undisguised sympathy for massive street protests in Russia in 2011 and 2012, and American backing for what Moscow called a "coup d'état," displacing Ukraine's president with a pro-NATO leadership in 2014.

Putin dramatically articulated these perceptions in a speech delivered in 2007 at the annual Munich Security Conference, in which he bitterly criticized American unilateralism and illegitimate interference in the sovereign affairs of other states.[98] Washington had repeatedly betrayed Russia, first by expanding NATO despite assurances to Gorbachev that it would not, and later by establishing permanent bases in Central Asia that it pledged would be temporary, all the while fighting against Russian influence despite purporting to be a strategic partner. The United States clearly could not be trusted. It wanted to weaken Russia and overthrow its government; the only question was how best to defend the country against this formidable foe. For Moscow, the best defense included a good offense.

THE REALITY GAP

How accurate are these mutual fears of existential threat? Does Russia really hope to hasten America's demise by fatally undermining its democracy and provoking internal conflict? Does Washington actually intend to encircle Russia with NATO forces and foment regime change, ultimately breaking Russia into pieces? It is difficult to tackle subjective perceptions in an objective way, to juxtapose feelings and opinions to concrete realities. But one sign that there is a gap between these perceptions and reality is the derision with which each side regards the perceptions of the other. Each dismisses the other's fears as mistaken at best, if not completely disingenuous. Each believes its intentions are misperceived.

Americans generally find Russian accusations that we have intentionally sought to ring Russia's borders with NATO allies and US military bases to be risible. Americans are of course aware that Russia has objected to NATO's eastward enlargement, but they tend to regard Russian concerns as exaggerations, frequently using the word *paranoia* in their discourse on the subject. *Washington Post* columnist Anne Applebaum discounts Russian fears of NATO expansion altogether. "There is no way that Putin believed that NATO was a genuine military threat," she states. "This is propaganda he has been using at home as a way to consolidate his power."[99] A former US ambassador takes a similar view. "NATO is good for Russia. NATO maintains stability on Russia's west, and that allows Russia to focus its attention on other places. As much as they complain about NATO, there's no threat that Poland is going to invade Russia, and they know that. I mean, they may not admit that, but deep down they know that." Others take a more nuanced view, accepting Moscow's fears as genuinely felt, but rejecting the notion that the United States and NATO have been implementing a master plan to encircle and weaken Russia. From the start, "NATO enlargement was driven by demand, not supply," according to another former State Department official.[100] The aspirant members sought NATO, not the other way around. And the alliance's objectives were, in fact, not aimed at hurting Russia. "Enlargement served Wilsonian goals of democracy promotion in central and eastern Europe, which was not detrimental but actually beneficial to Russia's long-term interests," according to Michael McFaul and James Goldgeier, a former Clinton administration official.

Americans are similarly dismissive of Russian claims that the United States is cynically employing democratization programs to foment regime change in and around Russia. Former CIA acting director Michael Morell denies the Russian accusation point-blank: "Russian president Putin believes that the United States was behind the protests in the streets of Kiev that began the Russia-Ukraine crisis. That is not true."[101] A former senior State Department official notes wryly, "Were the CIA half as effective as [Putin] seems to think, we'd run the world. In the Maidan revolution, at one point there were estimates of 300,000 to 700,000 people on the streets of Kiev, a city of less than 3 million. You don't organize that from outside."[102] A former Bush White House official relates that Putin "thought we were the puppet masters. Like, man, we are not that good. I even told Russian television once, when they were accusing me personally of being the 'gray cardinal' of the color revolutions, I said: 'I wish. How come you see America with a massive budget being unable to do anything much, to stop the political deterioration and security deterioration in Iraq, and you think, on no budget at all, we can overthrow Moscow-supported governments in Kiev and Tbilisi?' Are you kidding me?"[103]

Along similar lines, McFaul describes President Obama's unsuccessful efforts to dissuade Putin's belief that the United States was driving regime change in the Middle East and along Russia's periphery. "The president explained to him, he said, 'Look, we're not behind this. I'm not a regime-change guy. We are responding to these events, and in our view, we're better to engage, to try to push these things toward peaceful evolutionary change, because if we don't, they'll end up as violent revolutionary change.'"[104] America's advocates of Wilsonian democracy promotion candidly acknowledge that they have supported democratization in and around Russia, but they aver that, far from seeking Russia's demise, they have long envisioned a strong, prosperous, and well-governed Russia. "We believed close ties between Russia and the West would make both Russia and the West better off."[105] This belief, which contrasts so strongly with Russia's perceptions of American intent, reflects a strong general American tendency "to assume that the exercise of US power in places less enlightened than America means the betterment of those places and the people who live there."[106]

For their part, Russians are dismissive of American accusations that they seek to undermine democracy and fatally subvert the United States. The term *Russophobia* appears in Russian discourse about American perceptions nearly as often as *paranoia* occurs in US analysis of Russian views.[107] Even Putin detractors in Russia and in Russian émigré communities in the West claim not to recognize their country in American media descriptions of Russia's objectives. "Anything they publish about Russia is, as a general rule, total garbage," wrote Oleg Kashin, an opposition journalist, in 2017. "The image of Putin's Russia constructed by

Western and, above all, American media outlets over the past 18 months shocks even the most anti-Putin reader in Russia. . . . They flood [us] with a wave of accusations [that] sounds like a joke warranting no response except for a laugh of derision."[108] Maxim Trudolyubov, another Russian journalist who is a Putin skeptic, doubts US allegations that Russia is fighting a global battle against democracy. "What this hype is really doing is elevating the Kremlin to the position of the world's meddler in chief by reading a coherent strategy into isolated and disparate trolling and propaganda efforts by various Russian institutions and individuals. I am an agnostic as to whether a strategy aimed at undermining democracies all over the world exists. Everything I know about how Russia and its government work makes me doubt it."[109] Andranik Migranyan, a senior Russian foreign policy expert and a Putin supporter, similarly disparages the notion that Russia is fighting against democracy in the Middle East and other regions: "Only a blind man would not see that Russia and its diplomats are fixated not on preserving dictatorship, but on observing principles. Russia is aware that regime change could result in chaos and anarchy, as was the case in Iraq and Libya. More often than not, the road to hell is paved with good intentions."[110]

Dmitry Suslov, one of Russia's leading experts on the United States and Europe, calls allegations that Moscow seeks to stamp out democracy in the United States and beyond "completely bizarre."[111] Russia has strong relations, he points out, with Israel, India, and Japan, all of which are developed democracies, none of which has alleged any Russian interference in its internal affairs. Moreover, Russians scoff at the notion that they hope to crush democracy in such countries as Ukraine and Georgia. They do not regard the polities in Ukraine and Georgia, long plagued by cronyism and corruption, as democratic or on a path toward democracy, according to Suslov. Russians reason, therefore, that the appeal of these countries for Washington must lie not in their illusory democratic progress but in their willingness to subordinate themselves to the United States and serve as bulwarks against Russia. Russians are similarly dismissive of the argument that the Russian regime requires an external enemy—the United States—to justify internal repression. Dmitri Trenin, the director of the Carnegie Moscow Center, points out that during the era of Russian-Western cooperation, "the Kremlin was using good relations with the West to legitimize its rule. The Kremlin can thrive politically on both good and bad relations with the West."[112]

Given the pivotal role of Russian interference in the 2016 US presidential elections in shaping American perceptions of Russia as an existential threat, it is important to examine Russia's own perceptions of the motives behind those activities. Many Russians (though not the Russian government) candidly acknowledge the election interference, although most believe that Americans have overreacted to it, largely for domestic political reasons. "Yes, of course Russia has interfered in the internal affairs of the US and other Western countries, if you call the Facebook and Twitter campaigns and Russia Today broadcasts and so on interference," according to Suslov. "But the purpose of this interference is not to destroy or undermine Western democracy. This purpose is to send a message that the West is not immune when it interferes in Russia, when it supports regime change policies all over the Middle East."[113] Frolov makes similar points:

It is unlikely that the Kremlin really hoped to influence the results of the US presidential election or viewed Trump's victory as likely. That would have signaled a degree of incompetence that Moscow is still incapable of. Rather, the point of the exercise was to send a message that Russia mattered and could do bad things that the US, in Moscow's view, has been doing to Russia. It worked, but not exactly how Russia had hoped.[114]

Foreign Minister Sergey Lavrov, while not acknowledging election interference, hints that Moscow is looking for a change in America's approach to encouraging democratization around the world. "The founding fathers of the United States, they also spoke of their leadership, and they believed that the American nation was exceptional, but they wanted others just to take the American experience as an example and to follow suit. They never suggested that the United States should impose, including by force, its values on others."[115] In other words, contrary to American perceptions, Russians say they are reacting to what we do and how we do it, not to what we are.

Significantly, Russians largely disagree with the consensus American view that the interference was an unmitigated success—that, as Clapper puts it, "the Russians succeeded beyond their wildest expectations."[116] Many have been happy to see Washington get what they regard as a well-deserved comeuppance, and some are pleased that Russia matters to the United States in ways that it had not since the Cold War, even if negatively. Being feared is preferable, in many ways, to being ignored or disrespected. But very few believe that American disarray serves Russian interests. Frolov criticizes the Kremlin for "refusing to discuss with the US what soured our relations and blaming everything on the long-gone Obama administration," but he says that Russian officials have bemoaned, not celebrated, America's reaction to the election interference. "'Russian meddling' has become a snowball in the US. Now that it's been released, it's been rolling downhill, destroying everything in its path, including Russian foreign policy interests."[117] He explains, "Détente with America was a necessary condition for transitioning to a peaceful domestic development agenda [inside Russia]. Now it seems to have been postponed indefinitely. It's the sense of a historical impasse that is driving the panic [in Moscow]."[118]

Suslov claims that the American belief that Moscow is celebrating the success of its election interference campaign is "misperceiving the real Russian attitude. Russia did not anticipate such a great and negative backlash for US-Russian relations. 'Russiagate' has consolidated an anti-Russia consensus in the United States. It has doomed us to a long-term continuation of this confrontation. This is absolutely not what Russia wanted."[119] He argues that if Hillary Clinton had won the election, as Moscow expected, there would have been considerably less furor about Russia's activities. And if Moscow's goal was to demonstrate that American elections are charades, stage-managed by entrenched elites, it could hardly have been cheered by the outcome. As Kirill Martynov observed in the Russian opposition newspaper *Novaya Gazeta*, "For a year, 90% of US media outlets claimed that Trump was the spawn of the devil, and that his election would be catastrophic for the country. However, voters decided otherwise. Therefore, this destroys the notion that democracy is a mere spectacle put on by the elite to serve their interests."[120] All this suggests that Russia's election interference, if it was indeed the result of a conscious Kremlin strategy and not the product of uncoordinated steps taken at lower levels, flowed from a significant misestimation of the likely American response.

Another way to compare perception and reality is to explore whether there are instances of Russian and American behavior that are inconsistent with each side's purported intentions. Are there examples of American policies that contradict the belief that the United States is fomenting color revolutions to advance its global

hegemony and topple adversary regimes? Are there important instances in which Russia has not fought against democratic movements in geostrategically significant regions? In both cases, the
answer is yes. Washington's reaction to the protest movement in
Egypt in 2011 is an example not of American officials' mastermind-
ing regime change to outmaneuver an adversary nation but rather
struggling to keep pace with an unanticipated popular uprising in
an important ally. The US decision to press President Mubarak
to step down amid growing protests and to insist on legitimate
national elections—paving the way to the electoral success of the
anti-Western Muslim Brotherhood—could hardly be described as
a cynical effort to advance American hegemony. In many ways, it
proved to be a setback for US influence in the region and strongly
suggests that US officials were guided much more by a genuine
belief in the principles of democracy than by hegemonic aspirations as they attempted to navigate a messy and complex situation.

Similarly, Russia's response to the color revolution in Armenia
in 2018 suggests that it does not object to democratic movements
or popular protests per se but rather to the rise of anti-Russian
governments on its periphery, and particularly to those intent
on joining NATO. In May of that year, Armenian prime minister Serzh Sargsyan resigned after more than a week of fist-
pounding mass protests reminiscent of the uprisings in Georgia
and Ukraine. Simon Saradzhyan, a Harvard-based expert who has
closely followed Russian-Armenian relations, explains that Armenia rated at the time as more democratic than Russia, had friendly
relations with the West, had recently signed an EU Association
Agreement, participated in NATO's Partnership for Peace program, and had troops in the NATO-led campaign in Afghanistan. Had Russia sought reasons for worry, it would not have
been difficult to find them. But Moscow neither intervened in
Armenia nor displayed particular concern about the implications

of the political instability for Russia's national security. Why? Because Armenia's leadership evinced no ambition to join NATO, and its elites showed little antagonism toward Moscow.[121]

If they are to some degree distortions, what is the significance of these perceptions of deadly intent in Moscow and Washington? Despite deep mistrust and suspicion, neither side truly expects an imminent nuclear or conventional military attack designed to destroy the other. The stakes are too great, and the odds of success are too long, for anyone to contemplate such a suicidal course. But these perceptions nonetheless make unplanned disaster more likely. For one thing, when each side believes the essence of the threat derives from the very nature of the other side, which cannot change, there is little incentive to seek compromise. Indeed, aiming for a negotiated settlement is seen as dangerous appeasement. Such efforts are viewed as "worse than useless; they contribute to weakening of national will and reduce a country's readiness to win the inevitable conflict when it finally comes. By this logic, it seems more prudent and certainly more politically advantageous to abandon any effort to avoid that conflict."[122]

More ominously, these perceptions are reinforcing each other in a vicious cycle of interaction. They shape the narratives that determine how events are interpreted, and they provide the cognitive filters that determine which facts are salient and which are disregarded. This in turn drives statements and actions that reinforce the threat perceptions on each side and heighten each side's sense of vulnerability. Russia's great power aspirations fuel American concerns about imperialism, which strengthens US support for building West-leaning bulwarks against Russia's influence along the country's periphery. This stokes fears in Russia of hostile encirclement and regime change, which encourages Russian aggression in neighboring states and internal crackdowns on media and opposition groups, further convincing Americans that the Kremlin has imperial designs and sees democracy as an ideological foe. Russia tries to cool America's ardor for democratization crusades by cybermeddling, which the United States interprets as an existential threat and responds with punitive economic sanctions and stepped-up cyberactivity of its own, all meant to deter further Russian meddling. This, however, only further convinces Moscow that Washington is accelerating its aggressive bid to weaken and destroy Russia.

Left unaddressed, this cycle of perception is likely to deepen, increasing the likelihood that the two sides will misinterpret the signals each sends in a crisis and overreact to the actions of the other side. When a state believes its very existence is at stake, its resolve and willingness to take risks in conflict or crisis situations run startlingly high. Failure to appreciate that resolve can have serious consequences, as Europe and the United States experienced in 2014 in underestimating Moscow's likely response to the Maidan uprising in Ukraine, and as Russians encountered in 2016 in failing to anticipate the ways America might react to election meddling. And when this strong resolve and high risk tolerance are overlaid against a background of increasingly unconstrained shadow warfare between two nuclear powers in the cyber, military, economic, and information domains, they assume disproportionately dangerous implications.

3

Brake Failure

The Cold War was a bitter, high-stakes affair, but for most of its duration, it was fought according to a set of rules. Some of these were formalized as treaties, as in the numerous arms control agreements that limited the numbers and types of weapons systems the United States and Soviet Union could have. Some were political rather than legal commitments, as in the Helsinki Final Act, in which the United States, Canada, European states, and Soviet Union settled on a security arrangement for a divided Europe and launched a series of confidence-building and risk-reduction measures aimed at minimizing the prospects of conflict on the continent. Others were informal and even unspoken, as in the implicit understanding between the CIA and KGB that they would not target each other's officers for kidnapping or assassination.[1] Throughout the Cold War, the sides maintained both official and unofficial lines of communication with each other, despite the fact that mutual suspicions ran high, to help avoid or manage crises.

The Cold War's rules of the game were not established out of any fondness between the two combatants, nor were they conceived by either side as rewards for good behavior. Neither country succumbed to the illusion that diplomacy would by itself bring peace by eliminating genuine conflicts of interest between Washington and Moscow. Rather, the rules were meant quite simply to protect the Cold War competition from spinning out of control and posing unacceptable danger to both sides and to the world. Their goal was, as one historian put it, "to impose order on uncertainty."[2] One of the biggest ways that today's shadow war differs from the Cold War is that it largely lacks formal or informal rules of the game that might mitigate its dangers. Nearly all the old rules that governed the Cold War have either disappeared or are in the late stages of demise, and new rules have not emerged to replace them. And in a game in which anything goes, we run significant risks that anything might in fact happen.

ARMS WITHOUT CONTROL

On December 25, 1991, the last day of the Soviet Union's nearly seventy-five-year history, the list of bilateral and multilateral arms control agreements that bound Washington and Moscow legally or politically was long and impressive. An entire class of particularly destabilizing strategic weapons, ground-launched intermediate-range missiles like the American Pershing II and Soviet SS-20, had been banned. NATO and the Warsaw Pact had formally capped the levels of conventional weaponry in Europe and begun the large-scale destruction of weapons exceeding those limits. Washington and Moscow had pledged in parallel to eliminate all nuclear artillery munitions, short-range nuclear missile warheads, and certain other forms of tactical nuclear weapons. Both governments had codified unprecedentedly intrusive systems of verification and on-site visits that allowed for direct inspection of military units and facilities. These agreements served simultaneously as constraints on weaponry, frameworks for the two sides to air and manage points of dispute in their military relations, and landmarks in a journey toward building and affirming trust that each side was more interested in enhancing stability than in gaining unilateral warfighting advantage. A little more than twenty-five years later, most of these agreements have died or are on life support.

The Anti-Ballistic Missile (ABM) Treaty was the first and most significant of these agreements to end. The United States and Soviet Union signed the treaty in 1972, and it limited each country to the deployment of only two national missile defense sites, later amended in 1974 to restrict each side to only one site. In the treaty's preamble, the signatories noted that strict limits on anti-missile systems would serve as a "substantial factor in curbing the race in strategic offensive arms." The reasoning behind the treaty was clear: if either side improved its capabilities to shoot down incoming strategic missiles or warheads, the other would automatically be incentivized to build new ways to overcome these defenses. It would become a vicious cycle of offensive and defensive one-upmanship, with advances on one side fueling countermeasures on the other, threatening the assurance of mutual destruction on which stability rested. The best way out of that spiraling competition would be to end the race to build strategic defensive systems. For thirty years, the ABM Treaty served as the foundation upon which all subsequent bilateral strategic arms agreements were erected.

In late 2001, that foundation cracked. The United States announced it would withdraw from the ABM Treaty for reasons that had little to do with Russian actions or with US intentions toward Moscow. Rather, the treaty became a casualty of America's lost confidence in its ability to deter emerging nuclear powers such as Iran and North Korea. These countries, Washington believed, were fanatical, willing to risk the prospect of American nuclear retaliation in the event they were to launch nuclear-tipped missiles at the United States or its allies. The clerical rulers in Tehran, many thought, viewed the prospect of nuclear war in much the same way that Middle Eastern suicide bombers viewed their self-demolitions: they might actually welcome an apocalyptic scenario that would hasten the ascent of Allah's faithful to heaven.[3] The North Koreans, though not religious, were seen as equally radical, prone to irrational risk-taking under the cover of a nuclear umbrella. By 2001, the United States had already started to build two national missile defense sites in California and Alaska to defend against North Korea, and it could not contend with emerging Iranian capabilities on the other side of Asia without deploying new sites in Europe. To allow this approach to missile defense, Washington reasoned that it had to withdraw from the treaty and remove restrictions on what the United States could deploy. Deterrence might fail, but missile defense would provide supplemental insurance against disaster.

Moscow did not share Washington's assessment of the threat or the solution. In Russian eyes, both North Korea and Iran were a long way from developing even a conventionally armed long-range missile capable of striking the United States or Europe, let alone a viable nuclear warhead to go with it. There were ample diplomatic options for dealing with Iran and North Korea, as Moscow saw it. If diplomacy failed, the testing of such missile capability would be obvious long before any deployment, providing adequate lead time for countermeasures should the threat materialize.[4] Furthermore, reasoned the Russians, neither North Korean nor Iranian leaders had a death wish; deterrence would work with Tehran and Pyongyang as well as it had with Maoist China, Pakistan, India, and other emergent nuclear powers.

The Russians also objected to US plans to position ballistic missile defense (BMD) facilities in Poland and the Czech

Republic—which, in their eyes, seemed suspicious. Poland, in particular, had a history of hostile relations with Russia, and Moscow viewed potential BMD deployments there through the prism of NATO expansion and the potential westward march of US military bases toward Russian borders. Russian defense experts worried the BMD systems could be pointed at Russia and that the interceptors would eventually pose a threat to Russia's second-strike capability, potentially creating a destabilizing situation in which the United States could threaten nuclear attack against Russia with little fear of retaliation. Moreover, Moscow suspected that the launchers for America's ground-launched interceptors could be quickly modified to launch offensive as well as defensive weapons at Russia.

The United States viewed Russian concerns as overblown. The systems were designed to defend Europe as well as the United States, and Europe lay directly in the over-the-pole flight path that Iran would use to attack North America, so basing them in Europe made sense. US experts explained that American interceptor technology could not cope with advanced Russian ICBMs and that the planned number of ground-based BMD interceptors fell far short of what would be required to pose a threat to Russia's vastly greater arsenal of missiles and warheads. The system could contend with a handful of less sophisticated Iranian weapons, but it could not launch offensive missiles without major modifications, and there was no threat whatsoever to Russia's large and sophisticated second-strike capability. Russia, however, remained skeptical. Recalling disputes over what the United States had pledged to Gorbachev about NATO's eastward expansion, the Russians insisted that oral assurances about the size and sophistication of the American system were not enough; a legally binding treaty that capped US BMD deployments was required. Washington refused, reluctant to tie its hands in response to changing Iranian and North Korean threats, and loath to risk the political uncertainties of a Senate ratification process.

Russia's efforts to build a broader strategic partnership with Washington were in full swing in 2002, prompting Moscow to soft-pedal its rhetoric about ABM withdrawal. In the wake of the American announcement, Putin called US withdrawal a mistake and cautioned calmly that Russia would have to take countermeasures. Washington mistook Russia's muted tones for grudging acceptance, but Russia was far from resigned about BMD deployments in Eastern Europe. In 2007, as US-Russian relations turned openly sour and the prospect of BMD deployments in Eastern Europe drew near, Putin dramatically compared them to the Soviet decision to station nuclear missiles in Cuba. Absent a change of course, he implied, such a military threat near Russia's borders could provoke a modern crisis between Washington and Moscow, just as the threat near US borders had in 1962.[5] In 2011, then Russian president Medvedev reiterated the message, warning that "if we don't work [an ABM compromise] out, then we'll have to respond with appropriate measures, which we would not like to do. In this case, we would talk about boosting the strike potential of our nuclear weapons, which would be a deplorable scenario that would take us back to the Cold War era."[6]

Despite efforts by both the Bush and Obama administrations to find such a compromise over ABM—including changing base plans to substitute Romania for the Czech Republic—none satisfied Moscow,[7] and the demise of the treaty produced a cascading effect on both Russian countermeasures and other arms control treaties. In the immediate aftermath of the American withdrawal from ABM, Moscow announced its withdrawal from the signed-but-not-implemented START II treaty, which banned the use of multiple independently targetable reentry vehicles (MIRVs) on intercontinental missiles.[8] Russia accelerated efforts to counter the impending US BMD deployments by quietly developing advanced new strategic weapons systems—including hypersonic weapons that travel at speeds greater than Mach 10 and are all but impossible to intercept—that were ultimately announced in public by Putin in 2018.[9] Moscow apparently also reevaluated its adherence to the Presidential Nuclear Initiatives (PNI) undertaken in 1991, under which both countries had pledged in parallel to reduce or eliminate a variety of tactical and short-range nuclear weapons. In 2004, without public acknowledgment, Russia began reequipping its submarines with tactical nuclear weapons that it had renounced under the PNI, and numerous reports indicated that it had long been stockpiling other short-range nuclear weapons in Kaliningrad despite its pledges.[10]

The Treaty on Conventional Armed Forces in Europe (CFE) fell victim to similarly changing international circumstances. Once regarded as the "cornerstone of European security," CFE was nearly two decades in intermittent negotiation between the NATO alliance and the Warsaw Pact, having started somewhat acrimoniously in the early 1970s under the banner of "Mutual and Balanced Force Reductions" (MBFR) in Europe and concluded much more harmoniously in late 1990 as a capstone of what Gorbachev then called "new thinking" in Soviet foreign policy. The treaty codified equal numbers of conventional weapons stationed on NATO and Warsaw Pact territory, apportioned that weaponry in a series of nested zones structured to minimize threatening concentrations of force, and required the withdrawal and destruction of tens of thousands of conventional weapons from the European theater. When the Warsaw Pact dissolved months after the CFE treaty was signed, later followed by the incorporation of several ex–Warsaw Pact members into NATO, the signatories launched a process of adapting the treaty to base its ceilings on national and territorial rather than group limits, turning what had been essentially a bilateral negotiation between two alliances into a multilateral negotiation among thirty states-parties. Despite the inherent difficulties of such an unwieldy negotiation, the adaptation process concluded in late 1999 with the signature of the Adapted Treaty on Conventional Armed Forces in Europe (ACFE).

The ACFE treaty was short-lived, however. In the treaty's negotiations, the United States and its NATO allies had emphasized the importance of a host nation's consent for any foreign forces based on its territory, in part out of general principle, and in part to manage the tendency of the treaty's smaller states to hold broader negotiations hostage to their particular interests. Russia had inherited several deployments of Soviet troops and weapons in other ex-Soviet republics, including in Georgia and Moldova, that the host states wanted removed. Because these erstwhile Soviet forces were located in contested parts of Georgia and Moldova that were agitating for independence or greater autonomy from their central governments, Moscow argued that it could not withdraw them absent political settlements of what had become "frozen conflicts" without significant risk that fighting would resume. Moreover, as negotiations on the adapted treaty were concluding, Russia had launched a second military operation in Chechnya following its unsuccessful first war in the breakaway republic from 1994 to 1996, which involved large-scale deployments of Russian forces in the southern portion of the treaty's geography—part of the so-called flank zone—that far exceeded the numbers permitted. Signature of the ACFE treaty was therefore based on a delicate compromise under which Russia acknowledged that it must withdraw forces from Georgia and Moldova and reduce its holdings in the "flank," and the United States and other Western states indicated that they would not submit the adapted treaty for ratification until Russia came into compliance with its terms.

The ACFE treaty never came into force. In 2002, Russia

indicated that it had come into compliance with the flank limits, and in 2007, it announced that the last Russian military base in Georgia was closing,[11] but NATO states still refused to begin ratification absent Russian withdrawal from contested parts of Moldova, which had stalled following the collapse of the Kozak Plan for a settlement in 2003. NATO's refusal was particularly vexing to Russia because the alliance had accepted several new members (including the Baltic states) who were not parties to the original treaty, were not subject to any limitations, and could not join until the adapted treaty was ratified and entered into force. In frustration, Moscow announced in late 2007 that it was "suspending" implementation of the CFE treaty and would no longer provide required military data and notifications, allow inspections, or consider itself bound by the treaty's limits. The Obama administration attempted in 2010 to develop a new framework to rescue the treaty regime, but the talks stalled, and the United States announced at the end of 2011 that it would no longer carry out "certain obligations" under the treaty. Russia's intervention in Ukraine since 2014 has involved the deployment of military forces along the Ukrainian border that would have been constrained, if not prevented, by CFE limitations had they been implemented.

Changing international circumstances also drove the demise of the Intermediate-Range Nuclear Forces (INF) Treaty. Signed by Washington and Moscow in 1987, INF eliminated an ominous threat that had hung over Europe since the late 1970s. The Soviet Union had created this threat by deploying nuclear-tipped SS-20 intermediate-range missiles to target US military facilities in Germany and other parts of Europe. This prompted Western fears that Moscow could gain what strategists call "escalation dominance" in a European crisis: the Soviets could target Europe with theater-based missiles, while the United States had no intermediate-range theater-based missiles with which to respond. As a result, Wash-

ington might face a difficult choice between using its intercontinental missiles in a regional military crisis (thereby risking what
was seen as near-certain Soviet retaliation against the US homeland) or conceding the USSR's objectives in Europe. Some Europeans feared that the United States would be reluctant to put its
own existence at risk to defend Europe, a scenario that strategists
termed "decoupling" of the United States and its NATO allies.
NATO responded to this worrisome possibility by deploying advanced US Pershing II intermediate-range missiles to Europe in
1983 while simultaneously calling for arms control negotiations
that would address the SS-20 threat and eliminate the need for the
new NATO deployments.

The Pershing IIs solved the decoupling problem by ensuring
that NATO had theater-based nuclear missiles that could respond
to Soviet military aggression in Europe. But at the same time,
they created a new strategic stability problem that put the US-
Soviet nuclear balance on a hair trigger. Combining high velocity
with high accuracy, the Pershing IIs could reach their targets in
the western USSR within ten minutes, and in contrast to the US-
based ICBMs that would fly long distances over the North Pole,
their shorter flight paths posed significant challenges for Soviet
early-warning radars. This prompted Soviet fears that the United
States had gained a legitimate first-strike capability that could—
with little to no warning—"de-capitate" Moscow's political and
military leadership and cripple its retaliatory capability.[12] As one
American official put it, the Pershing IIs could hit Soviet leaders "before they got up from their sofas, let alone made it to their
command bunkers." The Soviets insisted that the new threat ne-
cessitated a "launch on warning" policy that still left little time in
which to get that warning and initiate retaliatory strikes. The INF
Treaty turned the page on this precarious situation by banning
ballistic missiles and ground-launched cruise missiles with ranges

between 500 and 5,500 kilometers and by—for the first time in the history of US-Soviet arms control—instituting a rigorous system of on-site verification of compliance.

The INF Treaty was well suited to a bipolar world in which the two superpowers were seeking strategic predictability and building mutual trust. It became increasingly inconvenient, however, in an emerging multipolar world in which China, India, and other non-signatories of INF were deploying unlimited numbers of intermediate-range missiles of growing sophistication. Moscow complained publicly in 2007 that China's expanding intermediate-range missile force posed a military threat that Russia could not easily counter under INF's restrictions, and Russia's defense minister told his American counterpart that Russia wanted to withdraw from the treaty and deploy intermediate-range missiles in Russia's south and east to counter Iran, Pakistan, and China.[13] And once it became clear that US BMD deployments were advancing during Obama's second term, the Russians proceeded with testing and—in 2014—deploying ground-launched cruise missiles that the US claimed were banned under INF and could both target American anti-missile batteries in Poland and Romania and ultimately deal with the Chinese threat if needed. As growing Chinese power posed greater problems for the United States and the prospects of direct military conflict loomed larger, the lack of land-based intermediate-range missiles became increasingly problematic for Washington. Launching intercontinental ballistic missiles from the US mainland over the North Pole toward China raised a vexing problem: in a war scenario with Beijing, would the Russians accept US assurances that the incoming missiles were targeted at China and not Russia? Building intermediate-range missiles and basing them on Guam or Hawaii might mitigate that thorny problem. The combination of China's unconstrained forces and Russia's violations drove Washington to announce in late 2018 that it intended to withdraw from the treaty. Should Russia or the United States reintroduce once-banned IRBMs into the European theater, veiled allusions to a new version of the Cuban missile crisis could easily become reality.

The last remaining vestige of strategic arms control between Moscow and Washington is the New START Treaty, which entered into force in 2011 as the cornerstone of the Obama administration's "reset" of bilateral relations. New START accelerated the reduction in strategic nuclear weaponry that had begun under the START treaty in 1991—which reduced overall inventories of strategic nuclear warheads to 6,000—and continued in the Strategic Offensive Reductions Treaty (SORT) of 2002, which reduced the total number of such warheads to between 1,700 and 2,200. New START superseded START and SORT and reduced each side's inventory of strategic warheads to 1,550 while simultaneously capping the number of ICBMs, SLBMs (submarine-launched ballistic missiles), and heavy bombers each side could deploy at 700. Although New START did not ban MIRVs like the never-implemented START II accord, the treaty's low ratio between warheads and delivery vehicles disincentivized heavy reliance on MIRVs. In a nod to Russian concerns about American BMD, the treaty's preamble notes the "interrelationship between strategic offensive arms and strategic defensive arms" and bans the conversion of launchers for missile defense interceptors into ICBM or SLBM offensive launchers and vice versa (but not, because the INF treaty already banned them, into IRBM launchers). At US insistence, the preamble also states explicitly that "current strategic defensive arms do not undermine the viability and effectiveness of the strategic offensive arms of the Parties." New START's ten-year treaty period is due to expire in 2021. The treaty can be extended by mutual consent for an additional five years, and it is not clear at present whether New START will be extended.

•   •   •

In retrospect, the 1970s, '80s, and '90s were the golden age of arms control, an era that is now over. Both Russia and the United States have largely forsaken the search for strategic stability and predictability through bilateral arms control that characterized their approaches during détente and the early post–Cold War period. The rise of China and India, together with the addition of North Korea and potentially others to the circle of nuclear weapons states, has prompted many in Washington to regard bilateral arms control accords with Moscow as anachronistic, despite the reality that the United States and Russia control more than 90 percent of the world's inventory of nuclear weapons. As a result, the popular American belief that the threat of US-Russian nuclear exchanges is an unimaginable relic of the distant Cold War past is wildly out of step with the thinking of war planners in both Washington and Moscow. In 2018, the Bulletin of the Atomic Scientists moved its infamous Doomsday Clock forward by thirty seconds, to two minutes before midnight, representing the greatest risk of apocalypse since Stalin ruled the Soviet Union in 1953.[14]

Experts on each side now believe the other is building a force posture designed to fight and win a nuclear war, not because either side wants to fight one but because both fear they might otherwise be checkmated in a crisis scenario and have to concede the match. Pentagon planners fear that Moscow is building a force capable of preemptively seizing NATO territory in Europe and then "escalating to de-escalate" by using its superior battlefield nuclear weapons to settle the war on Russian terms, "gambling that going nuclear will intimidate the United States into backing down."[15] Russia in turn has condemned the 2018 *Nuclear Posture Review* for envisaging the development of low-yield nuclear weapons, which it said could lower the threshold for nuclear use. "We will interpret any use of nuclear weapons against Russia and its allies no matter how powerful they are, of low, medium or any other yield, as a nuclear attack," Putin cautioned in 2018. "It will trigger an immediate answer with all the consequences stemming from it. No one should have any doubts about it."[16]

As arms control regimes have crumbled, technology has advanced. Highly accurate long-range conventional weapons are allowing advanced militaries to carry out rapid nonnuclear strategic strikes around the world, narrowing the capabilities gap between nuclear and conventional weaponry. Cybertechnology has the potential to disable strategic command, control, communications, and warning systems before any bombs detonate. Advanced nuclear fuse technology is making warhead accuracy and lethality greater than ever, reducing the number of warheads needed to destroy enemy ICBMs.[17] The development of hypersonic weapons threatens to add to the pressure that national command authorities would be under in a crisis to make near instantaneous "launch on warning" decisions, while putting enormous burdens on automated early warning systems to eliminate false alarms. As a result, the demise of arms control will not set the clock back to the dark days of the early 1960s, when fears of a missile gap fueled an arms race, and the two superpowers came eyeball to eyeball over Berlin and Cuba. Rather, it will contribute to shaping a strategic weapons environment that in many ways is more complex, more unstable, and more lethal than at the Cold War's peak hostility.

POOR FENCES MAKE BAD NEIGHBORS

On November 19, 1990, as thirty-five heads of state and government from Europe and North America gathered to sign the Charter of Paris for a New Europe, the walls of their conference room could barely contain the brimming optimism. If, in retrospect, the Yalta Conference of 1945 had turned out to be the founding act of the Cold War, the gathering in Paris would serve as its peace conference, laying down the guidelines that would prevent future military conflict and end ideological warfare. The charter was many years in gestation, with origins in an ongoing process that had begun nearly twenty years prior at the Conference on Security and Cooperation in Europe (CSCE) in Helsinki, which aimed at managing and containing the rivalry between the US-led NATO alliance and the Soviet-led Warsaw Pact. By the end of 1990, however, it had become clear that the Cold War was over. The ideological dispute and military rivalry that had long divided the continent looked like relics of the past. The future promised a new Europe "whole and free," nestled within a trans-Atlantic community that embraced common Enlightenment values and extended from "Vancouver to Vladivostok."

Fewer than three decades since the Charter of Paris was signed, however, that vision has been shattered. The Paris Charter looks in hindsight to be less like the epochal Congress of Vienna, which produced a century of peace on the continent, and more like the ill-fated Treaty of Versailles, which provided a mere two-decade respite between World Wars I and II. Rather than having an integral role inside a new European security architecture, Russia finds itself "outside the tent pissing in," to borrow Lyndon Johnson's colorful metaphor.[18] As a result, Europe is once again on the brink of new divisions, with the political principles and rules that were enshrined at Cold War's end honored more in the breach than in the observance.

The United States had entered into the CSCE talks in 1973 with mixed feelings. Kremlin leaders had long been eager for the West to recognize post–World War II borders in Europe as permanent features of the regional political landscape, thereby alleviating concerns that NATO would challenge Soviet rule in Eastern Europe,[19] and they were similarly keen on revving up the sputtering Soviet economy through access to Western trade and technology. Conversely, the Nixon administration saw much domestic political downside in recognizing the permanence of the Iron Curtain dividing Europe and Germany, as well as many potential dangers in providing the Soviets with access to Western technology. But the United States was certainly interested in pursuing détente with Moscow, seeing it as a way to handle the simultaneous challenges of extracting the United States from its failing war in Vietnam, limiting the USSR's rapidly growing strategic nuclear arsenal, and gaining a breathing spell abroad to deal with growing political and social instability at home. The Nixon administration thus began talks with the Soviets about European security cautiously, wary of accepting the permanence of Communist rule in the East, while still intent on reducing tensions and minimizing the prospects that military and ideological competition might erupt into a hot war.

The result of those negotiations, the Helsinki Final Act signed by President Gerald Ford and thirty-four other heads of state and government in 1975, was a delicate compromise between each side's key objectives. In signing the accord, the West tacitly acknowledged post–World War II borders in Europe by enshrining the principles of territorial sovereignty and integrity, abjuring the use or threat of force against another state's political independence, and agreeing that borders may change only through peaceful means. The accord also launched what became a series of increasingly intrusive military confidence-building measures among the participating states, mitigating the dangers of war by requiring advance notification of major military maneuvers and exercises, coupled with on-site inspections to verify transparency. In return, the Soviets had to commit themselves to an array of parallel obligations in the areas of human rights, information sharing, and environmental protection standards. These included pledges by all participating states to endeavor "jointly and separately" to respect "freedom of thought, conscience, religion, or belief" and to ensure the right of all people to political self-determination.

Security, the Final Act asserted, was a seamless web shaped not only by traditional "hard security" measures in the external relations of states but also by the ways that governments treated their citizens, dealt with media, managed economies, and protected natural resources inside their borders. The Soviets got their long-desired rules to govern the competition among contending military blocs in Europe, but not without opening the door to rules applying to internal governance.

The Final Act was controversial in the United States. The Ford administration suffered severe criticism, as anti-communist Democrats joined with Republican hard-liners to oppose what they saw as US capitulation to Soviet rule in Eastern Europe.[20] In response to such attacks, Ford officials pointed to the liberal principles embedded in what became known in CSCE parlance as "baskets" in the human and economic dimensions of the Final Act. Washington may have agreed to a cease-fire in the wrangling over control of European territory, they argued, but it had not ceased to oppose the ways that communism ruled on its home turf. These arguments had little impact on détente's opponents, however, even though history ultimately proved them correct. In many ways, the seeds of the American neoconservative movement that later had so much influence during the George W. Bush administration were planted during this period.

Kremlin leaders rationalized their concessions in the human and economic dimensions of the CSCE. Like the American neo-conservatives, they viewed their gains in the security dimension as concrete, while regarding their commitments in the human and economic baskets as little more than empty words. But it turned out that Soviet leaders had badly underestimated the impact of their "soft security" concessions. Almost immediately after the Final Act's signature, independent Helsinki watch groups formed in the Soviet Union and most of its Warsaw Pact allies, and they proved to be stubbornly relentless activists despite prosecution and persecution from their home governments. These groups focused on publicizing failures to live up to Helsinki commitments in such areas as freedom of speech, assembly, and association. Much to the Kremlin's surprise, the human dimension obligations provided "a powerful tool to promote democratic change in the closed societies of the Soviet Bloc, from both within and outside."[21] Although CSCE norms indeed reduced the threat of bloc-to-bloc military conflict as Moscow had hoped, they also helped to fuel a new threat to stability from inside the confines of the Warsaw Pact.

With the end of the Cold War and the signing of the Charter of Paris, the Cold War tussles over principles to guide internal governance seemed to have ended. The Soviet Union had explicitly agreed that liberal principles should govern both the internal and external activities of governments, and the CSCE began to transition from a norm-setting forum aimed at reaching agreements that promoted mutual security into an operational organization—the Organization for Security and Cooperation in Europe (OSCE)—capable of direct involvement in settling conflicts, protecting minorities, monitoring elections, and ensuring human rights. Post–Cold War Europe provided abundant opportunities for action in all these areas. In the political and economic realms, Western states were eager to share their wisdom and provide hands-on assistance in helping the newly liberated East to create liberal democracies like the ones that had served the free world so well. In the security sphere, old historical grievances reignited and new separatist wars flared as authoritarian regimes transformed.

But unlike NATO and the EU, which could bring guns and money to the evolving process of creating a new European security architecture, the OSCE had neither military capabilities nor economic might to offer in dealing with Europe's changing challenges.

Its sole comparative advantage was that it was the only European security institution in which Russia was a member with full decision-making power. That distinction proved of little value when it came to wielding power and influence in the new Europe, where the name of the game quickly became promoting economic growth in the East, dealing with separatist conflicts in the Balkans and former Soviet Union, and preventing the spillover of regional instability. Despite Russian hopes to transform the OSCE into a collective security organization that might supersede NATO and turn the page on the old Cold War threat, the OSCE could not supply peacekeeping capabilities or coercive force to compel an end to Balkan conflicts, protect participating states from attack, or supply leverage in negotiated settlements. Nor could it offer the lure of reconstruction assistance or trade benefits to encourage good behavior.

As a result, NATO and the EU increasingly dominated the continent's security landscape, and the OSCE gradually settled into a niche role focusing on compliance with human dimension obligations and cooperative approaches to security, including confidence-building measures and monitoring missions—areas where Moscow frequently found itself the target of criticism from other OSCE states. And this criticism came against a backdrop of growing Russian doubts that liberalizing reforms were in fact producing the good governance, political stability, and economic prosperity that their Western advocates believed they would. The 1990s had begun with Moscow hopeful that it could integrate into a new Europe united by common values and objectives; they ended with Russia's questioning whether the West genuinely wanted Russia to prosper and have a place at the European table.

In practice, this meant that an organization dedicated to cooperation turned increasingly suspicious and acrimonious. Through Russian eyes, the chaos Russia experienced in the 1990s, followed by the instability created by color revolutions in several ex-Soviet republics and by the Arab Spring in the next decade, called into question the wisdom of advancing liberal democratic reforms too quickly in authoritarian polities. Through Western eyes, Russia's growing resistance to Western counsel about internal governance reinforced suspicions that the Kremlin was intent not on building a free-market democracy but on returning to its authoritarian traditions. As the 2000s progressed, OSCE discussions devolved into stale repetitions of accusations and counteraccusations. Western states charged Moscow with stage-managing elections and persecuting political opponents. Russia countered that the United States and the EU seemed much more concerned with Russia's internal politics and human rights record than with their own performance in dealing with national minorities or protecting the rights of Russian speakers in the Baltic states and Ukraine. Through Russian eyes, Western officials came across as self-righteous and hypocritical lecturers; from the West's perspective, Russia seemed to be afflicted with an acute case of "what-about-ism" in pointing to the West's imperfections.

These dynamics created a vicious circle of hostility in European security forums. The more Russia resisted Western political counsel and insisted that NATO had no business operating in what Moscow called its "sphere of privileged interests" in the former Soviet Union, the more fearful Russia's neighbors and former Warsaw Pact allies became about Kremlin intentions, and the more they looked to NATO to protect them. The closer these states drew to the West, the more suspicious and fearful the Kremlin became about NATO's intentions and capabilities toward Russia. A new European security order was taking root, but it was one that Russia opposed, dominated by NATO and the EU, in which Moscow had no decision-making authority. Rather than being a cofounder of the new Europe with a stake in its success,

Russia found itself on the outside looking in, incentivized to disrupt the new order as its old adversary, NATO, crept ever closer to Russian borders.

The starkly different conceptions in Russia and in the West of the optimal European security order were laid bare in 2009, when Russian president Dmitry Medvedev formally proposed a new European security treaty to address many of Moscow's concerns. The Russian draft treaty would legally obligate all states to consider the interests of others before undertaking any actions "significantly affecting the security" of any other treaty signatory, and it would allow signatories to call for an extraordinary conference in the event of a crisis and take decisions by unanimous vote—giving any of its signatories potential nay votes over the actions of others. As one former American diplomat noted, the proposed treaty seemed to be "an attempt to put a limiting umbrella over NATO and the EU," and it completely omitted the "normative, humanitarian, and human rights content of the UN and OSCE documents to which it referred."[22] In response, the United States asserted that Europe's existing security institutions, including the OSCE and the NATO-Russia Council, were sufficient to handle the continent's security challenges without a new treaty. The West called instead for a special discussion on organizational reform inside the OSCE, while underscoring the importance of upholding all OSCE norms and principles, including those in the human dimension. "Moscow had sought a geopolitical pact on hard security that would restrain the United States and NATO and instead wound up with a comprehensive agreement with numerous intrusive provisions on governance and human rights."

With Russia's annexation of Crimea and its accompanying proxy war in eastern Ukraine since 2014, the failure of what was once known as the Helsinki Process and of Europe's broader security architecture has been made plain. The rules and structures put in place since the end of the Cold War not only failed to prevent war between Europe's two largest states but—in fostering the impression that Russia was locked out of decisions in the continent's primary security decision-making bodies and that the rules pertaining to human rights could be used cynically to encourage revolutionary regime change in other states' internal affairs—they may actually have made that conflict more likely.

When the United States agreed to enlarge NATO in the mid-1990s and early 2000s, thereby committing itself to regard an attack on any of the new members as an attack on the United States, it lacked corresponding military plans or capabilities to handle such a scenario and doubted they would be needed. American forces were drawing down substantially from their Cold War numbers, and the United States was destroying Treaty-Limited Equipment under CFE. Many Americans regarded expanding the alliance as more political than military, providing new members with confidence in their security that would facilitate their liberal domestic transformation and mitigate against the rise of militant nationalism that often afflicts unstable states. Washington and many other alliance capitals thought NATO security could be bought on the cheap, assuming that Russia lacked both the intention and the military strength to attack any NATO member, and that the prospect of a conventional or nuclear confrontation was so daunting for Moscow that it obviated the prospect of Russian aggression in any event.

Such assumptions are no longer sustainable, if they ever were accurate. As America's suspicions about Moscow's intentions have darkened, its concerns about Russia's military capabilities have grown. Pentagon planners now believe that Russia hopes to overthrow the post–Cold War security arrangement in Europe, by negotiation if possible but by subversion or force if necessary, and that it has begun acquiring the military and information warfare wherewithal to realize its ambitions. The healthy optimism about Europe's future that infused the signatories of the Charter of Paris in 1990 has mutated into malignant pessimism. By 2018, the "Common European Home" touted by Mikhail Gorbachev, built on a foundation of common rules and common purposes, seemed further from reality than at any time since the fall of the Berlin Wall.

PUSHING THE BOUNDARIES IN SPY GAMES

A few days after Thanksgiving in 1989, the CIA's chief of station (COS) in Moscow got an unusual phone call from the KGB. "This is Gavrilov," the caller said, and he proposed a meeting to discuss what he vaguely called a "matter of some importance." The COS immediately grasped what the caller was implying: *Gavrilov* was the code name of a secret communications channel that the CIA and KGB had established in 1983 to discuss particularly sensitive issues. Named after a nineteenth-century Russian poet, the channel had been used over the years to manage potential interservice crises and discuss cooperation in counterterrorism and other matters of mutual interest, but the channel had gone dark for more than two years. The COS relayed the approach to Washington, and the rival spy organizations quickly arranged to meet at a senior level in mid-December at the Soviet embassy in Finland.[23] The Soviets would be represented by Rem Krassilnikov, chief of KGB counterintelligence worldwide, and by Leonid Nikitenko, who oversaw counterintelligence operations against the United States. The American side would feature Milt Bearden, head of the Directorate of Operations' renowned SE Division (Soviet and Eastern Europe), and Gardner Rugg "Gus" Hathaway, chief of the agency's counterintelligence staff. As a rule in the Gavrilov channel, neither side was willing to risk a one-on-one meeting, fearful that a lone individual would be susceptible to accusations that the other side had recruited him, whether accurate or not.[24]

Bearden and Hathaway entered the embassy in Helsinki un-
sure of what the Soviets wanted specifically to discuss but convinced
generally that the renewal of the Gavrilov channel was worthwhile
and willing to listen. Once the two sides had exchanged pleasant-
ries, Krassilnikov came right to the point. "I would not suggest
that spying against each other will ever cease," he said, "but at
some point we should begin to look at what kinds of rules might
be incorporated into the conduct of our business." Coercion—the
use of drugs, kidnapping, or violence—should be out of bounds,
he insisted. Bearden and Hathaway exchanged puzzled glances.
The two organizations had long observed an unstated gentlemen's
agreement not to target the officers of the other side with violence. Recruitment through persuasion and even blackmail was
part of the game, but assassinations and other forms of violence
could easily spin out of control and devastate both sides. What
was prompting the Soviet concern? Perhaps it was the fact that the
trickle of KGB defectors to the West had turned into a flood in
the late 1980s, as perestroika and glasnost had advanced inside the
Soviet Union and the failings of the communist system had been
made plain. Was Krassilnikov casting blame for his system's own
faults by implying that the CIA was violently coercing these defectors to leave the motherland? This was completely untrue, they
countered, as the Soviets well knew. The Soviet officers denied
accusing the American side of anything specific; they were merely
suggesting a general understanding on rules of conduct that both
sides would observe. Bearden and Hathaway agreed there was
merit in keeping the Gavrilov channel's agenda open, but nothing
further came of the Soviet suggestion. The wheels were quickly
coming off the metaphorical Soviet vehicle of state. The animosity of the Cold War would soon end, and each side would be con-
sumed by more urgent matters than delineating rules to govern an
anachronistic spy competition.

Some thirty years later, the question of rules to circumscribe

the spy game is once again becoming relevant. High-level dialogue between the CIA and Russia's various intelligence services
has continued, including a well-publicized meeting in 2018 to discuss counterterrorist cooperation. The post–Cold War breakup of
the old KGB and the rise of new successor organizations, however,
have fostered the growth of interservice rivalries inside Russia that
have incentivized greater risk-taking and aggression in Russia's
intelligence activities. At the same time, the post-9/11 focus on
counterterrorism operations in the US Intelligence Community
has featured an increased emphasis on targeted killings, through
both drone strikes controlled from remote distances and special
operations activities at close quarters. Under circumstances in
which the United States and Russia sometimes back opposing sides
in regional proxy wars—as in Syria and Ukraine—American and
Russian intelligence officers are in danger of finding themselves
in the crosshairs of the other side's targeted killing operations,
whether intentionally directed at them or not. These trends are
pushing the boundaries of the old gentlemen's agreement about
violence toward the other side's personnel.

Some instances of this boundary-pushing have involved direct violence against American personnel. In the summer of 2016,
for example, Russian television broadcast video footage of a Russian security officer beating an American that it claimed was a
CIA undercover case officer attempting to enter the US embassy
in Moscow.[25] The American suffered a broken shoulder, but the
Russians refused to acknowledge any wrongdoing. It was not the
first time the Russians had targeted American officials with violence, but the use of national television to boast about the incident
added an ominous new twist.

Others have involved the targeting of former Russian intelligence officers living in the West. The poisoning in 2006 of
Alexander Litvinenko, a veteran of Russia's Federalnaya Sluzhba

Bezopasnosti (FSB, the service responsible for domestic Russian intelligence operations) who was living in London and working with exiled Russian businessman and Putin opponent Boris Berezovsky, sent a chilling message about Russian willingness not only to carry out assassinations in the heart of the West but to use exotic weaponry—in this case, radioactive polonium—in particularly gruesome and intimidating ways. While Litvinenko was not an American or British intelligence officer, he was engaged in two activities that would have drawn the ire of both Chechen government leaders and Russian intelligence: he was working closely with the Chechen government-in-exile in London to support their war effort back in Chechnya, and he was on the payroll of the British MI6 service.[26] The combination proved deadly for him.

Russia appeared to stray even further across the line that proscribed violence against rival Western intelligence services in 2018. In March of that year, Sergei Skripal—a former Russian military intelligence officer who was living in the UK following an exchange of captured spies between Russia and the West in 2010—was targeted for assassination allegedly using a chemical nerve agent, along with his adult daughter, who was visiting from Russia. Both Skripals survived, but two other Salisbury residents were sickened by the poison, and another died. Closed-circuit video footage showed that two Russian men had visited Salisbury, Skripal's city of residence, on the weekend of the attack, and online research into their backgrounds indicated that they were Russian military intelligence officers traveling under alias. Swab tests discovered traces of the nerve agent in their hotel room. Russian television broadcast an interview with the men in which they denied attacking the Skripals and insisted that they were humble fitness instructors on a simple tourist jaunt. Few outside Russia believed their story.

Skripal's background as a former Russian military intelligence officer made it likely that the Russians considered him *nashi*—"one of ours" rather than "one of theirs"—and, as Putin colorfully put it, a traitor and a "bastard." Western intelligence organizations had long assumed that Moscow might target defectors resettled in the West, and US intelligence had regularly taken precautions to protect them dating back to the Cold War.[27] Still, officers exchanged in spy swaps were regarded as a special, less vulnerable category for the simple reason that targeting them would make recovering captured agents in any future spy swaps less likely. And it was shocking that Russian military intelligence officers had recklessly and sloppily attacked a naturalized British citizen on UK territory using a nerve agent banned under the international chemical weapons treaty, endangering not only their intended targets but numerous other Brits unlucky enough to come into contact with the poison, an action almost guaranteed to be discovered and attributed to Russia. At a minimum, it appeared that Russian military intelligence was operating without many bureaucratic constraints, perhaps to show the Kremlin that it was more willing to take risks than were its rival civilian services. But it was also possible that the Kremlin had decided to take the gloves off in an intensifying intelligence war with the West—a war in which the old rules of the game no longer applied.

In 1962, the Cuban missile crisis—known to Russians as the Caribbean crisis—served as a wake-up call to both Soviet and American leaders about how easily unconstrained rivalry could lead to a potentially apocalyptic conflict. In its aftermath, the two sides gradually put in place a series of formal and informal rules and procedures meant to prevent or manage any future crises and minimize the chances of catastrophe. A few of those rules and procedures— including the so-called communications hotline linking senior US and Russian officials, and agreements on "Incidents at Sea" and "Dangerous Military Activities"—remain in place and continue to serve the two militaries well. The OSCE-sponsored "Vienna Document" on military confidence and security-building measures is still in effect, although American diplomats accuse the Russians of selective implementation. Many others, however, have withered or disappeared. The Helsinki Process that began during détente and flourished in the early post–Cold War years has all but died. The bilateral arms control agreements that constrained the arms race during the latter phases of the Cold War and in its immediate aftermath are largely gone, and the channels of regular US-Russian communication and contact required for their implementation have gone dark. Even the informal understandings that constrained violence between the rival intelligence services are under grave threat.

Today, the pervasive fear that was prompted by staring into the abyss of the Cuban missile crisis has evaporated. In its place is a fear on each side that it is not doing enough to counter the other's aggression, mixed paradoxically with confidence that neither side would go so far as to risk a nuclear exchange. That confidence is misplaced, however, not because either side wants a conflict but because the brakes that might stop an unintended escalatory spiral in a potential US-Russian confrontation are failing. And the range of events that could trigger a dangerous new crisis is wide and growing.

4

Triggers

What happens when a state attempts to squeeze a rival power into submission, choking off its access to financial flows, resources, technology, and trade? Washington is betting heavily that it produces concessions. American policy toward Russia since 2014, after Russia annexed Crimea and initiated a separatist war in eastern Ukraine in response to the pro-Western Maidan uprising, has been premised on the belief that if the United States and Europe put Moscow under sufficient economic pressure, the Kremlin will recalculate the costs and benefits of its aggressive actions against its neighbors and the West and adopt a less threatening, more accommodating course. At worst, it is thought, Moscow might resort to economic retaliation in response to American sanctions, but given Russia's relative economic weakness, such retaliation is not regarded as a significant danger.

History, however, provides us with a sobering example of an alternative reaction: Pearl Harbor. Most people are familiar with the events of December 7, 1941, the "day that will live in infamy," when Japan attacked US naval assets in Hawaii. The Central Intelligence Agency was created largely as a result, with the primary goal of guarding against future surprise attacks by a determined foreign adversary. But fewer know the events that led up to that attack. There were really two intelligence failures that led to the surprise at Pearl Harbor. One was tactical, the failure to know where and when the Japanese would attack, despite numerous pieces of accurate intelligence that, in retrospect, showed clearly that the targeting of American naval assets in Hawaii was looming. The second was strategic. Dean Acheson, who was then US assistant secretary of state, described it:

> Everyone in the Department—and in the government generally—misread Japanese intentions. This misreading was not of what the Japanese military government proposed to do in Asia, not of the hostility our embargo would excite, but of the incredibly high risks General Tojo would assume to accomplish his ends. No one in Washington realized that he and his regime regarded the conquest of Asia not as an accomplishment of an ambition but as the survival of the regime. It was a life-and-death matter to them. They were absolutely unwilling to continue in what they regarded as Japan's precarious position surrounded by great and hostile powers—the United States, the Soviet Union, and a possibly revived and restored China.[1]

In the years leading up to the Pearl Harbor attack, the United States had put Japan under increasingly severe economic pressure in response to Japanese military conquests and expansionist policies in Asia. Washington terminated its commercial trade agreement with Tokyo in 1939, restricted the export of iron and steel in 1940, and then froze all Japanese assets in the United States in 1941 and placed a full embargo on oil exports. As an island nation whose industrial production and military capability were almost wholly dependent on the import of oil, steel, and other commodities, Japan viewed these measures as nothing less than an existential threat, but it had few economic cards it could play in response. A few days before the attack on Pearl Harbor, Japan's ambassador to the United States delivered a diplomatic note that plainly set out his government's perspective: "The Japanese people believe that economic measures are a much more effective weapon of war than military measures; that . . . they are being placed under severe pressure by the United States to yield to the American position; and that it is preferable to fight rather than to yield to pressure." Despite that warning, Americans were stunned by what they regarded as an unprovoked attack on American territory.

One of the lessons of Pearl Harbor is the importance of alertness to the danger of secretly planned "bolt from the blue" attacks by hostile foreign actors, such as the Japanese in 1941 and al-Qaeda in 2001. During the Cold War, this American intelligence mission most often took the form of ascertaining Soviet intentions, plans, and capabilities to attack the American homeland or to mount an assault against important objectives in the European theater, such as the Fulda Gap. In the early post–Cold War years, it refocused on preventing attacks by terrorist groups or hostile states such as Iran and North Korea. Now, in an era defined by "the return of great power competition," as the US National Security Strategy put it in 2018, intelligence alertness to the prospect of Russian or Chinese surprise attack, either against the continental United States or our friends and allies abroad, is once again coming to the fore.

Another lesson from Pearl Harbor, though, is the importance of sensitivity to the ways that adversaries can misread each other's perceptions and take steps that trigger unexpected escalations into unsought, full-fledged kinetic warfare. Intentions are simultaneously the most important and most difficult thing to understand about one's adversaries. And history is littered with examples of wars that involved the misreading of intentions, sometimes escalating even when their leaders tried to avoid them. World War I is perhaps the most notorious and impactful example, but it is far from the only one. The Seven Years' War between France and Britain in North America arose unexpectedly out of small skirmishes because each side incorrectly believed that the other knew its aims were limited. The Korean War began in large part because the Soviets and North Koreans mistakenly believed that Washington did not regard the Korean peninsula as important to its interests and thus would not oppose conquest of the South. China later entered that war, much to American surprise, because both Beijing and Washington misunderstood the other's key concerns, and each sent signals that inadvertently misled the other.

Today, a secretly planned military attack on the American or Russian homeland is not the primary danger posed by the extreme hostility in US-Russian relations, even though both nations have been taught by traumatic national experience to expect one—America by Pearl Harbor, Russia by Hitler's betrayal of the German-Soviet nonaggression treaty in launching his savage Operation Barbarossa. Neither state wants to initiate what it knows would be a mutually devastating, apocalyptic war. While Russia is under increasing economic pressure from the United States, American sanctions have not (yet) reached the crippling level that Japan suffered prior to Pearl Harbor, and Russia in any event has a range of less dangerous, alternative responses to Western economic warfare.

Nonetheless, we are each in grave danger of misreading the other's intentions and inadvertently triggering an escalatory spiral that neither side can control. Each side has convinced itself that the other is intent on its destruction. Each accuses the other of destabilizing the international order, with the United States defending the post–Cold War, NATO- and EU-dominated order in Europe, and Russia arguing that America's oft-touted "responsibility to protect" is undermining Westphalian conventions that have underpinned the international system since 1648. Within this context, each side is increasingly confronting the other in regional proxy wars, in probes of air and maritime boundaries, and in cyberspace. In Syria, US and Russian air forces are operating in the same airspace on opposing sides for the first time since the Korean War. Each country is directly backing opposing sides in the fighting in Ukraine, potentially bringing US and Russian forces into the other side's line of fire, or tying their fate to the actions of local proxies they only loosely control. In tense, politically and emotionally charged situations in regional military arenas, accidents or limited local clashes can force statesmen to choose not between all-out war and peace but between incremental escalation and humiliation—a dynamic process that is difficult to control once it begins.[2] An examination of near-miss US-Russian incidents, as well as hypothetical but realistic escalation scenarios, reveals just how easily local events could spin out of control, leading Washington and Moscow toward a nuclear confrontation that neither wants.

BULLETS DODGED

Many people remember the Cuban missile crisis and recall how close Washington and Moscow came to nuclear catastrophe at that time. Fewer are familiar with what is now known as the Able Archer incident, a much less public affair that took place in the secret confines of NATO and Soviet military commands in November 1983. The events played out as the culmination of a tension-filled year. In March, US president Ronald Reagan had made a high-profile speech describing the Soviet Union as "the evil empire" and called for a rollback strategy that would "write the final pages of the history of the Soviet Union," followed only a few days later by his announcement of the "Star Wars" strategic defense initiative. In September, Soviet air defenses in the country's far eastern region had shot down a civilian airliner, Korean Air Lines flight 007, believing it to be an American intelligence collection plane crossing into Soviet airspace, resulting in the deaths of 269 civilians, including a US congressman. Meanwhile, NATO was proceeding with plans to deploy American Pershing II intermediate-range ballistic missiles in Europe to counter the Soviet SS-20s targeting the alliance, stoking fears on each side that the other might attack. Trust between the United States and the USSR was at rock-bottom levels.

Against this backdrop, the United States and NATO carried out a regular annual military exercise designed to test command and control procedures for nuclear weapons use. It was framed around a hypothetical Warsaw Pact reaction to unrest in Yugoslavia, which led to a conventional clash with NATO and escalated quickly into the use of chemical and nuclear weapons. But unlike past exercises, "Able Archer 83" involved high-level US government policymakers, used new and different encrypted message formats, included dummy nuclear warhead handling procedures, and placed forces participating in the exercise on a notional high alert. Soviet officials, already primed by KGB reports to suspect that the United States might use the cover of a military exercise to mask preparations for a nuclear attack, detected these changes and became alarmed, unable to distinguish actual from notional activity. They responded by placing Soviet forces on high alert, loading planes in Poland and East Germany with bombs, preparing seventy SS-20 missiles for launch, and sending submarines armed with ballistic missiles under the Arctic ice to await attack orders. Years later, the President's Foreign Intelligence Advisory Board (PFIAB) wrote in a subsequently declassified report that the

Soviet fear of attack was genuine and that the United States "may
have inadvertently placed our relations with the Soviet Union on a
hair trigger."[3] War may have been averted, the report said, largely
due to the actions of one American official, Lieutenant General
Leonard Perroots, who "acted correctly out of instinct, not in-
formed guidance" in deciding not to elevate the alert of Western
military assets in response to the Soviet actions. The fact that the
affair played out largely in secret, outside the pressure of headlines
and the glare of television cameras, probably facilitated its peaceful outcome.

Even in their current somewhat weakened state, confidence-
building measures put in place in the context of the OSCE that
allow for direct observation of large military exercises make such
misinterpretations less likely today. But the renewed rivalry and
heightened mistrust between Moscow and Washington in the past
several years have made other escalation scenarios a realistic possibility once again. According to the American Security Project,
which tracks military incidents between Russia and the United
States, there have been over two hundred instances of Russian
military aircraft flying across or close to Western airspace since
2012, apparently probing the West's ability and willingness to
intercept the Russian sorties.[4] These aggressive offensive operations have been paired with equally aggressive defensive maneuvers, including several incidents in which Russian interceptors
have flown at high speeds within a few feet of American military
aircraft or naval ships approaching Russian airspace or territorial
waters. The margin for error in these encounters is slim. American
officials have accused Russian aircraft of reckless and irresponsible
actions, flying without transponders that would facilitate detection
by radar.

While these maneuvers unquestionably appear reckless, they
are also rational in the context of Russia's broader security in-

terests, which means they are likely to continue. The American strategist and deterrence theorist Thomas Schelling famously compared deterrence in the nuclear age to teenagers engaged in a game of chicken, driving their hot rods directly toward each other on a narrow strip of road, daring the other to turn aside. Like that senseless game, he observed, nuclear deterrence is dependent on convincing the other side that one has the nerve not to yield to the other's will, to defend one's line in the face of looming self-annihilation. Such a posture requires the demonstration of a certain degree of recklessness to make one's resolve clear to the other side. Forays into the other side's airspace and "buzzing" its aircraft and "shouldering" its ships are meant in part to gain insight into the military procedures and capabilities that an adversary will employ in actual warfare. But they are also intended to take a measure of the opponent's mettle and send signals about one's own fortitude, not despite the dangers but because of them. When two nuclear powers face off across borders, these close encounters—and the risk of accident that goes with them—are an almost unavoidable part of the game.

The dangers of such "rational recklessness" were made clear in a direct clash between US and Russian forces in Syria in February 2018. Each side was backing opposing forces in Syria's civil war; Moscow was supporting a coalition of pro-government forces, including the Syrian military, while the United States was assisting a mix of anti-regime opposition forces, including a large contingent of Kurdish fighters. Both sides were fighting a common foe, however, in ISIS (the Islamic State of Iraq and Syria) and had recently made significant gains against the ISIS stronghold in eastern Syria near the city of Deir al-Zour, an area that housed valuable oil and natural gas reserves and a gas production facility known as the Conoco plant.

As ISIS was driven out of the area, the question of who would control the Conoco plant and surrounding fields rose to the fore. ISIS had used black-market gas sales to help fund its activities, and the plant could potentially help to sustain other opposition forces in the wake of ISIS's defeat. Up to this point, the two militaries had done a good job of communicating regularly about deconfliction, careful to notify each other about flight plans and ground maneuvers, sensitive to the danger that the other's forces could come accidently under fire. As part of that effort, they had agreed that neither would cross the Euphrates River near Deir al-Zour, which separated Russian and Russian-backed forces on the west bank from American and American-backed forces in the east. But US commanders grew increasingly concerned as they observed pro-regime forces massing to the river's west, seemingly poised for a crossing. Through the deconfliction channel, they warned about the approaching forces and reminded the Russian commanders about the agreement to remain on opposite sides of the Euphrates.

Despite US warnings, the pro-regime forces launched a sustained tank, mortar, and artillery attack on the night of February 7 and began crossing the river. The Americans fired warning shots and inquired again through the deconfliction channel about whether the approaching forces included Russian personnel. The Russians, however, denied participating in the attack and claimed to have no control over the forces involved. As artillery shells and Russian-made T-72 tank rounds rained down on American special forces personnel, the US command faced a choice between fighting back and falling back. It chose to fight. "The Russian high command assured us it was not their people," Defense Secretary James Mattis subsequently testified to US senators, so he directed "for the [attacking] force, then, to be annihilated. And it was."[5]

US forces fired back at the attackers using anti-tank missiles and machine guns and then called in massive air strikes. The resulting four-hour battle killed more than two hundred of the attackers, according to documents released by the Pentagon, against no reported American casualties. But Russia's denial about having any personnel in the attacking force turned out to be misleading. The casualties included fighters from Evro Polis, a private mercenary army of Russian and pro-Russian veterans of the war in Ukraine known informally as the Wagner group, after the nom de guerre of its commander. The Russian foreign ministry acknowledged after the fact that five Russian citizens—but no official Russian military personnel—had been killed and dozens more injured. Independent Russian media reports suggested that the death toll was actually eighty or more.

Whether the Wagner group was acting at the behest of the Russian government is unclear.[6] Evro Polis certainly had reasons of its own to target the Conoco gas plant with or without any official blessing, as it had signed an agreement with the Syrian energy ministry in 2016 entitling it to 25 percent of the production from gas and oil facilities it helped to liberate, protect, and develop.[7] However, a *Washington Post* report suggests that Wagner had at least some level of Russian government approval for the operation; it cites an alleged intelligence intercept in which the owner of Evro Polis told a Syrian official that he had secured the approval of an unnamed Russian government minister for a "fast and strong" initiative in early February.[8] This suggests several possible explanations for the attack. A government official resentful of Wagner's growing role may have okayed the attack in the hope that a rout by the Americans would undermine an influential rival to Russia's uniformed military forces, or alternatively, the promise of a personal share in gas proceeds may have won the blessing of a corrupt minister. It is also possible that the Kremlin had full knowledge of the planned attack and used it to test America's resolve while maintaining some level of plausible deniability about its involvement.

Regardless of the explanation for Russian actions or the absolute numbers of Russian citizens killed or wounded, the gravity of the event remains clear. Whether officially blessed or not, Russian forces in significant numbers had attacked US military personnel on the battlefield. And for the first time since the Cold War, that clash had produced appreciable casualties. The amazing lack of American losses in the attack was at least as important in avoiding a genuine crisis as was the Kremlin's choice to disavow any official involvement.

AN INCREASINGLY BLURRY NUCLEAR LINE

It is one thing to risk localized military encounters between ships and planes or small expeditionary ground forces. It is quite another to move from limited conventional clashes to the use of nuclear weapons. No country has crossed that threshold since the United States dropped atomic bombs on Japan in 1945, and all recognize the immense dangers of doing so. That recognition played a big part in keeping what Cold War historian John Lewis Gaddis has called "the long peace" between the United States and Soviet Union, despite their mistrust, military rivalry, and ideological animosity.[9]

But technology has evolved since the post–Cold War period in ways that make escalation from conventional to nuclear conflict more likely once fighting starts, even if the combatants try to avoid crossing that threshold. James Acton, a physicist working on deterrence and nuclear policy issues at the Carnegie Endowment for International Peace, has been sounding the alarms about what he calls "nuclear entanglement," the intermixing of the command, control, communications, and intelligence warning systems that oversee nuclear and conventional weapons systems in the militaries of the world's great powers, coupled with new nonnuclear capabilities that can threaten an opponent's nuclear retaliatory force. The bright line separating nuclear and conventional conflict is in reality not bright at all, he argues, and national command authorities in Russia and the United States probably have less control than they think over whether any conventional military clash turns into a catastrophic nuclear conflict.[10]

During the Cold War, the only viable means of countering an opponent's strategic nuclear forces was a nuclear strike against the weapons themselves or against their hardened command and control systems. Each country's satellites—used both to communicate with nuclear weapons systems and for early warning of an adversary's nuclear launches—were largely safe from ground-based attacks. Unless one of the superpowers detected the other preparing or launching any of its nuclear forces, it could rest assured that its strategic retaliatory force was safe, able to serve as a reliable nuclear deterrent.

Today, that is no longer the case. The world's great powers have grown more and more dependent on satellite-based systems to detect launches of nuclear and nonnuclear missiles, to guide ever more accurate weaponry through global-positioning systems, and to communicate with both nuclear and nonnuclear weapons systems. But these satellites have also grown more vulnerable than ever to nonnuclear anti-satellite (ASAT) weapons.[11] And highly accurate long-range conventional weapons, not to mention cyberweapons and ballistic missile defense systems, hold the potential to undermine an opponent's nuclear capability without resort to nuclear strikes.

As a result of these new capabilities and vulnerabilities, both Washington and Moscow have officially announced that they might launch a nuclear attack in response to conventional threats. The United States has lapped the field of global competitors in developing and using long-range sea-launched and air-launched conventional cruise missiles, with an inventory of several thousand.

Russia's concerns about these conventional capabilities had years ago prompted it to announce that it might use nuclear weapons to counter a conventional threat. But Russia has recently deployed a smaller number of similar weapons, most notably the Kalibr cruise missile that it has employed in the Syrian war. As Russian and Chinese conventional weapons, anti-satellite technology, and cybercapabilities have evolved, the United States has grown more concerned about nonnuclear threats to its nuclear arsenal. Its 2018 *Nuclear Posture Review* declares that in the event of "significant nonnuclear strategic attacks . . . on US or allied nuclear forces, their command and control, or warning and attack assessment capabilities," the United States would consider the use of nuclear strikes.[12]

Even more alarming, according to Acton, is the fact that such nonnuclear threats to nuclear capabilities might be inadvertent, flowing from activities not meant to be escalatory.[13] Today, a significant number of weapons systems are dual-use, capable of delivering either nuclear or conventional warheads. Thus, whereas the command, control, communications, and intelligence surveillance and reconnaissance systems (C³ISR) that govern the nuclear arsenal were once largely separate from those of conventional weaponry, those systems today are increasingly networked and overlap. As a result, if Moscow were to grow concerned in a crisis situation that the United States might target its forces with conventionally armed Tomahawk cruise missiles, it would have strong incentives to counter those weapons preemptively by crippling the American C³ISR satellites controlling them through anti-satellite weapons or cyberattacks or some combination thereof. Washington might interpret an attack on dual-purpose satellites, however, as a threat to American nuclear capabilities—causing US authorities to believe they must choose between launching nuclear weapons immediately or losing their ability to use them altogether. This would constitute a highly escalatory situation driven by misunderstanding and fear rather than by any desire to initiate a nuclear exchange. Some Russian experts share Acton's concerns, cautioning that "entanglement erodes the traditional delineation between nuclear and nonnuclear arms, as well as between offensive and defensive systems, and creates the threat of a swift and unintended escalation of a local conventional armed collision between the great powers into a nuclear war."[14]

TWO SCENARIOS FOR WAR

Dry tinder does not produce a fire absent a spark of some kind, and sparks do not always result in a conflagration. Conditions that are ripe for an escalatory spiral—deep mistrust between adversaries, ongoing cybersparring, a mutual belief that the other side is intent on one's own destruction, and deteriorating organizational and procedural frameworks that might normally contain conflicts and manage crises—do not necessarily lead to disaster, as the encounter in February 2018 between Russian mercenaries and American special forces in Syria demonstrated. Still, an examination of two hypothetical conflict scenarios, an exercise in imagination based on actual conditions that are ripe for escalation, illustrates how easy it would be for Washington and Moscow to find themselves in a nuclear confrontation neither wants.

RELIGIOUS VIOLENCE IN UKRAINE

The 2014 Russia-Ukraine crisis has precipitated one of the largest schisms in Orthodox Christian history. Millions of worshippers are caught in the middle of a struggle for political control between Moscow and Kiev. The present conflict has its roots in 1686, when the Ecumenical Patriarch of Constantinople granted the Russian Orthodox Church (ROC) conditional jurisdiction over the Kiev Metropolis. This arrangement has remained unchanged for over three centuries, but the Soviet collapse and Ukraine's subsequent attainment of statehood have elicited a host of difficult political questions dividing Ukrainian public opinion: How does nationality intersect with religious identity in an overwhelmingly Orthodox state? Does fealty to the Moscow Patriarchate compromise Ukrainian national sovereignty?

The majority of Ukraine's Orthodox parishes currently belong to the Ukrainian Orthodox Church under the Moscow Patriarchate (UOC-MP), subordinate to the ROC. In 1992, a faction led by the newly proclaimed "Patriarch of Kiev," Filaret Denysenko, broke off from the UOC-MP to assert its autonomy from Moscow. This spiritual project has proved popular with Ukrainian nationalists, who have long expressed displeasure at the political messaging scattered throughout some Russian Orthodox liturgies; most strikingly, these include prayers for the health and safety of the Russian armed forces. The schism came to a head with the annexation of Crimea, when Ukrainian president Petro Poroshenko took up the cause of the Kiev Patriarchate (UOC-KP) as an assertion of Ukrainian "spiritual independence" from Russia.

But over the span of its existence, the UOC-KP has not been recognized by any other Orthodox church; the Russian-aligned UOC-MP remained the sole Orthodox authority in Ukraine. In a bid to secure international legitimacy, Ukraine lobbied the Constantinople Patriarch for a certification of autocephaly, or full self-government. It was granted this document, a Tomos in Orthodox terminology, in January 2019. Shortly afterward, the UOC-KP and smaller Ukrainian Autocephalous Orthodox Church (UAOC) were merged into the new Ukrainian Orthodox Church.

The UOC-MP, with its twelve thousand parishes across Ukraine, is regarded by Ukrainian nationalists as a national security threat and stands on the verge of being branded as an illegitimate sect within Ukraine. Around seventy parishes have opted to join the Ukrainian Orthodox Church, but what will become of the less willing? Several UOC-MP priests have unequivocally stated their resolve to die in defense of their churches and monasteries. Meanwhile, the Russian Orthodox Church is accusing Ukrainian authorities of seizing and vandalizing UOC-MP property with increasing frequency. The Ukrainian Rada has already passed an unprecedented law allowing church allegiance to be switched by majority vote, further increasing the likelihood of conflict within UOC-MP communities.

From this point, it is easy to imagine how events might begin to spiral out of control. Ukraine's president is unlikely to seek outright physical confrontation with the UOC-MP, but Ukrainian nationalists to his right have proved themselves less restrained. Right Sector, a prominent nationalist coalition, sees the UOC-MP leadership structure as wartime traitors, hostile foreign agents who cynically undermine Ukrainian national sovereignty under the cover of religion. Over the past year, Right Sector has staged several large street confrontations outside of UOC-MP churches to disrupt ongoing religious services. These ongoing efforts are likely to intensify and become more frequent, as the granting of autocephaly has cast the dispute over UOC-MP church property in a new political light.

Imagine, then, that a large group of Ukrainian nationalists blockades yet another UOC-MP church, as they have recently done in the Volyn Oblast of northwestern Ukraine. The priest arrives shortly thereafter, accompanied by a small congregation. Against a cacophony of jeers and threats of violence, he insists on entering his church to hold regularly scheduled services. As he pushes his way through the crowd, someone throws a stone at the back of his head. He collapses at the footsteps of his church. An ambulance is called, and responders pronounce him dead on the spot from a fatal concussion.

The religious cold war in Ukraine begins to turn hot. Tens of thousands of Russian Orthodox believers march in protest against the violence in Ukraine. Hundreds of private Russian citizens cross the border armed with pistols, rifles, and other small arms, intent on preventing further Ukrainian attacks and defending what is seen as Russian Orthodox property. The US State Department attempts to defuse tensions with a statement condemning violence, affirming the importance of religious freedom, and supporting Ukraine's right to handle its own internal affairs in accordance with democratic principles.

The Russian response does not prove nearly as restrained. Since the presidential election of 2012, Russian president Putin has had to contend with growing Communist and nationalist movements on his political right flank. They accuse Putin of not doing enough to defend Russian interests with military force and complain that he naïvely seeks compromise with the West when he should instead be taking aggressive measures to roll back NATO influence in Russia's legitimate sphere of interest. According to one particularly popular Communist critique, Putin has failed to protect the predominantly Russian-speaking people of Donbass from what is portrayed as a Ukrainian ethnic-cleansing campaign.[15]

The Communists charge, with overwhelming popular support, that this killing of a priest demonstrates the need to act immediately and decisively to protect Russian compatriots in Ukraine. They use this opportunity to again demand formal Russian recognition of the Donetsk People's Republic (DPR) and the Luhansk People's Republic (LPR), something that they have sought since 2015. Putin has to this point resisted calls for open and direct Russian military involvement in Donbass, a move that would invite serious international repercussions. But doing nothing in the face of the Ukrainian religious violence would play into the hands of his detractors, whose hawkish calls to action reflect the country's mood better than Putin's caution. Actively preventing Russian mercenaries from defending their co-religionists would be seen as an act of betrayal. The Kremlin settles for a response that stops just short of recognizing the Donbass: Russian emergency ministry units, supported by the Russian national guard, will cross into Donbass to establish a safe zone around the Luhansk area, replete with field hospitals to treat Ukrainians wounded over the course of the civil conflict.

Kiev calls this move not merely an invasion but an act of war, and it appeals to Washington for immediate military aid. Poland supports this call and offers to host additional American military forces to respond to Russia's aggression. With Congress and influential segments of American public opinion demanding a forceful response, the White House has neither the political capital nor the diplomatic tools to de-escalate with Moscow. American tactical missile defense systems, air assets, artillery, and heavy armor pour into western Poland over the next several weeks. The US president announces that he has ordered US military personnel that had been rotating through Poland on temporary assignments to be increased in number and stationed along the border with Ukraine, ready for action should Russian military forces move toward the western portions of Ukraine. He explains that this show of force is not to help Kiev retake Donbass but to be ready to defend the rest of Ukraine against Russia. Moscow views the US announcement with alarm. Despite Washington's denials, Russian military leaders conclude that Washington and Kiev are preparing for joint military action against Donbass.

From here, both sides become constrained by an increasingly narrow field of policy options. Moscow officially recognizes Donetsk and Luhansk as independent of Ukraine in a desperate last bid to deter what it sees as an imminent invasion. To protect what it has now acknowledged as two sovereign states, Russia establishes and enforces a no-fly zone across Donbass while stationing military forces across the border from Kiev-controlled territory. The United States, in turn, has no choice but to support a Ukrainian military buildup on the other side of the Donbass border, putting the two sides within a hair's breadth of kinetic conflict.

A single shot across the unofficial border serves as the spark to war. It was not ordered in Moscow, Kiev, or Washington, however. Rather, it comes from the many "volunteer" forces active in and around the Donbass region, including the Kuban Cossack Host, which had long threatened to "come to the defense of our homeland and mother church" in response to acts of persecution against Russian Orthodox believers, and from ultranationalist paramilitary groups within Right Sector that had long been convinced that the Ukrainian government is unable or unwilling to take the steps necessary to retake Donetsk and Luhansk. As limited conventional skirmishing between Russian and Ukrainian forces begins, the United States does its best to avoid being drawn directly into the fighting, providing intelligence, arms, and advice to Ukrainian forces while keeping its own forces far from the line of contact, ready to defend against a Russian offensive. But a Ukrainian-operated antiaircraft unit shoots down a Russian fighter plane on combat air patrol over the Donbass, and Russian aircraft and artillery retaliate against several sites where US advisers were assisting Ukrainians, killing four American military personnel. A direct US-Russian military conflict starts climbing the ladder of escalation.

THE FOG OF CYBERWAR

The highly sophisticated, Russia-generated NotPetya malware attacks in Ukraine in 2017 quickly spilled out of control beyond Ukrainian borders and into networks across the world, inflicting more than $10 billion worth of damage and constituting the most destructive malware attack in history. The American response—indicting some named Russian individuals and adding new economic sanctions to those already in force against Russia, struck many cyberprofessionals as incommensurate to the severity of the damage. "The lack of a proper response has been almost an invitation to escalate more," commented one.[16] The next time Russia launched an attack, many advised, the United States should actively disrupt Russian cybercapabilities and impose much higher costs for such reckless aggression.

Imagine, then, a scenario in which a new cyberweapon is unleashed on Ukraine that targets gas pipeline control systems. Its effect is nearly instantaneous, shutting down valve control systems and pumping stations and bringing the flow of gas through Ukrainian pipelines to a halt. Because the halt is brief, and because the attack occurs in summer, the impact on European gas supplies is not nearly as severe as it would be in cold weather, but the intended message seems clear.

Ukrainian, European, and American governments issue immediate condemnation of the attacks and all but officially accuse Russia of responsibility. Moscow denies any involvement. Russia's foreign ministry spokesperson suggests that Ukrainian hackers had launched the attack themselves in what she calls a "provocation." Russian cybersecurity experts say Ukrainian criminal hackers who had been part of a transnational cybercrime group had initiated the crisis using Russian botnets and imitating Russian techniques. Their aim had been nothing more than extortion against Ukrainian government officials. US and European audiences find the Russian counteraccusation risible.

The perception of bald-faced Russian lying only reinforces American determination to act. Leaders at US Cyber Command urge the White House to draw a firm line. Issuing toothless legal indictments that have little chance of putting any Russian hackers behind bars would only underscore American powerlessness in the face of such attacks, they counsel. They ask for authorization to mount a reciprocal and proportionate attack on Russian infrastructure, reverse engineering the Russian malware and redirecting it against valve control systems and pumping stations in Russia. The White House agrees. Within weeks, Russia experiences a brief disruption of gas flows. The economic impact is minimal, but the psychological effect is significant. The United States, it seems, has removed the gloves on offensive cyberoperations.

Events soon begin to accelerate. As markets open on Wall Street several weeks later, traders experience a series of short "flash" outages of their online systems that result in the loss of several trillion dollars. Intermittent trading outages continue over the course of the few days, and trading is halted as stock and bond markets begin to plunge. FBI investigators strongly suspect that Russia is behind the attacks. The US Treasury secretary warns that sustained Wall Street losses could have a devastating domino effect on the American economy, producing a collapse of confidence from which it might be difficult to recover. If investors lose faith in the stability of the American economy, the foreign credits on which the financing of America's massive national debt depends could grow dangerously more expensive.

In response, the American president draws a firm redline. He telephones the Russian president and states that cyberinterference with the US financial system constitutes an attack on critical American infrastructure that poses an existential threat to US national security. US policy allows for a kinetic response to such cyberattacks. He has no desire to attack Russia, he says, but unless Russia's cyberattacks stop immediately, he will be forced to take military action, which he insists will be narrowly targeted and proportional. He counsels his counterpart to remove personnel from the Internet Research Agency building in Saint Petersburg as a precaution to minimize the chances of civilian deaths.

In Moscow, the Russian Security Council convenes a meeting on the growing crisis. One official recalls the critical role that an informal back channel between Bobby Kennedy and the Soviet ambassador had played resolving in the 1962 Caribbean crisis, but others point out that Russia's current ambassador has long been frozen out of contact with anyone who matters in the US administration. Russian military officials, fearing the possibility of conventionally armed Tomahawk or drone attacks on key cyberunits, urge the Kremlin to authorize a "demonstration" event to discourage American aggression. Since many of America's precision-targeted munitions depend on satellite-guidance systems, they argue, Russia should use ground-based weapons to temporarily disable a US global positioning system (GPS) satellite. By "escalating to de-escalate," the action would show Washington that Russia can and will defend itself against attacks and bring US decision-makers to their senses. The Russian president approves the operation.

But the "temporary" disabling of a single GPS satellite proves to be more damaging and more enduring than the Russians had expected. The satellite remains out of service for three days, and its outage has a cascading effect on the twenty-three other satellites in the US GPS constellation. Synchronization failures disrupt the entire system. Though it is popularly regarded as a mapping system, GPS in fact is an enormous space-based timing device vital to a wide range of government and commercial functions. Telecommunication networks rely on GPS clocks to allow cell towers to transfer calls. Electrical power grids use GPS to balance current flows. ATMs and credit cards cannot function without GPS time-stamping. Even computer network synchronization depends on GPS clocks.[17] And much to Moscow's surprise, its disabling of a single satellite brings all of this activity and more to a grinding halt. Americans are shocked to learn that the US government has no effective backup system in place.

Outrage over the Russian satellite attack quickly mounts. Congress demands that the White House respond, and it passes an immediate authorization for the president to use any and all means he deems necessary to end the Russian aggression. Pentagon officials tell the president that under the circumstances, they cannot be confident that Russia will not target even more critical C³ISR satellites next, which might cripple the United States' ability to receive early warning of a Russian missile attack or to communicate with its conventional or nuclear forces. Piggybacking on the Pentagon warning, the NSA and CIA report that they have detected what they believe is a Russian cyberpenetration of a C³ISR communications network, and they cannot determine whether the intrusion is meant to monitor or disable the system. All concur that unless the president strikes back against the Russians immediately, he might lose the ability to defend the United States altogether. They urge an immediate retaliatory attack on all Russian ground-based ASAT facilities, in addition to targeting Russia's cyberunits and its GLONASS counterpart to the US GPS system.

The march up the ladder of military escalation begins skipping rungs.

These hypothetical scenarios are far from inevitable. At each rung in their particular notional escalatory ladder, American and Russian leaders had options they failed to exercise that could have reduced tensions, cooled off emotions, and mitigated the dangers of spiraling into a disastrous confrontation. Individuals matter in the affairs of state, in addition to national interests, perceptions, technologies, alliances, behavioral norms, and the balance of power. Wiser leaders could have taken more responsible decisions that might have produced a much less alarming outcome. The fog of war and the "slings and arrows of outrageous fortune" could have shaped developments in substantially different ways.

But neither are the scenarios far-fetched. To one degree or another, each of the elements in the scenarios are based on current trends, actual recent events, the tendencies of leaders now in power, and genuine military capabilities. Nor are they the only set of events that could trigger an escalatory spiral. Unrest in the Baltic states, a clash in Syria, and a US-China confrontation in the South China Sea that Russia seeks to exploit are among a wide range of realistic situations that could produce unsought catastrophe.

No matter its origins, any escalation scenario is likely to have some features in common with the events illustrated in this chapter. The adversaries show themselves willing to run risks in the interest of gaining a competitive advantage, but they prove unwilling to take risks in the interest of peace. Both sides in the scenario fall into the same cognitive trap, the unexamined assumption that incremental escalation at each stage of the dispute will cause the other to reconsider its actions and back down, that "escalating to de-escalate" will prove to be a winning strategy. Both eventually discover that they are not dealing with what international relations scholar Robert Jervis has labeled a "deterrence model," where a tough response to an ambitious aggressor state ends its aggression, but rather with a "spiral model," in which coercive steps against a state that already sees itself as threatened wind up magnifying perceptions of vulnerability and triggering a dangerous escalatory reaction.

But both reach that discovery too late to change course.

PART II

Synthesis: Managing the Problem

Everything simple is false. Everything complex is unusable.
—Paul Valéry

Escaping the Simplicity Trap

How does one handle what management experts call a *wicked problem*—one that is not rooted in a primary cause but rather results from dynamic interactions between a multiplicity of vexing technological, psychological, political, societal, institutional, and international factors, few of which individually are prone to solutions?[1] There is no universal recipe for success. Like Tolstoy's observation that every unhappy family is unhappy in its own way, every wicked problem exhibits its own peculiar qualities that require particular approaches. But failures in dealing with such systems problems tend to have some important common features. One way to begin grappling with the complexities of the current US-Russian dynamic and mitigate the dangers of escalatory spirals is to examine past failures in dealing with other complex systems problems, to understand what not to do. And looking outside the realm of statecraft, toward such fields as ecology, is a good place to start.

PROBLEMS IN MANAGING SYSTEMS

The path toward wisdom in managing our Russia problem begins in Yellowstone National Park. Created by an act of Congress in

1872 as the first formal nature preserve in the world, the park encompasses more than two million acres of the American West, an area larger than the states of Delaware and Rhode Island combined. At the time of its establishment, Yellowstone teemed with wildlife. One naturalist characterized the early park as "an unfenced zoological garden for the enjoyment and enrichment of visitors who rarely saw such animals elsewhere."[2] Visiting the park in 1903, President Teddy Roosevelt observed many thousand elk, hundreds of antelope, and numerous cougar, mountain sheep, deer, and coyotes. Overwhelmed by the abundance and natural beauty, he wrote, "Our people should see to it that this rich heritage is preserved for their children and their children's children forever, with its majestic beauty all unmarred." And for more than a century, American law has required the US government to do exactly that, protecting the park against damage to its geological and botanical wonders and preventing "wanton destruction of fish and game found within." Yet within a few decades of Roosevelt's visit, Yellowstone was in steep decline. In 1934, an official US government publication announced that "white-tailed deer, cougar, lynx, wolf, and possibly wolverine and fisher are gone from the Yellowstone." In the mid-1980s, one of the park's foremost chroniclers declared, "As a wildlife refuge, Yellowstone is dying."[3] The tale of what produced this decline is not one of neglect or corruption or ill intentions. Rather, it is the story of a complex systems problem.

When the park's new rangers set to thinking about how they would preserve its wonders, they quickly realized that they had been handed an enormous challenge. The park's elk and bison populations were becoming endangered. At their peak, millions of bison and elk had roamed the American West. But for decades, Native American tribes and Euro-American settlers and game hunters had aggressively hunted the herds. In the years following the

Civil War, the proliferation of modern rifles had greatly improved the efficiency of hunters, while new tanning technologies had generated huge markets for wildlife hides around the world.[4] This combination devastated the bison and elk populations throughout the West. The Yellowstone herds were no exception. Hunting in Yellowstone was still legal through the 1870s, although the ill-defined "wanton destruction" of wildlife was banned. Hunters killed some four thousand elk in the park in the spring of 1875 alone, and they had reduced the Yellowstone bison herd to a mere twenty-five by 1894.[5]

To arrest the herds' decline, the United States government banned the hunting of game in the park and literally called in the cavalry. Beginning in 1886, US Army personnel took over management of the park and invested considerable resources in feeding its elk and bison, driving out their poachers, and killing their natural predators. "Buffalo" Jones, appointed as the park's first game warden, oversaw what effectively became a dedicated bison ranch within the park, devoted to the herd's breeding, feeding, and care. These efforts were strikingly successful. By the late 1880s, Yellowstone's elk population had started to rebound. Within a few more decades, the Yellowstone elk herd had grown to some thirty-five thousand, and bison had once again become a significant tourist attraction for the park.[6] Moose began to establish themselves in Yellowstone for the first time, and the bear population increased. By early in the twentieth century, nearly everyone associated with Yellowstone, in and out of government, viewed the park as a grand success. More and more visitors were coming, and the park was regarded as a true national treasure.[7]

Just as old problems were being solved, however, new problems emerged. By the 1920s, it was becoming clear that something was going very wrong with park wildlife. Elk and bison continued to thrive, but the park's antelope, deer, and bighorn sheep populations went into steep decline. White-tailed deer were gone altogether by 1924. Most alarmingly, beaver grew scarce:

> Perhaps no animal was more important in Yellowstone than the beaver. By building his dams, he slowed spring runoff in the streams, discouraging erosion and siltation, keeping the water clean for the spawning trout. By building ponds, the beaver raised the surrounding water table, adding moisture that promoted vegetation—willow and aspen, forbs (broad-leaved plants such as aster, yarrow, and clover), berries and lush grass—that were essential foods for other animals. The ponds themselves provided habitat for waterfowl, mink, and otter.[8]

The National Park Service, which had been established in 1916 and had taken over management of Yellowstone from the US Cavalry, was convinced that it knew what was causing the problems: predators. Beavers were the primary staple of wolves, and cougar and coyotes preyed on deer, antelope, and bighorn sheep. Rangers redoubled their antipredator efforts, declaring "open war" on mountain lions, wolves, and other predatory animals.[9] They eliminated the wolves and cougar altogether from the park. But instead of helping the deer, sheep, beaver, and antelope, these corrective steps only made the situation worse. "The more predators they killed, the greater the decline of the game; and the greater the decline of the game, the more predators they killed."[10]

Perplexed, the park service called in experts to study the problem. The biologist Adolph Murie reached his conclusion after a two-year study in 1939. Predators, he said, were not the cause of the declining herds. Rather, the elk population "is unquestionably too large." Hungry elk herds had devastated the park's once abundant aspen and willow trees, which in turn left little for deer and antelope to eat. With the aspen in decline, beavers had fewer and fewer trees with which to build dams, and the beaver population declined. Without beaver dams, meadows lost a critical factor in their water management, and vast areas of the park that were once a source of native grasses, waterfowl, and small mammals dried up. This cascading effect was devastating the ecosystem.

As the origin and scale of the problem became increasingly evident, the National Park Service began to grasp the damage that well-intentioned but ill-informed park management had caused. They hired range specialists to study the park and invited more research by independent biologists. They followed elk movements, measured spring runoff and soil erosion, and carefully monitored tree and vegetation growth to gauge the impact of grazing. The more they learned, the worse things looked. Not only were the large herds overgrazing, but they were trampling vast areas of the park, compacting the soil and diminishing its porosity. When it rained, the water ran off the surface of the soil rather than soaking in. The soil dried out, and the water table dropped, decreasing plant growth. This, in turn, contributed to soil erosion, which exacerbated the other problems. Range decline had become a vicious cycle.

To break out of this cycle of devastation, park rangers embarked on a new program to contain the size of the elk and bison herds by trapping and transferring them to other parts of the country. They launched an ambitious reseeding effort to restore vegetation and native grasses. They encouraged the hunting of elk outside the confines of the park. But they made only limited progress; the elk population still remained too high. Trapping and transferring could only go so far in containing the herd, as demand for elk in other parts of the country was saturated. So rangers reintroduced cougar and wolves into the park and began to view coyote as allies rather than enemies. Elk would be "naturally controlled" by a combination of native predators and periodic harsh winters.

But the addition of natural predation still failed to control the herd.

Absent alternatives, the National Park Service ultimately determined that it would have to kill a large number of elk annually in Yellowstone. A little over a century after the park's dedication, its management approach had come full circle. The hunters and predators once thought to be the primary threat to the park's wildlife were determined to be critical parts of its survival. Park managers had gone from regarding Yellowstone as the sum of its individual parts, each posing problems to be addressed segmentally, to viewing the park as an integrated ecosystem, a superorganism whose parts are interrelated and must be managed as such.

Through trial and a lot of error, the National Park Service had discovered in Yellowstone one of the main tenets of dealing with complex adaptive systems: you can never do merely one thing.[11] In a complex system, multiple individual elements are connected to and interact with one another in ways that change over time. Relationships in such a system are not arithmetic, and good intentions do not necessarily bring success. Combining two and two seldom produces four; sometimes it produces twenty-seven or negative eight. Every individual step that you take inevitably has effects on other parts of the system, some of which may be damaging. And recognizing in advance what those cascading effects will be is immensely difficult.

RUSSIAN REFORMS: GOOD INTENTIONS GO BAD

Around the time that the National Park Service was coming to grips with failed efforts to fix the problems in Yellowstone, government officials in Russia and experts from the United States were embarking on an ambitious new effort half a world away: to build a free-market democracy in Russia on the ruins of the Soviet Union's failed communist system. Their intentions were noble.

Both Russian and American reformers wanted those who had suffered under the Soviet system to have better, freer, more prosperous lives. Each side believed that successful reforms would enable Russia to be "at peace with itself and with the world."[12] But while there were many free-market democracies in the world at the start of the 1990s, nearly all of them had evolved gradually over time, growing out of the rich soil of a substantial middle class and long experience with private enterprise and rule of law that the Soviet Union lacked. And when the recipe that the reformers devised for Russia's rapid transformation produced an unanticipated cascade of negative effects—a handful of crooked insiders owning billions of dollars of former state assets, an unprecedented 40 percent decline in gross domestic product, a shocking plunge in male life expectancy to some fifty-seven years—each side pointed fingers at the "predators" they deemed culpable rather than admitting misplaced confidence in their ability to reengineer a complex societal system. Learning lessons from what went so wrong with reforms in the 1990s is a critical part of taming the vicious cycles of US-Russian hostility that threaten to spin out of control today.

Russia's new leaders faced a daunting task as they surveyed the wreckage of the Soviet Union on its last day of existence, December 25, 1991. The newly independent Russian Federation had almost none of the attributes of a viable state, let alone a free-market democracy. First, the Soviet economy had collapsed. Store shelves had emptied, budget deficits had ballooned, and hard currency reserves had dwindled. The ruble was nearing worthlessness. Starvation threatened. Second, the levers of government that a normal state might employ to deal with this crisis barely functioned. Key government operations had been in the hands of the highly centralized but dysfunctional Soviet state, and Russia lacked the ability to collect taxes, coordinate monetary policy, control borders, regulate trade, enforce laws, or oversee military activity on its own. Directives were given but not carried out. Third, although the state had imploded, civil society was all but nonexistent. People were bewildered, demoralized, and spiritually exhausted. There was next to no private property or private enterprise. Genuine political parties and nongovernment civic organizations did not exist. Religious life had long been hollowed out. Decades of KGB informant networks had bred deep mistrust among Russians toward both the government and each other. The Russian republic had held its first legislative elections in 1990, but the newly created Russian Congress of People's Deputies had little experience with the business of passing actual legislation or representing the views and interests of its constituents. Under the circumstances, how were Russia's leaders to pull the country out of its rapidly worsening crisis?

A small team of young Russian economists, led by Yegor Gaidar and Anatoly Chubais, insisted that they had the answer. Russia's crisis, they argued, had its roots in Soviet leader Gorbachev's refusal to adopt true market-based reforms. Gorbachev had hoped to preserve some elements of the Soviet state-owned and state-run economic system, but his timid half measures had only made matters worse. The Soviet economy could not be tweaked, they argued, only destroyed and replaced. Putting the old system out of its misery would be painful, but "shock therapy"—Harvard economist Jeffrey Sachs's term for the immediate elimination of price controls, rapid privatization of state-owned enterprises, extreme tightening of the money supply, and radical reduction of government spending—would minimize the duration of that pain. Classical capitalism would restock Russia's empty shelves, reduce budget deficits, stabilize the currency, and begin to restore growth and prosperity within as little as a year.[13]

American experts largely agreed. There was a broad consensus in Washington at the time of the Soviet collapse that the fate of liberal reform in Russia would be a critical factor determining whether Moscow would make a decisive break with its old imperial ways. Senior officials strongly believed that the United States had a compelling interest in Russia's liberalization; the only question was how it should liberalize. A few lone voices warned that radical economic disruptions could produce a societal backlash and endanger the survival of Russia's fragile democracy, and they cautioned that the post-Soviet transition to capitalism should proceed carefully in accordance with local Russian traditions.[14] But the vast majority of American experts, including several Harvard economists who advised the Russians and later joined the Clinton administration, regarded Russian traditions as the problem, not the solution. A gradual transformation of the Soviet command economy would only allow benighted revanchists to choke reform in its cradle. Rapid market reforms, on the other hand, would produce a growing Russian middle class that would become the foundation for an enduring capitalist democracy.

President Yeltsin was no economist, but he liked the approach Gaidar and Chubais advocated. It not only promised an economic turnaround relatively soon, but it also contrasted nicely with Gorbachev's indecisiveness and resonated with the world's wealthiest and most powerful nation. And Yeltsin was not a patient man. As he put it in his memoirs, "I couldn't force people to wait once again, to drag out the main events and processes for years. If our minds were made up, we had to get going!"[15] He put Gaidar and Chubais in charge of economic stabilization and privatization, and they launched "shock therapy" on January 2, 1992. Overnight, most state-controlled prices were freed.[16] Then, in rapid succession, old import barriers were lifted, and private retail trade was legalized.

Much as the shock therapists anticipated, the pain was immediate: prices skyrocketed almost instantly. But they soon reached unexpectedly high hyperinflationary levels of 2,500 percent annually. Russians had only recently lost their empire and then their country, and now inflation caused them to lose their savings. "A scientist, whose salary in Soviet times may have been two hundred rubles a month, who may have saved five thousand rubles over a career, saw the value of his entire life savings shrink to a loaf of bread."[17] Consumer goods eventually returned to shelves, but by the time they did, no one could afford them. Stores became, as one observer put it, "museums," where Russians came to look but not buy. Protests spread across Russian cities, and people resorted to bartering and selling personal possessions on the streets to get by. By April, Gaidar had become Russia's most unpopular figure, and by year-end, he was forced to resign from his post as acting prime minister and play a less public role on Yeltsin's team.

The problem was not that Gaidar was a bad economist. He understood the workings of a classical market economy well, probably better than any other economist in Russia. But he failed to grasp the limits imposed by the complexities of the broader social and political system in which he was operating,[18] so he was surprised when his narrowly focused technocratic prescriptions produced unintentional cascading effects. Ending state price controls was necessary, but freeing prices without first breaking up the Soviet economy's numerous monopolies to create market competition had invited an uncontrollable inflationary spiral. Monopolists, not markets, started dictating prices. Tightening Russia's money supplies made sense, but it was impossible to do when the other newly independent former Soviet republics also had the ability to print rubles and when the chairman of Russia's own central bank was not on board with the reform team. As one humorist put it, Russia was like a man who had fourteen bitter ex-wives, each of whom still had a credit card billed to his account.[19] And imposing radical market reforms from above without erecting a social safety net or building political support from below created the impression that the Yeltsin team was indifferent to popular suffering. Reformers who were attempting to save Russia quickly came to be seen as wreckers who were trying to destroy it.

Yeltsin's team adjusted tack amid the storm. They launched an ambitious privatization effort to break up state monopolies, create market competition, and incentivize investment. They tried to explain their approach to the public and build political support. Yeltsin named an experienced Soviet industrial manager, Viktor Chernomyrdin, as prime minister. And Yeltsin's team worked even more closely with American advisers and government officials to think through their next steps, win large infusions of credit from the World Bank and International Monetary Fund, and cushion the blows of reform.

But while each of the steps they adopted helped to ease some problems, they created others in the process. Establishing new privately owned banks to replace the Soviet state bank, for example, was an important step toward building a functioning financial sector supporting genuine markets. But where would the banks get their capital? In a country where the state owned nearly everything, only the state had money. So several new banks convinced government ministries to deposit their money in special accounts within specific "authorized banks." And once the banks had state funds on hand, they quickly found lucrative ways to make easy money off of it. Rather than lending money to new entrepreneurs or to old enterprises that needed to retool, the banks made big money off currency speculation.[20] And by delaying disbursements, they could keep funds available to invest in high-yield government bonds and reap huge profits.[21] But that meant that "coal miners, pensioners, teachers, and nurses [among others] went without pay" because the banks would not release the funds to pay them in a timely fashion.[22] Enterprises could not pay their suppliers and went into arrears. That had a domino effect on other enterprises, creating a massive inter-enterprise debt problem.

So an economy that had been running on fumes for the waning years of Soviet rule did the only thing it could under the circumstances: it demonetized. People dumped their rubles and turned to dollars, gold, silver, and barter. Transactions increasingly went off books and underground. "Authorized banks" making huge profits off government deposits shipped their earnings to secret accounts in offshore tax havens denominated in dollars, safe from the reach of the state. With enterprises conducting fewer and fewer transactions officially, and accumulating more and more of their income off-book, the Russian government collected even fewer taxes. The less it collected, the weaker the state grew, and the less it was able to provide the basic services of government. Citizens lost any remaining respect for state officials, and the country's ethnic republics—including Chechnya—spun increasingly out of Moscow's control. Corruption and lawlessness spread. Organized crime exploded. Countless Russians desperate to escape poverty fell prey to cynical get-rich-quick scammers.

The Yeltsin reformers sought two ways out of this vicious circle. The first was to lean even more heavily on American help. Borrowing from the World Bank, International Monetary Fund, and other lending institutions became Russia's primary means to cover its massive budget deficits. Cultivating close relations with official and unofficial Washington heavyweights, in turn, became the Yeltsin team's best way to convince those institutions to keep lending money. America formed "a strategic alliance with Russian reform," as President Clinton put it. And the more money the West lent, the more political pressures mounted to show success for its effort. Washington leveraged Russia's need for debt relief and infusions of capital to push for policies aimed at "transforming almost every aspect of Russian economic, political, and social life."[23] A top

Russian diplomat commented at the time that "among ourselves, we call Talbott [the top American official overseeing Russia policy] 'Proconsul Strobe.' He has all the answers and rarely hesitates to tell us what to do, as if we were small children in need of instruction."[24]

Yeltsin's second approach was to consolidate power to overcome political resistance. As Russia's living standards plummeted and popular opposition to "shock therapy" exploded, the Yeltsin team sought a renewed popular mandate by holding a national referendum in April 1993 asking four questions: whether Russians had confidence in Yeltsin, whether they supported his reforms, whether Russia should hold an early presidential election, and whether early legislative elections should be held. American advisers created a high-profile, Western-funded public relations campaign for the referendum, urging Russians to vote "Da, Da, Nyet, Da" on the four questions.[25] Yeltsin prevailed narrowly in the referendum, but Russians would not forget such overt American involvement in Russia's politics.[26]

Despite the temporary political boost provided to Yeltsin by the referendum, it had become clear by the fall of 1993 that the tension between economic reform and democratic governance had reached a breaking point. Russia could not continue radical market reforms without dissolving the democratically elected Russian legislature, which had openly rebelled against Yeltsin's rule. In October 1993, he ordered tanks to shell the legislative building, killing more than one hundred of its occupants. In the aftermath of the violence, the Kremlin engineered the approval of a new constitution that dramatically increased Yeltsin's executive power and diminished that of the new parliament, the State Duma. When the Clinton administration backed Yeltsin's moves against what it termed "reactionaries," many Russians concluded that Washington cared little for their economic plight and even less for genuine democratic governance. According to gradualist reformer Grigory

Yavlinsky, "The Russian people expected to hear something like this: 'We Americans understand the difficulties you are facing. America has been through the Depression, has dealt with crime and corruption. Please do not think that crime and corruption are normal attributes of democracy.' Instead, all they heard was unstinting praise for the [Russian] government."[27]

Russian voters made their unhappiness clear in the December 1993 elections to the new State Duma. Gaidar led a pro-Yeltsin reform party called Russia's Choice, but the "shock therapists" garnered a disappointing 15 percent of the vote. The anti-reform nationalist party of the bombastic Vladimir Zhirinovsky took first place with nearly a quarter of the vote, and the Communists and other anti-reform parties won another 20 percent, with a sprinkling of votes for gradualist-reform and special-interest parties accounting for much of the remainder. Washington was stunned. Almost no one had seen Yeltsin's popular rebuke coming.[28] In a press conference following the vote, Strobe Talbott suggested that the results reflected the need for "less shock and more therapy for the Russian people."

But many of the shocks had already been administered, and backing off reforms could stall Russia's transformation in a catastrophic no-man's-land between capitalism and socialism where nothing functioned at all. In the face of a hostile legislature, Yeltsin increasingly resorted to imposing reforms by executive decree, and Chubais pressed the accelerator on his privatization program, worrying that Russia had to make privatization irreversible before revanchists recaptured the reins of power. To get a vital piece of legislation through the Duma, he reluctantly agreed to a provision that would allow workers and managers in state enterprises to buy 51 percent of the shares of their new privatized companies at a nominal price.[29] Chubais reasoned that it was the best he could do under the circumstances and that market forces would eventually force the privatized companies to retool and restructure no matter who ran them. But in practice, this meant not only that the government failed to earn much revenue selling ownership shares but also that the old Soviet factory managers under communism became the new Russian managers under capitalism. They pressured workers to sell their shares to management for a pittance and had none of their own skin in the game. Rather than rebuild their companies into efficient producers, many of these "red directors" simply stripped them of assets and embezzled funds. A program aimed at progress produced regression.

The reformers' most fateful compromise came in 1995 and 1996, as legislative and presidential elections approached. By that time, Yeltsin's once robust popularity had cratered, his approval ratings consistently registering well below 10 percent. The Communist Party was clearly Russia's strongest political organization, and Communist presidential candidate Gennady Zyuganov's polling numbers dwarfed those of Yeltsin. Unless Yeltsin somehow pulled some election magic out of his hat, the reformers looked to be on the way out. To conjure up that magic, Chubais struck a backroom deal with a handful of Russia's leading bankers and media moguls. In return for lending their financial and media support to the Yeltsin campaign, the moguls would be granted large shares in the crown jewels of the Russian economy, the prized state-owned enterprises in the oil and gas and extractive industries worth billions of dollars. It was a win-win deal for the bankers. The "loans for shares" deal would make them instant billionaires while minimizing the chances that a Communist government might seize their ill-gotten gains and jail them. Chubais recognized that he was making a Faustian bargain, selling the state's most valuable assets for a tiny fraction of their worth, but he saw no viable alternative.

The deal worked as both sides had hoped. The bankers poured millions of dollars into the Yeltsin campaign to produce television advertising that blanketed the airwaves. American political experts advised the campaign on tactics and messaging. And the Russian media moguls provided the campaign with the equivalent of many more millions in unpaid advertising by focusing network news coverage relentlessly on Yeltsin, lavishly praising his accomplishments and virtues. On the few occasions when television did devote airtime to Zyuganov, news coverage lambasted him. Yeltsin won reelection, Washington breathed a sigh of relief, and the moguls won both instant billions and instant power.

Afterward, some moguls officially joined the new Yeltsin government as ministers and presidential administration members. Others exercised their political power unofficially in what became known as the *semibankirshchina*, or "reign of the seven bankers." Some were part of a shadowy group of Yeltsin relatives and close aides that became known as the "Family," which served as a substitute presidency to compensate for the fact that Yeltsin could no longer govern, having suffered an unpublicized heart attack during the presidential campaign and undergone bypass surgery thereafter, while increasingly succumbing to alcoholism. Russia had privatized and staved off the communist threat. But it had not become a free-market democracy. It had become an oligarchy, with a handful of obscenely wealthy businessmen presiding over a government that could not function, underpinned by a corrupt, semi-criminal economy.

When an ailing Yeltsin resigned the presidency in 1999, apologizing to the Russian people for his failures and turning his administration over to his prime minister, Vladimir Putin, two questions loomed large: Who was to blame for the mess Russia found itself in? And what should be done about it? A few Russians, and many Americans, felt that the Yeltsin team had backed off reforms too soon, watering them down quickly when they met popular resistance, not paying enough attention to democratic reforms, and never completely following through on the reform agenda. The reforms that they did implement accomplished a lot, according to this school of thought, and a stronger reform team would have done a better job of explaining its approach to the public and building support in Russian society. For these die-hard believers in shock therapy, the villains in this tale were those ignorant of market economics and democratic principles who stood in the way of history's inevitable progress. This only prolonged the pain that Russia would sooner or later have to endure. Getting reform back on track was the only viable path to success in post-Yeltsin Russia.

Others viewed the 1990s not as a narrative of disrupted reforms but as a story of the decline and destruction of the Russian state, a process that had started in the Soviet period, and which accelerated under reforms designed, as Ronald Reagan might have put it, to get the state off the people's backs.[30] Absent that state, however, no private enterprises or civic institutions existed in Russia that could encourage virtuous behavior and respect for the law. In an anything-goes atmosphere, anything went. Democratic and market reforms were both possible and desirable, according to this school of thought, but they should be advanced slowly and carefully over time in accord with Russian history and long-standing traditions, and they could not take place without restoring the state's authority and capacity for governance. Putin and other *gosudarstvenniki*—loosely translated as *statists*—strongly advocated such an approach.

Still others adopted a different diagnosis. Like the Yellowstone park managers who blamed decline on predators, some pointed fingers at Yeltsin's reformers, at the "oligarchs," and at the Americans thought to be their allies. Ousting these malefactors was the key to progress. Gaidar came to be regarded suspiciously as a foreign agent. Chubais became the most unpopular man in Russia. The oligarchs were seen as robber barons, stripping the motherland of its riches while ostentatiously flaunting their stolen wealth and frequenting luxury resorts in the West. And because American officials had played such a public and intrusive role in Russian policies, many Russians assumed that the United States, the world's most powerful nation, had "lured us into a trap, that this was done intentionally. They wanted us weakened."[31] The "fundamental attribution error"—the assumption that bad outcomes are the result of bad intentions or bad character, not difficult circumstances—was evident in Russian perceptions.

Viewed through the prism of Yellowstone National Park's complex mix of interacting problems a century ago, however, Russia's catastrophic experiences in the 1990s look more like good intentions gone bad than malfeasance on the part of key individual actors. Attempting to reengineer such a complex and delicate social organism was an enormously ambitious undertaking, prone to precipitating a wide range of knock-on effects difficult to anticipate. The shock therapists of the 1990s may have been guilty of overconfidence, but not of bad intentions. Their failures showed that creating a free-market democracy from scratch is neither a linear process nor a mere matter of will and perseverance. The legacy that decade left behind, however, is an important part of another set of complex system dynamics, one that today threatens to pull the United States and Russia into an unwanted, disastrous spiral of confrontation.

These brief overviews of Yellowstone's travails in the late nineteenth and early twentieth centuries and Russia's collapse in the 1990s provide a key lesson in what not to do when faced with a complex systems problem: do not treat it as if it were a linear problem, rooted in a single or primary cause that can be resolved through a determined effort. The Yellowstone managers initially believed the park was suffering primarily from predation—the more predation, the fewer elk, bison, and other game. Thus, they reasoned, reducing predation should solve the problem. But it did not; it caused even greater problems. Their diagnosis failed to consider the dynamics of the broader ecological system encompassing the park. The shock therapists in Russia encountered similar surprises for similar reasons, zeroing in on the economy as the primary cause of Russia's problems, which they attempted to address with a Herculean campaign. But pressing the accelerator of economic reform did not hasten Russia's journey toward greater prosperity and better governance, and in some ways diverted it.

This has important implications for the ways the United States has attempted to deal with Russia since the Cold War's end. We have tended to look for primary causes of what we believe are essentially linear problems, recently attributing the growing dangers in the US-Russian relationship to the nature of Putinism and Russia's endemic expansionism, believing resolute counterpressure will quell Russian appetites for aggression. We have attempted to seek progress through incremental steps, in the hope that making headway on some discrete problems can build momentum toward larger success. We have habitually sought to compartmentalize issues, preferring to focus on those driven by domestic politics or those that we think hold the best hopes for progress.

This incremental and compartmentalized approach makes abundant sense intuitively. Why complicate things, when one can break the problem down into its component parts and focus on what is most salient or easily achievable? It is also driven by the bureaucratic silo effect, which encourages narrow specialization while discouraging cross-organizational integration. But it has not worked in practice.[32] For example, we have attempted to tackle complex issues such as Ukraine in isolation of broader factors, only to find that putting off such thorny subjects as how to structure Europe's security architecture and how to deal with the controversies over interfering in internal governance renders progress on Ukraine all but impossible. We have hoped that US-Russian cooperation against terrorism or joint efforts to deal with the Iranian nuclear problem might build momentum in other areas, only to find in frustration that success has not proved contagious. We have largely treated Russian cyberintrusions as a technical security issue, and Russia's subversive influence operations as an aggression challenge, only to find that cybersecurity measures cannot keep pace with the offense and that our punishments of aggression are not resolving the problem and may be making it worse. Meanwhile, our attempts to isolate and pressure Russia have had unexpected secondary effects, reinforcing Russian incentives to deepen security cooperation with China and subvert NATO and the EU. As planning expert Russell Ackoff has observed about "messes," his term for complex systems problems, "if we do the usual thing and break up a mess into its component problems and then try to solve each one separately, we will not solve the mess." The fundamental dictum of complex systems, that one "can never merely do one thing," means not only that our actions will always have secondary effects but also that in order to bring about desired change, we must do several things at once.[33]

A more holistic approach to dealing with our complex set of problems with Russia would make for a greater challenge in managing the US interagency process, necessitating a larger number of players and deeper integration of regional and functional issues, but without one, we are likely to find ourselves continually slipping backward as we struggle for progress. The simple recognition that we are dealing not with a linear Russia problem but rather with the dangers posed by a complex system may by itself have a salutary effect on our approach. Awareness that we must change course could stimulate creative efforts to find new (albeit less direct) paths to success.[34]

Recognition that our problems with Russia are not linear has other implications as well. It suggests that we should approach our ambitions with a good deal more humility, acknowledging the limits of our knowledge and our capabilities, while remaining alert to the risks of unintended knock-on effects from our policies. This has particular relevance to the question of promoting democratization, an issue that has plagued the US-Russian relationship for nearly the entire post–Cold War period. George F. Kennan, the father of America's Cold War containment policy and among the most insightful experts on Russia that our country has produced, warned against ambitious attempts to reshape foreign societies some four decades prior to the disastrous Russian reforms of the 1990s: "The ways by which peoples advance toward dignity and enlightenment in government are things that constitute the deepest and most intimate processes of national life. There is nothing less understandable to foreigners, nothing in which foreign interference can do less good."[35] His advice was premised not on disputation of the virtues that enlightened governance abroad might bring but rather on the recognition of our own limitations in diagnosing and treating the ailments of other countries. "This whole tendency to see ourselves as the center of political enlightenment and as teachers to a great part of the rest of the world strikes me as unthought-through, vainglorious and undesirable," he later cautioned.[36] Realist scholar John Mearsheimer recently put it even more plainly: "Social engineering in any country, even one's own, is difficult. The problems are multifaceted and complex, resistance is inevitable, and there are always unintended consequences, some of them bad."[37] To this, one might add that good intentions and high ideals are not the only yardsticks by which to assess virtue; implicitly promising the attainment of outcomes that America lacks the power to effect is a moral hazard in its own right.

Reconsidering how we have approached democratization does not and should not require the United States to abandon its ideals or change its nature. Advancing the causes of liberty and justice in the world is an inherent part of what America is and what it represents. But *how* we advance these ideals matters immensely. If liberalization is not a linear process but one shaped within the contours of a complex, interacting set of factors, most of which we do not and cannot control, then a more humble approach is warranted. Identifying those factors in which the United States can play the most beneficial part, while attempting to minimize the prospects of counterproductive actions, might improve our dismal results in encouraging liberalization abroad. Serving as a powerful example, the "shining city on the hill" that attracts the world's respect and emulation can be an effective way to advance democratic ideals, and it is a factor that the United States most directly controls. Attempting to impose liberal governance through pressure or coercion, however, in the belief that democratization is a linear process that follows a universal recipe for success, can lead to failures that provoke opposition abroad and prompt doubts at home about our system of governance.

Washington's foreign policy culture is biased toward action. When problems arise, our first impulse is to "do something," which at times can foster the impression that we regard any action as better than none. By contrast, this chapter has focused on what not to do, acknowledging the vast potential for unintentionally compounding problems in the context of complex systems dynamics. Avoiding such errors will not by itself restore US-Russian relations to health or eliminate the dangers of escalatory spirals. It will not settle genuine conflicts of interest over Europe's security architecture, resolve fundamental differences in US-Russian values, or address the problems flowing from cybertechnology. But in a relationship woefully short on trust, a focus on learning from the common threads running through our past mistakes is something each side can do independently, without need of the other reciprocating or making concessions. The old dictum, "When you find yourself in a hole, stop digging," contains valuable wisdom. Once we have stopped, we can begin to lay the foundation for new rules of the shadow war game and new mechanisms for absorbing future shocks to the system.

6

Absorbing Shocks

Shock absorbers are the pessimists of the automotive world. Their very existence is premised on the belief that roads and highways will inevitably include some bumps and potholes and debris of various kinds, no matter how hard our road designers and construction engineers and maintenance crews work to avoid them. Their purpose is not to correct these defects but to make them less damaging to vehicles and less painful to drivers and passengers. They reflect a recognition that imperfect roads are a chronic condition of transportation, one that we can minimize but not eliminate.

Our interwoven and dynamic world makes shocks—surprise developments that diverge sharply and suddenly from the trends preceding them, sometimes producing disastrous outcomes, sometimes not—all but inevitable. In recent decades, these shocks have included the disintegration of the Soviet Union, the 2008 financial crisis, and the Arab Spring, all discontinuous "black swan" events resulting from complex systems dynamics. The exact form and timing of these shocks are nearly impossible to predict, but their impact can be cushioned, their effects managed. If the first order of dealing with complex systems problems is to avoid treating them as if they were linear problems, susceptible to piecemeal resolution, the second is to build resilience into the system, rendering shocks, when they come, less damaging than they would otherwise be.

A focus on resilience differs in significant ways from efforts to promote stability. Stability is, all things being equal, usually a desirable thing. But in some contexts, the search for stability can be counterproductive. Buildings that are too rigid will crumble under the stress of an earthquake. Similarly, stability strategies that emphasize preventing danger and eliminating risk in the realm of foreign affairs can become too rigid to withstand shocks, too unimaginative to adapt to challenges, too protective of the status quo to adjust to change.

When stability strategies fail, as in the prelude to World War I, their failure can be catastrophic.

In the second half of the nineteenth century, the European system grew increasingly rigid, unable to adjust incrementally to new geopolitical challenges and changing domestic politics. Europe devolved into a system of rival alliances focused on reinforcing the bonds within each camp rather than maintaining broader equilibrium on the continent. Diplomacy lost touch with new technologies and their implications for warfare, and proved unable to cope with the imperatives that were driven by the advent of the railroad and the advantages that would flow from preemptive attack. As a result, the system amplified rather than buffered disturbances and became highly susceptible to shocks generated by relatively minor disputes.[1]

Resilience strategies, by contrast, acknowledge the inevitability of change and the probability of shocks, and they focus on more general capabilities to respond to hazards when they occur, regardless of what they are.[2] California's Loma Prieta earthquake in 1989, for example, caused the iconic fifty-two-story Transamerica building in San Francisco to sway wildly but produced no lasting damage to the flexible structure, while more rigid buildings not far away collapsed altogether. The early nineteenth-century Concert of Europe featured similar resilience. Prior to the shocks of the Crimean War in 1853 and German unification in 1871, it had been an adaptable and flexible system, able to make incremental adjustments as needed to manage disturbances. It was aimed not at preventing conflicts altogether but at limiting their impact and containing their dangers. How might we build such resilience into the system that is both shaping and shaped by US-Russian relations, improving its ability to bend but not break under stress?

COMMUNICATIONS RESILIENCE

The successful management of any crisis begins with communications. In the wake of the Cuban missile crisis, the United States and Soviet Union established the so-called hotline linking leaders in Washington and Moscow, because it was evident that direct and timely communications were vital to managing crises in ways that minimized prospects for escalation. A similar recognition about the need for American and Russian military commanders in Syria to avoid accidental clashes between their forces led them to establish an official deconfliction channel there in 2016. Extending this narrow channel into broader US-Russian discussions of how we might handle possible security crises in Europe and beyond would be an important preparatory step toward better crisis management. There is much potential danger to discuss in Ukraine, North Korea, Iran, and elsewhere, in our parallel efforts to battle terrorists, and in how we handle the thorny issue of cyberoperations, including false-flag cyberattacks designed to deflect blame or even spark US-Russian conflict.

Communications are not only useful in avoiding accidents and misunderstandings; they are also the best means available for contending with two unavoidable problems that flow from twenty-first-century technology: time and ambiguity. Time played a critical role in the tragedy of World War I, as military leaders pressed to mobilize forces quickly to outflank the enemy rather than be outflanked, and diplomacy relying on the slow transmission of letters and telegrams could not keep pace.[3] Time is even more problematic today. News and information flow at light speed across the globe, and the demand for almost instantaneous commentary on cable television and in social media and other digital forums puts enormous pressures on governments to issue statements and adopt policy positions well before the facts of an emerging conflict situation—or their meaning in larger context—are evident. The rapidity with which high-precision weapons systems can strike targets half a world away could force national leaders to make fateful military launch decisions in minutes, rather than hours or days. Moreover, the inherent ambiguity of the cyberworld, coupled with the entanglement of nuclear and conventional weapons systems and the vulnerability of satellite networks, means that they might have to make such decisions with little clarity about the origin or intention of devastating digital attacks. The combination of shrinking time, increasing ambiguity, and burgeoning streams of data is driving increased reliance on artificial intelligence and automation to assess and respond to threats. This can potentially reduce the role of human decision-makers, increase the chances of accidents, and narrow the opportunities for compromise. The time for discussing how to handle such dangers is now, not in the suffocating heat of a crisis.

For maximum resilience, formal lines of communication are not enough. In high-stakes crises, emotions can run hot and the mooting of compromises can be a most delicate matter. Lower-level representatives engaging in off-the-record discussions have greater freedom to explore possible off-ramps and convey the limits of flexibility than do heads of state. In the Cuban missile crisis, the "confidential channel" between US Attorney General Robert Kennedy and Soviet ambassador Anatoly Dobrynin played a crucial role in averting disaster. In fact, the ultimate resolution to the crisis—a secret understanding that Kennedy would remove American nuclear missiles stationed in Turkey after the Soviets dismantled missile sites in Cuba, an understanding that would not be put in writing or acknowledged publicly—was brokered between Kennedy and Dobrynin.[4]

The fact of a confidential channel is less important, however, than the quality of the communication within it. That quality, in turn, depends both on the skills and wisdom of the specific personnel involved and on the recognition by leaders in both Washington and Moscow that they must invest in building and safeguarding the relationships that the channel requires for effectiveness. Dobrynin observed in his memoirs that a channel that ensured "possibilities for a candid if not always pleasant dialogue between the leaders of both countries . . . appeared to be the only way of preventing the Cold War from turning into a hot one." But to work, he added,

> [the confidential channel] has to be permanently available, and its immediate participants must possess a certain level of diplomatic and political experience and knowledge. Above all, the channel should never be used by any government for the purpose of misinformation. Of course, a diplomatic game is always being played, but deliberate misinformation is inadmissible, for sooner or later it is going to be disclosed and the channel will lose all its value.[5]

Dobrynin's caution against transmitting misinformation in the channel reflects the critical but fragile role of trust in its effectiveness. The belief that one's interlocutor is lying can quickly prove fatal to a relationship, particularly one in which the stakes are as great as those in the US-Russia relationship. A certain degree of personal trust—including that conversations in the channel will remain confidential—is a prerequisite for using the channel to clarify intentions, to communicate key redlines and vital interests, and to moot potential formal and informal understandings that might be too risky to explore directly at the presidential level. Sound relationships take time to establish, however; they cannot be created on the spur of the moment during a crisis. Incorporating that feature as an enduring element of the system is a critical part of enhancing resilience.

One of the factors contributing to systemic fragility is ambiguity about the sides' strategic intentions. As discussed in this book's first two chapters, part of this ambiguity derives from the inherent uncertainties involved in cyberoperations, and part is a result of each side's growing conviction that the other is intent on its destruction. These perceptions are fueling escalatory spirals of suspicion and distrust and increasing the likelihood that each side will overreact in a crisis. There is no way out of this perceptual spiral other than strategic dialogue that directly addresses each side's intentions and its perceptions of its most important national interests. Such a dialogue cannot eliminate genuine conflicts of national interest, but it could conceivably narrow ambiguity and help to minimize the role of misperception in driving each side's actions. Given the present domestic political obstacles, pursuing a direct dialogue between the White House and Kremlin is not a near-term possibility, but so-called Track II discussions of prominent nongovernment experts could nonetheless help.

This approach to building systemic resilience through formal and informal channels of communication stands in contrast to the approach the United States has employed in recent years, which has treated official contacts with Moscow as something to be turned on and off in response to Russian behavior, either as a reward or punishment. Following the Russian-Georgian war in 2008, for example, the Bush administration took a step that was unprecedented in the post–Cold War period, cutting off all official US-Russian contacts above the level of deputy assistant secretary, in order to show the Russians "that they could not get away with something like invading Georgia."[6] Only a handful of years later, after full diplomatic contacts had been restored under Obama's "reset" policies, Washington again attempted to send Moscow to the diplomatic sidelines following its annexation of Crimea and covert war in eastern Ukraine, joining other G8 states in kicking Russia out of that great power club, suspending cooperation with Russia in the NATO-Russia Council, and imposing travel bans and economic sanctions on named individuals in and out of the Russian government. These policies have largely continued under the Trump administration in the aftermath of the 2016 election-meddling controversy. The newly appointed Russian ambassador to the United States complained of difficulty getting meetings in Washington,[7] and media reports that presidential son-in-law Jared Kushner attempted to create a "secret channel" for discussions with Moscow produced an avalanche of criticism.[8]

However justified the United States has been in imposing a price for Russian aggression, attempting to isolate Russia in our globalized world has failed in practice. Judging from Moscow's continued belligerence against NATO in general and Ukraine in particular, banning Russia's presence at the European "adults' table" has done little to prompt reconsideration in Moscow, but it has almost certainly reinforced Russian perceptions of Western hostility and added to its incentives to subvert the Western alliance. And as doors have shut to Russian diplomats in Europe and the United States, Russia has responded with such steps as deepening ties to China, intervening militarily in Syria, and using undeclared agents of influence to establish relationships with prominent Americans, circumventing its diplomatic isolation—none of which has served US interests.[9]

TECHNOLOGICAL RESILIENCE

Part of designing resilience into the system involves identifying critical "single point of failure" features and building backups that can compensate for their damage or loss. As processes that were once performed by humans have increasingly grown more automated, we have realized stunning efficiencies. Automated inventory and delivery systems allow "just-in-time" provision of food and consumer goods and massively reduce waste. Modern ports employ automated cargo-handling to improve capacity and reduce the costs of manual labor. These systems are not only vulnerable to cyberinterference from Russia and a range of other state-sponsored and individual cyberactors but also to extreme weather events flowing from climate change.

The American Global Positioning System (GPS) is but one example of a system on which numerous critical military and commercial functions depend, but which is highly vulnerable to disruption and at present is not adequately backed up by emergency alternative systems. Plans have recently been put in place to provide such a backup, but they have been moving slowly. Most experts have long agreed that the "eLORAN" system (Enhanced Long-Range Aids to Navigation), developed by the US Coast Guard, can provide an effective non-GPS-dependent timing and navigation system that can sustain critical national communications and other GPS-related functions in the event of a sustained outage, and provision for its further development and use was signed into law by President Trump in 2018.[10] But discussions about the need for a backup system have been under way for nearly twenty years,[11] and even now the new legislation makes implementation "subject to the availability of appropriations." The pace of progress has lagged vastly behind the urgency of the problem.

Electoral systems are another area where we have been slow to grasp the magnitude of our vulnerability and slow to put backup systems in place. Research by cybersecurity professionals has long revealed numerous electoral system vulnerabilities, dating back more than a decade. "Ethical hackers" investigating system problems have been able quickly to penetrate voting machines even when they are air-gapped from the internet, suggesting that hostile "black hat" hackers could, if they chose, alter the casting of votes inside polling places.[12] Despite belated efforts to improve election system security since the revelations of Russian interference in the 2016 election, voter databases remain susceptible to intrusions and data corruption, and the tabulation and reporting of vote tallies remain vulnerable to interference. There is no single fix for these problems, but one low-cost step that would significantly improve the resilience of our electoral process is the use of paper ballots to back up electronic voting and the employment of low-cost scanners to record and tally those ballots. Many—though far from all—state electoral commissions have begun to adopt this approach.[13]

Other parts of America's critical national infrastructure are in similar need of greater resilience. Many of our power plants, water systems, ports, and energy supply networks are dependent on automated industrial control systems (ICS) and supervisory control and data acquisition (SCADA) systems that are highly vulnerable to cybersabotage. Too few of them have independent backup systems in place that could function in the event of an emergency. One of the factors that allowed Ukraine to limit the impact of Russian cyberattacks on its power grid in 2015 and 2016 was that its relatively unsophisticated network could function manually when automated systems failed.[14] Building such fail-safes into America's power grid and other critical infrastructure would require a high-cost, long-term effort.[15] Without one, however, our vulnerability to potentially paralyzing cyberdisruptions will continue.

One of the domains most at risk—yet designed as if it were immune to threats—is not on the ground but in space. The United States is increasingly dependent on space-based assets for both civilian and military communications, early warning of missile launches and other military threats, and delivery of precision-targeted weapons to their targets. Nearly every aspect of America's "smart warfare" capabilities on which our military superiority depends is in turn dependent on space. But our potential adversaries, including the Russians, have begun to regard this dependence as America's Achilles' heel, and they have been rapidly increasing their ability to target our space-based assets, turning one of our biggest assets into a problematic vulnerability.[16] Ground-based kinetic anti-satellite weapons can increasingly threaten satellites in a variety of orbits, laser weapons and other high-technology devices can disable or disrupt them, and cyberweapons potentially can corrupt or interfere with their operations. Moreover, much of this satellite network is dual-purpose, supporting both conventional and nuclear operations. This commingling means that Russian actions meant to undermine our conventional military effectiveness in a regional conflict by targeting vulnerable satellites could, by accident more than design, threaten our strategic systems and spin into a broader nuclear confrontation. According to General William Shelton, former commander of US space forces, "Our satellites were not built with such threats in mind."

New threats to our space-based assets are a reality that we cannot eliminate. Building greater resilience into our systems could help, however. Since the end of the Cold War, our satellite technology has grown more capable and better able to endure the stresses of a nuclear war, but to save scarce budgetary dollars, this has come at the cost of redundancy.[17] According to Elbridge Colby, a former deputy assistant secretary of defense in the Trump administration, building separate space-based systems to handle nuclear and conventional applications could not only add valuable redundancy but also reduce the chances of inadvertent escalation from conventional to nuclear war, and provide tactical warfighting advantages to the United States in a potential confrontation with Russia.[18] Such an effort would necessarily require an expensive, long-term program, but the benefits could be well worth the costs.

This overall approach to building technological resilience would represent a significant shift in the way the United States has approached its critical infrastructure. During the Cold War, our infrastructure was largely invulnerable to attack outside the context of an unlikely nuclear war. We were able to treat our space-based assets as secure, and we viewed our ground-based infrastructure as an essentially economic asset beyond the reach of our adversaries. But the advent of the cyberage requires a change of perspective, so that we begin to see our critical infrastructure as a key component of national security even when the connection to military operations is indirect, in much the same way that the federal government decided in the 1950s that the country required an interstate highway system as a matter of national security to help move troops and weapons, not just for more efficient personal and commercial transportation.

RESILIENT RULES

A system without rules is inherently fragile. The US-Soviet relationship was most vulnerable to instability during the early Cold War period when rules to govern it had not yet been clearly established. The crises over Berlin and Cuba had their roots in Soviet probing of the limits of America's tolerance and of its willingness to run risks. As those limits became evident, a set of formal and informal rules began to take shape that reduced the chances that third world proxy wars and other forms of superpower competition in the 1970s and 1980s might escalate into broader conflict. Today, both the cyberworld and the space domain are in an analogous state to the early Cold War period, with no consensus among the great powers on rules that might contain dangers.

But a system with rules that are too rigid can fail to adapt to change and manage shocks. The arms control regimes and Helsinki Rules that characterized the mid-to-late–Cold War world have crumbled in recent years because they failed to adjust to the stresses of emerging multipolarity, new technologies, and political change. Europe's security architecture and the governance of international financial institutions are current examples of areas in which America's preferred norms are under challenge by Russia, China, or other emerging powers. Finding a balance between too much rigidity and too little structure is critical to enhancing systemic resilience in the twenty-first century.

Formal arms control arrangements can continue to have a place in an evolving set of resilient rules, but they are unlikely to play as large a role as they did during the Cold War. A weapons-based arms-control approach is ill-suited to the cyberworld, where malware is constantly evolving and where states have enormous disincentives to put their capabilities at risk by unveiling any specific features. Even in the nuclear domain, traditional approaches to arms control are growing more impractical as the lines between nuclear, cyber, and conventional warfare blur. Limits on weapons systems were effective during the Cold War, when each party to a bilateral treaty could balance its arsenal against the other, and anti-ballistic missile systems that might otherwise fuel an arms race were rudimentary and sure to be overwhelmed. But in a multipolar world, in which the United States and Russia must each contend not only with the other's nuclear weapons but also with those of China and other nuclear powers, such a balance starts to break down. Modern ballistic missile defense systems can play a meaningful role in contending with the small arsenals of emerging nuclear powers, but in so doing, they inevitably affect the perception of balanced bilateral capabilities and mutually assured destruction that underpinned Cold War arms control. If one side can effectively shoot down at least some portion of the other's missiles, the rival side is incentivized to improve its arsenal both quantitatively and qualitatively to compensate, complicating prospects for treaty-based limitations. Moreover, when the United States, Russia, and China all see each other to varying degrees as rivals, attempting to limit their nuclear arsenals to common numerical ceilings becomes unviable absent a mutual willingness to adopt a "minimal sufficiency" approach to deterrence rather than a "war-fighting" approach, based on the belief that deterrence depends on the ability to fight and win a potential nuclear war against any combination of opponents. As defense expert Andrew Krepinevich put it, "In a world with three nuclear great powers, none can maintain parity with the combined forces of the other two."[19]

Where formal treaty limitations might fail, however, informal understandings and agreed codes of conduct might help. Following the Cuban missile crisis, both sides implicitly recognized the dangers of stationing strategic nuclear missiles near the other's borders, in large part because short distances to targets would greatly abbreviate the warning times within which to make counter-launch decisions and leave them dangerously prone to war by accident. The exception to that norm—the American deployment of Pershing II missiles in Europe in the early 1980s—proved the rule and ultimately produced the INF Treaty's formal ban on intermediate-range missiles. A geographic restriction on the deployment of strategic weapons today could be helpful in reducing tensions.

Similarly, although legally binding limits on cybercapabilities are not feasible, a proscription against cyberintrusions or other forms of cyberattack on critical infrastructure—including electoral infrastructure, nuclear command and control systems, and nonmilitary satellite systems—should be possible, particularly if it were backed up by credible threats of retaliatory punishment should it be violated. Both in the cyberworld and in space, the United States and Russia share an interest in protecting their critical assets from damage or destruction, and each is largely dependent on the self-restraint of the other in refraining from attacks. Negotiating where the lines are drawn can be a basis for establishing and enforcing a resilient set of rules.

Agreeing on rules to govern cyberinfluence efforts, in addition to those involving cyberintrusions and attacks on critical infrastructure, should also be possible. Joseph Nye, a Harvard scholar who once chaired the National Intelligence Council, argues that the United States and Russia could draw a line between the "permitted soft power of open persuasion and the hard power of covert information warfare."[20] Openly acknowledged and properly labelled content would be declared in-bounds; deceptive, illegally procured, or covertly produced content would be out of bounds.

Skeptics in both the United States and Russia scoff at the notion that rules might somehow limit the actions of either side, which they see as having little respect for rules or treaties, while harboring deadly intent toward its adversary. And it is indeed true that when states believe their vital national interests at stake, neither formal nor informal rules will stand in the way of actions that they regard are necessary. Russia bemoans NATO's bombing of Serbia during the Kosovo war, accusing the United States and its allies of end-running UN charter requirements for Security Council approval for such action, and ultimately changing established international borders by force.[21] The West in turn charges

Russia with flouting both the UN charter and OSCE principles in annexing Crimea and launching covert warfare in Ukraine. For the skeptics on each side, these perceived violations demonstrate the futility of pursuing a rules-based order.

But history shows that even deadly enemies can reach understandings that encourage mutual restraint and reduce the likelihood of a crisis arising from misinterpretation or miscommunication. Moscow and Washington certainly viewed each other as untrustworthy adversaries during the period of détente, yet both saw their interests served by understandings that limited and contained the dangers of their rivalry. Even if rules ultimately carry little weight in a conflict, they can reduce the chances of winding up in that conflict, particularly if they are bolstered by strategies to incentivize their observance.

When engineers design a building, bridge, or dam, they typically plan against past catastrophes. Constructions are sometimes built to withstand a "one-hundred-year storm" or worse, depending on the consequences of failure and the parameters of their budgets. Today, we live in a world of increasing ferment in which extreme events, the equivalent of five-hundred-year storms, are becoming increasingly common. And as these threats have multiplied, technological advances have made the consequences of disaster existential. Designing resilience into the complex system surrounding US-Russian relations is rapidly becoming more difficult, even as it grows in importance.

The common temptation amid periods of rapid change and growing peril is to attempt to "stand athwart history, yelling, 'Stop!'" to borrow William F. Buckley's memorable turn of phrase. But history has repeatedly been unkind to uncompromising defenders of the status quo. Looking back on modern history, one can see a steady pattern of one-hundred-year extreme geopoliti-

cal events among the world's great powers, including the bloody
Thirty Years' War, the Napoleonic conquests, and World Wars I
and II. And while these events have come with impressive regu-
larity, they have also increased in their destructiveness over time.
That the United States and Soviet Union managed—through a
combination of good policies and good luck—to avoid such destruction during the Cold War is an anomaly historically. Those
attempting to engineer our complex post–Cold War system would
be wise not to base their designs on the assumption that our relatively recent string of good fortune will long continue.

7

Working the System

Shock absorbers may be pessimists, but Americans are not. The notion that complex systems problems can only be managed, not solved, that we must plan for failure and seek to cushion the blows inflicted by inevitable shocks, sits poorly with the optimistic American psyche. The country was founded in a determination to leave behind the conflicts and world-weary cynicism of the Old World. As Alexis de Tocqueville observed nearly two centuries ago, Americans "have all a lively faith in the perfectibility of man . . . They all consider society as a body in a state of improvement."[1] The American spirit almost instinctively pushes back against the argument that nothing can be done about the Russia problem beyond trying to mitigate dangers, avoid missteps, and contain damage.

One of the characteristics of a *wicked problem* is that efforts to break the problem down into its component parts and solve them incrementally are counterproductive. Addressing one aspect of the problem makes others worse and often adds new dimensions of difficulty. The United States and Russia have crashed repeatedly into these shoals over the past twenty-five years, declaring a series of relationship "resets" that attempted to build a strategic partnership by focusing on specific areas of cooperation such as liberal reforms or counterterrorism or arms control, only to see the situation continually spiral further into hostility despite each side's intentions. With each failed reset, the prospects for repairing the relationship have dimmed, cumulatively resulting in great reluctance on both sides to take political risks for the sake of uncertain progress. Domestic circumstances in the United States and Russia are compounding this reluctance. American politics are currently embroiled in domestic political controversies that rule out any high-profile initiatives aimed at better relations with Moscow. And as the end of Putin's constitutionally limited presidential term approaches in 2024, the Kremlin is growing increasingly focused on ensuring a stable leadership transition, guarding against anticipated American political interference, and insulating itself from attacks by nationalist and communist forces eager to accuse Putin of weakness in dealing with the United States.

The good news is that while the picture is bleak, it is not hopeless. We may not be able to solve our Russia problem, but there are things that we can do to work the system to advance our interests. Just as ill-considered actions can trigger negative feedback loops and cause a damaging cascade of unintended effects, other moves can do the opposite, kicking off virtuous circles of improvement. In a system, the path toward success is often not direct. What can seem to be lateral or even regressive steps can counterintuitively initiate processes that help us to reach desirable destinations not attainable through frontal assaults or incremental moves forward.[2] The US deployment of Pershing II missiles in Europe in the early 1980s was decried at the time for stoking Soviet fears of nuclear "decapitation" and heightening the dangers of war, but it helped to initiate a virtuous circle that brought Moscow to the INF negotiating table and eventually led to improved US-Soviet relations. Similarly, the 1975 Helsinki Final Act was painted as "the biggest hoax in postwar history" that would entrench Moscow's domination of Eastern Europe, but its provisions unexpectedly wound up playing a large role in improving humanitarian conditions, undermining Soviet control in the East, and providing a common reference for improved East-West relations.[3] Traversing the long trail up the mountain of US-Russian relations will require some switchbacks, but progress is possible. How, then, might we take some steps in a new direction that help to break out of the escalation cycle in which the United States and Russia are now trapped?

AN UNCONVENTIONAL PATH TO PROGRESS

The first step toward improving US-Russian dynamics is to move backward. American and Russian leaders since the early 1990s have repeatedly avowed strategic partnership and cooperation on shared interests as their guiding vision for bilateral relations. A series of American presidencies has tended to focus on what the two sides can agree on, preferring to set aside our nettlesome disagreements for future work at a more opportune time, presumably when the momentum of positive cooperation makes our differences easier to tackle or when leadership change in Moscow makes breakthroughs possible. This approach has failed. To arrest the downward spiral in relations, the two sides should acknowledge candidly that they are competitors and declare that their goal is not to build a partnership but to keep their competition within safe, mutually respected bounds. Rather than focusing on what little we can agree on, we should enumerate our many areas of disagreement and expose our contrasting perceptions.[4]

Why would such a backward step help? Its biggest virtue is that it both reflects reality and resonates with the domestic politics of both countries. The United States and Russia are not strategic partners, nor is there much remaining desire in either country to pursue this goal given their deep mutual suspicions and their bitter disappointments over the past two and a half decades. Acknowledging this reality keeps expectations for progress sensibly low. It does not require quixotic efforts to change perceptions of the other side's hostility, as distorted as they may be. It does not make progress contingent on resolving intractable problems that have torpedoed past efforts at cooperation, or on grand bargains that neither side is in a position to consider. And it reduces the temptation to employ economic sanctions as political tools to register our disagreements with Russia. But at the same time, it also forces the sides to reckon with the danger of inadvertent conflict, to make clear that they do not desire war, to lay the groundwork for discussions on how to keep their competition within safe and mutually acceptable bounds.

By contrast, continuing to employ a bottom-up approach to relations will only continue to demonstrate that we have not yet reached rock bottom. Bottom-up approaches require working-level experts in both governments to implement concrete steps to manage or resolve discrete problems, but the reality is that there is little appetite in either the United States or Russian bureaucracy for cooperation or compromise, and much desire for inflicting pain on the other side. Absent a broader agreement on a strategic framework for relations, a focus on reaching a settlement in Ukraine or negotiating a cease-fire in the cybersphere— the two areas of greatest activity and danger in the US-Russian shadow war—would not only fail but might actually set back the cause of improved ties. Conversely, without an understanding on the boundaries of our competition, a focus on bolstering US and NATO deterrent capabilities in Europe and taking the fight to Russia in the information war would only add even more fuel to our escalatory spiral of hostility.

BROADENING OUR FOCUS

Step two is to look beyond Russia. For systems thinkers, "the more of the context of a problem that a scientist can comprehend, the greater are his chances of finding a truly adequate solution."[5] US-Russian system dynamics operate within a larger set structural and psychological changes under way in the international system that have important implications for bilateral relations. Structurally, the distribution of power in the world is in motion, shifting from a post–Cold War period in which the United States had no peer or even near-peer competitors, toward a more multipolar arrangement. The swift rise of China as an increasingly capable rival to the United States is the biggest factor in this dynamic, supplemented by the assertiveness and deepening cooperation of a number of second-tier states—including Russia, India, and Brazil—that wield uneven mixes of military, economic, global, and regional clout but share varying degrees of concern over unconstrained US power. Japan and the European Union remain influential American partners combining first-rank economies with much more limited military capabilities that may or may not grow over time. The capabilities of third-tier regional players and non-state actors have also grown as globalization and digitalization have facilitated access to advanced technologies. But while its relative power is declining, the United States remains the preeminent player within this increasingly multipolar system, able to project unmatched military firepower across the globe, serving as the world's unrivaled engine of economic innovation, and maintaining a unique network of partners and allies in all of the world's regions. The United States still dominates the international financial system despite China's growing economic heft, although there is increasing frustration with American stewardship.

Not only is the distribution of power within the international system shifting, but the nature of power itself is also changing.

Military capability still plays a significant role in the digital age, but these capabilities are flowing more from the development of advanced information technology and automation and less from industrial capacity and troop strength. Mastering artificial intelligence, defending telecommunications networks on the ground and in space, and securing and exploiting data will increasingly separate the world's leading powers from the also-rans. Advances in machine learning and artificial intelligence are not dependent on large state-funded research organizations or massive financial inputs, however. Small groups of mathematically talented individuals can make enormous strides in artificial intelligence and have disproportionate impacts on national and international security. Climate change, in turn, will have significantly varied effects on countries across the globe. All these factors make international standing more fluid than in the past. Today's rising power can be yesterday's news tomorrow.

Psychologically, there is a growing sense around the world that US clout is waning as China's is rising. Few doubt that American military and economic capabilities remain robust, but many suspect that the United States has lost its dynamism, its sense of purpose, and its appetite for global leadership. Many observers view the United States as mired abroad in numerous unwinnable wars and racked at home by social and political dysfunction. At the end of the Cold War, the American idea was in clear ascent, and it was widely assumed that its model of free markets and individual liberties and popularly elected governments would inexorably spread through the world and bring increasing prosperity and order. But if the American idea were a corporate stock, investors would be shorting it today. America's rivals have grown increasingly determined to counter its power and influence. Even friends and allies who share US values fret that Washington has been wielding its raw military and economic power profligately, inviting a backlash.

These changing circumstances argue for corresponding shifts in American objectives. Pax Americana is no longer a realistic objective, if it ever was. The goal in dealing with any system in which there is no acknowledged hegemon, there are wide gaps in values and perceptions, multiple peer and near-peer players compete to advance their preferences and assert their prerogatives, and many factors operate beyond the control of any of its participants, must be systemic equilibrium. Aiming for primacy rather than order in such circumstances will produce neither. But that balance need not be—indeed, should not be—solely a balance of power, because such a narrow focus would be blindsided by important moral and psychological factors at work in the system. An aspirational equilibrium that fails to account for both power and values will prove to be no equilibrium at all. The inspiration of high ideals is no less important than the dread of disaster in driving systemic progress.

Broadening our focus allows us to put the troubled US-Russian relationship within the larger context of US objectives in the international system. It proceeds from the premise that our bilateral relations both affect and are affected by world dynamics. How, then, might we look for areas where a step or two in a new direction might have a cascading effect that subtly but significantly improves the workings of the system, reframing perceptions in ways that increase the possibilities for progress toward a balance of power that manages China's rise and Russia's assertiveness while also advancing core American values?

One opportunity lies in Central Asia. Putin's help in establishing American military bases in Central Asia in 2001 was an important indication of his desire for strategic partnership with the United States. Washington's insistence that these allegedly "temporary" bases would remain firmly in place for an extended period of time, even after the initial American success in driving the Taliban out of power, contributed to Putin's growing disillusionment with that partnership. This played a small but significant role in poisoning Russian perceptions of American intentions and trustworthiness. The continuing US military presence in the region also served as a unifying factor in cooperation between Russia and China, encouraging them to subsume what might otherwise become a growing bilateral competition for influence in the region to their shared concerns about Washington's activities. US withdrawal from Afghanistan and shuttering of its surrounding military bases in Central Asia might not only encourage regional players to take greater responsibility for combatting extremism and maintaining order but also allow the forces of Russian-Chinese rivalry for Central Asian influence to come to the fore. This step might begin subtly to rebalance the triangular US-Russia-China relationship, currently tilted heavily toward cooperation between Moscow and Beijing against the United States. It might also prompt Russia to appreciate anew the role of Washington as an offshore balancer in Central Asia, as Moscow lacks the economic muscle to compete with Chinese dynamism in the region, and the legacy of Soviet-era ties with the Central Asian states is fading.

Another opportunity lies in Europe. As Chinese power waxes and Russian assertiveness grows, Europe must play a key role as a systemic counterweight to establish and maintain international equilibrium. It cannot play that role, however, if fissiparous forces continue to rend NATO and the EU, threatening to hasten European disintegration and trans-Atlantic decoupling. A situation in which Russia sees itself as locked out of European security decision-making, incentivized to exacerbate the continent's divisions and widen its fissures, reduces the chances that a strong and healthy Europe can play that balancing role. The threat of American disengagement from Europe has a similarly damaging effect, exacerbating divisions on the continent by stoking fears in eastern and northern European states that NATO might not be willing or able to defend them against Russian aggression, while resurrecting old fears of German hegemony.

Within what appear to be discouraging European trends, however, lies potential for gain. Whereas not long ago, both NATO and the EU thought of themselves figuratively as sharks, requiring the forward motion of expansion to sustain their functions in the absence of a unifying external threat, such expansion is no longer viewed as necessary or even desirable. The illusions that Russia can be integrated into European institutions on Western terms—or somehow transformed into a variation of Sweden, a once formidable military power now focused on creating a great standard of living for its people, content to defer to American stewardship of a rules-based international order—have disappeared. Moreover, the appetite in the United States and other NATO members for using the alliance in expeditionary activity has long since dissipated. These changes open the door to new approaches that until recently were impractical.

A renewed NATO focus on its original purpose, collective defense, might produce several advantageous effects. It would reassure Poland, the Baltic states, and other NATO members fearful of Russian aggression that the alliance is committed to their security, and in so doing, reduce intra-alliance tensions. It would also provide a secure basis for sending a balanced message to the Russians about NATO's intentions, underscoring resolve to defend member states and drawing a firm line against Russian involvement in internal alliance affairs, while at the same time signaling reluctance to stray beyond current NATO borders to add members or undertake out-of-area missions. The corollary to these signals would be that Europe and Russia share an interest in working to contain and manage instability in the unaligned states in between NATO and Russia, to minimize their incentives to seek an alliance that might threaten either side, and to reduce the chances of being drawn inadvertently into direct conflict. Such signals would facilitate bilateral and multilateral discussions of the ground rules for interaction in these in-between states, a prerequisite for any progress in settling the volatile, ongoing conflict in Ukraine and frozen conflicts in Moldova and the Caucasus.

Broadening our focus should include addressing the ongoing dispute over the principles that define legitimate international behavior. Moscow accuses the United States of illegitimate interference in the internal affairs of Russia and other states, of willfully bypassing UN charter requirements for Security Council approval for the use of force against states that have not attacked the United States, and of illegally orchestrating changes to international borders in Kosovo at the expense of Serbian territorial integrity. The West accuses Russia of using force to change borders in Georgia and Ukraine, of aggressive cybermeddling in the internal affairs of Europe and the United States, of flouting international arms control treaties, and of cynically enabling savage violations of human rights. Russia touts the Westphalian order based on respect for state sovereignty; the West highlights the "responsibility to protect" endangered citizens subjected to government abuses.

The suggestion that the West might attempt to find common ground with Russia and other non-Western states on normative issues immediately provokes charges of naïveté. These issues are not open for discussion, the critics contend, having been ably enshrined in the Helsinki Final Act and the Paris and UN charters. The challenge is to administer and enforce these principles, they say, not to debate them. But the reality is that while these principles should not be subject to renegotiation, there always have been inherent tensions between the tenets recorded in these foundational documents. Sovereignty and territorial integrity are relative rather than absolute values. They must be weighed against the importance of defending human rights and allowing for the self-determination of peoples, among other things. Cybertechnology and artificial intelligence have also added new dimensions to the problems of balancing these contending principles. Reconciling these tensions, as a result, requires ongoing discussion, give-and-take, and balance—in other words, a diplomatic process. Pretending that there is a clear and objective formula for striking this balance—or that the United States and NATO should be the sole arbiters of this balancing act—is not only disingenuous but dangerous. Henry Kissinger observed:

> Whenever the international order has acknowledged that certain principles could not be compromised, even for the sake of peace, stability based on an equilibrium of forces was at least conceivable. Stability, then, has resulted not from a quest for peace but from a generally accepted legitimacy. "Legitimacy" as here used should not be confused with justice. It means no more than an international agreement about the nature of workable arrangements and about the permissible aims and methods of foreign policy. It implies the acceptance of the framework of the international order by all major powers, at least to the extent that no state is so dissatisfied that, like Germany after the Treaty of Versailles, it expresses its dissatisfaction in a revolutionary foreign policy. A legitimate order does not make conflicts impossible, but it limits their scope.[6]

PHYSICIAN, HEAL THYSELF

Step three is to tend the weeds in our own garden. Ronald Reagan famously advocated dealing with adversaries from a position of strength, a position that facilitates favorable compromises where possible and victorious outcomes where not. Such strength is more than a military or economic matter; it also derives from such in-tangible factors as self-confidence and societal vitality. George F. Kennan, one of the Marshall Plan's conceptual fathers, saw the post–World War II Soviet challenge as more psychological than military in nature, and his recommendations for dealing with it tended to be largely political and psychological. He wrote in 1947 that "our policy must be directed toward restoring a balance of power in Europe and Asia," and that the best means of accom-plishing this were "the strengthening of the forces of natural re-sistance within the respective countries which the communists are attacking." This natural resistance, however, was threatened by a "profound exhaustion of physical plant and of spiritual vigor." A long-term aid program in which the aid recipients themselves were responsible for planning and implementation would go far toward restoring self-confidence in Western Europe and Japan, he thought, bolstering their resistance to Soviet political and psy-chological pressure. "Remember," he told a National War College audience in 1947, "it is not Russian military power which is threat-ening us, it is Russian political power."

Americans have long benefited from the geographic protec-tion of two large oceans, the blessings of abundant natural re-sources, and a set of inherited political habits and beliefs refined over centuries of British history. In many respects, we are the most secure great power the world has known. Over the course of the past two decades, however, America has transformed from a nation brimming with self-confidence, eager to lead the world and spread its values and system of governance, into a country vexed by societal divisions and political dysfunction, afraid that Russian social media trolling might destroy the foundations of American society. Soviet disinformation campaigns were a constant feature of the Cold War, but the United States typically regarded them as troublesome complications rather than as deadly threats to the nation's survival, and for the most part it was able to deal with them from a position of strength and self-assurance. But America recently has become infected with an acute sense of internal vulnerability.

> The country's political establishment, for the last 120 years a model of self-assuredness and solidity, has begun to lose self-confidence. The elites' sagging self-esteem is evident in their bewildered acceptance of the idea that the US democracy is vulnerable to outside meddling and ineradicable suspicion that the elected president and those loyal to him may have colluded with a foreign country. The establishment's prevalent anxiety that Russian propaganda, in the form of the media outlets RT and Sputnik, little known as they are in the United States, could sway the American public's attitudes betrays a lack of confidence in the US electorate.[7]

This lack of confidence is playing an important role in distorting American perceptions of the Russian threat and increasing the dangers of escalatory spirals. Projecting America's internal problems onto its perceptions of Russia is, in fact, a long-standing Western tendency. In his classic study of US and European views of Russia over the centuries, historian Martin Malia observes that "Russia has at different times been demonized or divinized by Western opinion less because of her real role . . . than because of the fears and frustrations, or the hopes and aspirations, generated within European society by its own domestic problems."[8] Westerners have too often, he says, "produced our images of Russia out of ourselves."[9] To no small degree, that is as true today as it was during the eighteenth and nineteenth centuries.

Addressing this growing self-doubt will not be an easy matter. It will require grappling with the problems of economic inequality, political partisanship, and societal fragmentation that began plaguing America long before the 2016 election. And looming in the background is a disturbing question: Can America's deep-rooted political tradition of constrained government meet the new challenges posed by the loss of institutional authority within atomized and disaffected societies, not only in the West but increasingly across the world? The United States defended freedom against the threat of tyranny in the twentieth century. Can it maintain both liberty and order against the threat of dysfunctional governance in the twenty-first?

CONCLUSION

The primary mission of intelligence is to warn of approaching danger. But the nature of the gathering storm in this case is neither easy to discern nor simple to convey. Despite our deepening shadow war, the biggest threat we face from Russia is not on the battlefield or in the cybersphere. It is in our understanding of the problem.

In the twentieth century, the United States defended freedom against the threats posed by tyrannical government. American military power prevented conquest of the world's key industrial regions by fascist regimes in World War II, and US nuclear muscle and ideological might helped to establish and maintain the "long peace" between the West and the Soviet bloc that protected our freedom and prosperity during the Cold War. It is tempting given our history to see our current struggles with Russia through a similar prism, as a battle between liberal democracy and aggressive authoritarianism. But such a lens distorts the nature of the challenge we face today.

John McLaughlin, who rose through the ranks of intelligence analysts during the 1970s, '80s, and '90s to become acting director of central intelligence in 2004, for many years displayed a placard in his office that read, "Subvert the Dominant Paradigm." It was a glib saying with a serious purpose behind it. Many analytic and policy failures stem from flawed paradigms, the conceptual frameworks that we all use, consciously or unconsciously, to make sense of events and distinguish relevant from irrelevant information. Paradigms help to shape our expectations, and those expectations in turn condition what we look for and what we perceive. The evidence that Japan would attack Pearl Harbor was there to see prior to December 7, 1941. Our expectations, however, prevented us from recognizing the significance of that evidence. Getting our paradigms right is a critical prerequisite to avoiding intelligence surprise and averting policy failure.

This book has attempted to subvert the dominant American paradigm regarding Russia. That paradigm treats the Russia threat as a linear problem, rooted in a fundamental aggression against liberal democracy that flows from the nature of Putinism itself. The preceding chapters have argued not that this formulation is entirely incorrect but that it is incomplete, that it misunderstands the drivers of Russian behavior, and that it is based on a flawed assumption that the primary danger we are facing is essentially a deterrence problem, rather than an escalation spiral that our own actions, along with Russia's, are helping to fuel rather than tame. The book's alternative diagnosis of the ailment produces a much different prescription from what current American policies are administering. It argues that we are far too fearful of Russia's intentions to destroy democracy, but not nearly wary enough about the chances that a broad mix of systemic factors could combine to create a disaster we do not see coming. All the pieces are in place for a World War I–type tragedy that few anticipate.

Our dominant paradigm would not in fact be dominant,

nor would it have remained unchallenged for so long, were it not deeply rooted in our politics, our bureaucracy, our media, and our industry, as well as our psychology. To varying degrees, each of these sets of players has a stake in its defense and perpetuation. The rapidity with which those who question it are labeled apologists, appeasers, or worse is one indicator of its strength. Subverting the dominant paradigm is generally not a path to professional success in Washington, despite McLaughlin's placard. In the case of Russia today, one challenges the conventional wisdom at particular peril.

But the dangers attending our Russia problem have grown so great that subverting the dominant paradigm may well be necessary for our survival. In science, paradigms tend to fall into disfavor when they predict outcomes that do not materialize or when they miss important developments that do. That failure is typically gradual, and they often linger stubbornly in popular use well beyond the point at which their flaws have started to become evident.[1] In the case of Russia, however, we cannot afford simply to let nature take its course and trust that the validity of the dominant paradigm will be proved or disproved over time; the proof of its flaws might well turn out to be catastrophic. The discovery that we have a problem is only beneficial if it occurs in time to deal with it. Challenging our popular conceptions of the dangers posed by Russia is a critical part of avoiding disaster before it is too late.

The book's subversive aims, therefore, are neither political nor academic in nature. They are meant to serve the higher purpose of warning, the most important mission of intelligence. In providing warning, intelligence analysts are taught to address three key questions: How soon might the developments occur? How bad might the damage be? How likely is the threat to materialize? Answers to these questions arm decision-makers with the information required to triage problems. Threats that are potentially very damaging and very likely, but which will not happen soon, might be relegated to second-tier priority as policymakers deal with more urgent matters. Low-probability, high-impact events might not seize the attention of decision-makers at all, depending on the particulars. The nature of the threat posed today by spiraling US-Russian hostility, however, is urgent, potentially catastrophic, and disturbingly likely. The indicator lights behind all three of the key warning questions are flashing bright red.

Warnings are meant to impel action. Awareness of a problem is nearly always a prerequisite to managing or resolving it. Fear can be a powerful motivator. Electoral campaign professionals have long known that playing upon voters' fears is one of the best ways to stimulate turnout at the polls. One of the reasons the Cold War remained cold, despite several close calls, was each side's growing awareness of the almost certainly catastrophic consequences of its turning hot. The Cuban missile crisis served that fear-inducing function in the early 1960s. Staring into the abyss of nuclear Armageddon ultimately produced a wide range of stabilizing and confidence-building measures that helped reduce the chances of disaster and provide a secure framework in which an improved US-Soviet relationship could evolve.

Today, our fear of US-Russian nuclear catastrophe has all but disappeared, replaced by worries that we are not doing enough to punish the other side's aggression. We cannot rely on a new variation of the Cuban missile crisis to shake us into sobriety, however. It is doubtful that contemporary American and Russian leaders could manage a modern variation of such a crisis successfully. The role of the media has changed in ways that greatly narrow the room for diplomatic maneuver, compress the timescales for decision-making, and reduce the likelihood of private understandings that allow leaders to compromise with their dignity intact. Statesmanship in foreign affairs is being overtaken by grandstanding for domestic political effect. Each side is flirting with "escalate to de-escalate" doctrines. And we cannot trust that plain old luck—which was a significant part of our avoidance of disaster in 1962—will continue to hold. This book, then, attempts to serve the same sobering role played by this crisis many decades ago. Despite its warnings, the book is fundamentally an act of optimism. It is premised on the hope that an "action-arousing gloomy vision"[2] will cause both Americans and Russians to reflect on the dangers looming before them and ensure that the coming years of US-Russian competition remain contained within safe bounds.

In summing up her classic study of the tragic descent into World War I, *The Guns of August*, the historian Barbara Tuchman wrote, "The nations were caught in a trap . . . a trap from which there was, and has been, no exit." Unlike the perils of the trap in which the European powers unwittingly found themselves in 1914, the dangers of the Russia trap are far from inevitable. It is well within our power to escape from the nascent escalatory spiral in which the US and Russia find themselves today. Opening our eyes to its dangers is the first step toward that escape.

ACKNOWLEDGMENTS

Assembling a list of those who have helped in conceiving, researching, writing, and refining this book, as well as supporting me through the emotional ups and downs of the experience, is humbling. I owe special thanks to Eric Haseltine, who recommended me to Thomas Dunne Books, and to my editor, Stephen S. Power, for his willingness to take a chance on a first-time author. Mark Episkopos provided exceptional and wide-ranging assistance. Daniel Hanson and Blake Laytham helped with research and served as sanity checks on my drafts as they progressed. I am indebted to Graham Allison, Milt Bearden, Chuck Boyd, Richard Burt, Susan Eisenhower, James Ellis, John Evans, Jim Goodby, Greg Govan, Tom Graham, Chip Gregson, Jacob Heilbrunn, Martin Hellman, Steedman Hinckley, David Holloway, Edward Ifft, Raymond Jeanloz, Sabira Jumanalieva, Bob Legvold, Anatol Lievan, Dave Majumdar, Wayne Merry, Keith Mosser, Roger Nebel, Steve Pifer, Paul Saunders, Robert Spaulding, Jim Timbie, and Bruce Turner for their invaluable ideas, insightful reviews, steadfast encouragement, and candid criticism of the manuscript as it evolved.

This book would have been impossible without the support of

Dimitri Simes, president of the Center for the National Interest, and Paul Saunders, the center's former executive director, who not only understand in principle the importance of mounting sensible challenges to conventional wisdom but also demonstrate in practice the essential corollary of protecting those who enter the fray. Above all, I am grateful for the immeasurable contributions of my wife, Sarah Miller Beebe, whose courage has inspired me, whose perspicacity amazes me, and whose love has sustained me. Work that we did together served as the book's intellectual foundation. Needless to say, I am solely responsible for any errors and shortcomings in the final product.

NOTES

INTRODUCTION

1. One notable exception was Pyotr Durnovo, a former Russian interior minister who became a member of the tsar's State Council. He wrote a prophetic memorandum to the tsar in February 1914, arguing that a European war would not remain limited, would not offer any concrete benefits to Moscow even if victorious, and would impose such enormous costs on Russia that it would ruin the economy and provoke a social revolution.

2. Henry Kissinger, *Diplomacy* (New York: Simon & Schuster, 1994), pp. 168–169.

3. Kissinger, *Diplomacy*, p. 194.

4. "Hillary Clinton Says Vladimir Putin's Crimea Occupation Echoes Hitler," *Guardian*, March 6, 2014, https://www.theguardian.com/world/2014/mar/06/hillary-clinton-says-vladimir-putins-crimea-occupation-echoes-hitler.

5. Aaron Blake, "All of These People Have Compared Vladimir Putin to Hitler," *Washington Post*, March 5, 2014, https://www.washingtonpost.com/news/the-fix/wp/2014/03/05/all-of-these-people-have-compared-vladimir-putin-to-hitler/?utm_term=.764188d526c2.

6. Terrence McCoy, "Here's 'Putler:' The Mash-Up Image of Putin and Hitler Sweeping Ukraine," *Washington Post*, April 23, 2014, https://www.washingtonpost.com/news/morning-mix/wp/2014/04/23/heres-putler-the-mash-up-image-of-putin-and-hitler-sweeping-ukraine/?utm_term=.8101da5af7da.

7. Thomas Donnelly and Gary Schmitt, "Could 'Zapad' Be a Trojan Horse?," CNN, September 13, 2017, https://www.cnn.com/2017/09/13/opinions/zapad-opinion-donnelly-and-schmitt/index.html.

8. Larisa Brown and Chris Greenwood, "Russian Cyber Attacks 'Could Cripple UK': Intelligence Chief Warns Kremlin Agents Have the Capacity to Shut Down Power Supplies, Hijack Air Traffic Control and Even Disable Air Conditioning," *Daily Mail*, March 7, 2018, http://www.dailymail.co.uk/news/article-5475325/Russia-cripple-UK-intelligence-chief-warns.html.

9. *Assessing Russian Activities and Intentions in Recent US Elections* (Washington, D.C.: Office of the Director of National Intelligence, 2017), https://www.dni.gov/files/documents/ICA_2017_01.pdf; "Remarks as Prepared for Delivery by the Honorable Dan Coats, Director of National Intelligence," Office of the Director of National Intelligence, https://www.dni.gov/files/documents/Newsroom/Testimonies/2019-01-29-ATA-Opening-Statement_Final.pdf.

10. Christopher Mele, "Morgan Freeman Angers Russians Over Video About 2016 Election," *New York Times*, September 22, 2017, https://www.nytimes.com/2017/09/22/world/europe/morgan-freeman-russia-video.html?mtrref=www.google.com&gwh=6901E1DC7DF87A2ACC182E69FBFB9D84&gwt=pay.

11. See Anne Applebaum's arguments in Stephen F. Cohen, Vladimir Pozner, Anne Applebaum, and Garry Kasparov, *Should the West Engage Putin's Russia?: The Munk Debates* (Toronto, ON: House of Anansi Press, 2015).

12. Dan Kovalik, "Rethinking Russia: A Conversation with Russia Scholar Stephen F. Cohen," *Huffington Post*, updated July 7, 2017, https://www.huffingtonpost.com/dan-kovalik/rethinking-russia-a-conve_b_7744498.html.

13. John J. Mearsheimer, "Why the Ukraine Crisis Is the West's Fault," *Foreign Affairs*, August 28, 2014, https://www.foreignaffairs.com/articles/russia-fsu/2014-08-18/why-ukraine-crisis-west-s-fault.

14. Thomas L. Friedman, "Foreign Affairs; Now a Word from X," *New York Times*, May 2, 1998, http://www.nytimes.com/1998/05/02/opinion/foreign-affairs-now-a-word-from-x.html.

15. For further explanation of the "spiral model" argument, see Robert Jervis, *Perception and Misperception in International Politics* (Princeton, NJ: Princeton University Press, 1976), pp. 58–113.

16. Ronald Asmus, *A Little War That Shook the World* (New York: St. Martin's Press, 2010).

17. Andrew Rettman, "EU-Sponsored Report Says Georgia Started 2008 War," *EUobserver*, September 20, 2009, https://euobserver.com/foreign/28747.

18. Ben Smith, "US Pondered Military Use in Georgia," *Politico*, https://www.politico.com/story/2010/02/us-pondered-military-use-in-georgia-032487.

19. Cohen, Pozner, Applebaum, and Kasparov, *Should the West Engage Putin's Russia?*

20. Mearsheimer, "Why the Ukraine Crisis Is the West's Fault."

21. "Russia Sends Two Nuclear-Capable Bombers to Venezuela," Associated Press, December 10, 2018.

22. Kissinger, *Diplomacy*, p. 174.

23. Ankit Panda, "Actually, Russia's Population Isn't Shrinking," *Diplomat*, May 1, 2014, https://thediplomat.com/2014/05/actually-russias-population-isnt-shrinking/.

24. Doing Business 2019, World Bank Group, http://www.worldbank.org/content/dam/doingBusiness/media/Annual-Reports/English/DB2019-report_web-version.pdf

25. Russell L. Ackoff, "The Corporate Rain Dance," *Wharton Magazine*, winter 1977, pp. 6–41.

26. Noteworthy examples include Angela Stent's *Limits of Partnership* and Robert Legvold's *Return to Cold War.*

27. The term *wicked problem* originated in the 1960s in the field of management science. It refers to a situation in which numerous interlinked systemic factors combine and reinforce one another to produce a problem bordering on insolubility, where efforts to address one part of the problem tend to create or exacerbate others. *Wicked* connotes the difficulty of grappling with the problem rather than any evil nature.

1. WAR BY OTHER MEANS

1. Andy Greenberg, "Hackers Gain Direct Access to US Power Grid Controls," *Wired*, September 6, 2017.

2. Andy Greenberg, "How an Entire Nation Became Russia's Test Lab for Cyberwar," *Wired*, July 25, 2018.

3. Ellen Nakashima, "US Officials Say Russian Government Hackers Have Penetrated Energy and Nuclear Company Business Networks," *Washington Post*, July 8, 2017.

4. Adam Segal, *The Hacked World Order: How Nations Fight, Trade, Maneuver,*

and Manipulate in the Digital Age (New York: Council on Foreign Relations, 2016), p. 113.

5. *National Cyber Strategy* (Washington, D.C.: White House, 2018), https://www.whitehouse.gov/wp-content/uploads/2018/09/National-Cyber -Strategy.pdf.

6. Michael Sulmeyer, "How the US Can Play Cyber Offense," *Foreign Affairs*, March 22, 2018.

7. *Simple Sabotage Field Manual* (Washington, D.C.: Office of Strategic Services, 1944), http://www.gutenberg.org/files/26184/page-images/26184-images .pdf?session_id=5cc0d158d771c1fc4d22b8548a44a3ae4928268d.

8. Pavel Sudoplatov and Anatoli Sudoplatov, *Special Tasks: The Memoirs of an Unwanted Witness—A Soviet Spymaster* (Boston: Little, Brown, 1994).

9. Department of Defense Science Board, *Task Force Report: Resilient Military Systems and the Advanced Cyber Threat* (Washington, D.C.: US Department of Defense, 2013), p. 6.

10. Brian Grow, Keith Epstein, and Chi-Chu Tschang, "The New E-spionage," *BusinessWeek*, April 8, 2008.

11. Grow, Epstein, and Tschang, "The New E-spionage."

12. Cybersecurity expert Mark Espinoza, in a video lecture entitled "The Five Laws of Cybersecurity," argues both that everything is vulnerable in some way and that every cybervulnerability will be exploited without doubt.

13. Dan Goodin, "How 'Omnipotent' Hackers Tied to NSA Hid for 14 Years—And Were Found at Last," *Ars Technica*, February 16, 2015.

14. Fred Kaplan, *Dark Territory: The Secret History of Cyber War* (New York: Simon & Schuster, 2016) pp. 78–82.

15. Kaplan, p. 83.

16. Neri Zilber, "The Rise of the Cyber Mercenaries," *Foreign Policy*, August 31, 2018.

17. Nick Lewis, "Is Equation Group Malware a Game Changer for Advanced Attack Defense?," SearchSecurity, https://searchsecurity.techtarget.com /tip/Is-Equation-Group-malware-a-game-changer-for-advanced-attack-defense.

18. Michael Riley, "How the US Government Hacks the World," *Bloomberg Businessweek*, May 23, 2013, https://www.bloomberg.com/news/articles /2013-05-23/how-the-u-dot-s-dot-government-hacks-the-world.

19. Cliff Stoll, "Stalking the Wily Hacker," *Communications of the ACM* 31, no. 5 (1998): pp. 484–497.

20. Sanger, p. 140.

21. Sanger, p. 91.

22. Sanger, p. 84.

23. Kaplan, *Dark Territory* pp. 3–5.

24. Sanger, p. 199.

25. Nathan Hodge, "Inside Moldova's Twitter Revolution," *Wired*, April 8, 2009.

26. Natalia Morar, "I Am Not a Communist!" LiveJournal, April 7, 2009, https://natmorar.livejournal.com/36886.html.

27. Ellen Barry, "Protests in Moldova Explode, with Help of Twitter," *New York Times*, April 7, 2009.

28. Neil MacFarquhar, "A Powerful Russian Weapon: The Spread of False Stories," *New York Times*, August 28, 2016.

29. "Andrei Soldatov," PBS, https://www.pbs.org/wgbh/frontline/interview /andrei-soldatov/.

30. "Edict of the Russian Federation President," Instituto Español de Estudios Estratégicos, http://www.ieee.es/Galerias/fichero/OtrasPublicaciones /Internacional/2016/Russian-National-Security-Strategy-31Dec2015.pdf.

31. Clay Shirky's book *Here Comes Everybody: The Power of Organizing Without Organizations* provides a good overview of the optimism common in the United States at the time about how the internet and social media would facilitate the liberalization of societies across the world.

32. "Alliance for Youth Movements: Using Technology to Change the World," *Be*, September 28, 2010, http://www.bemagazine.org/alliance-for-youth -movements-using-technology-to-change-the-world/.

33. Tim Rutten, "Tyranny's New Nightmare: Twitter," *Los Angeles Times*, June 24, 2009, http://articles.latimes.com/2009/jun/24/opinion/oe-rutten24.

34. Evgeny Morozov, *The Net Delusion* (New York: Public Affairs, 2011), p. 128.

35. Andrei Soldatov and Irina Borogan, *The Red Web* (New York: Public Affairs, 2015), p. 116.

36. Morozov, *The Net Delusion*, p. 126.

37. Will Stewart, "Putin's Poster Girl: Pin-Up Politician Hates the West, Loves Thatcher," *Daily Mail*, March 14, 2009, https://www.dailymail.co.uk/news /article-1161977/Putins-poster-girl-Pin-politician-hates-West--loves-Thatcher .html.

38. Soldatov and Borogan, *The Red Web*, p. 117.

39. Morozov, *The Net Delusion*, p. 125.

40. In a 2014 article, "SMI i Informatsionnie Voini [Mass Media and Information Wars]," Ekaterina Yakushina argues that censorship is a crude tool to

be used only as a last resort and that blatant fabrication of facts is unsustainable in an age where information is easily verifiable via the internet. The best long-term strategy, she argues, is to allow a wide range of views and to reframe negative news in the government's preferred narrative.

41. "Number of Social Media Users Worldwide from 2010 to 2021 (in Billions)," Statista, https://www.statista.com/statistics/278414/number-of-worldwide -social-network-users/.

42. James Farwell, a longtime political campaign professional, interview with the author, June 5, 2018.

43. Thomas Rid, *Cyber War Will Not Take Place* (New York: Oxford University Press, 2013) pp. 120–121.

2. DEADLY PERCEPTIONS

1. Henry Kissinger, *World Order* (New York: Penguin, 2014), p. 234.

2. "Ivan Krastev: Russia Is 'Reverse Engineering' Western Foreign Policy," Graduate Institute, Geneva, November 18, 2015, http://graduateinstitute .ch/home/relations-publiques/news-at-the-institute/news-archives.html/_ /news/corporate/2015/ivan-krastev-russia-is-reverse-e.

3. Fyodor Lukyanov, "What Russia Learned from the Iraq War," *Russia in Global Affairs*, March 19, 2013, http://eng.globalaffairs.ru/redcol/What-Russia -Learned-From-the-Iraq-War-15897.

4. Robert Legvold, *Return to Cold War* (Malden, MA: Polity Press, 2016), p. 32.

5. Pavel Yevdokimov, "Russkaya Pravda Generala Leonova," Spetsnaz Rossii, May 2001.

6. See for example, *Russia Engages the World, 1453–1825*, Cynthia Hyla Whitaker, ed., (Harvard University Press, 2003).

7. Edward Keenan, "Muscovite Political Folkways," *Russian Review*, Vol. 45, number 2 (April 1986): pp. 115–181.

8. Douglas Schoen and Evan Ross Smith, *Putin's Master Plan* (New York: Encounter Books, 2016), p. vi.

9. "Statement by the Press Secretary on the United Kingdom's Decision to Expel Russian Diplomats," White House press release, March 14, 2018, https://www.whitehouse.gov/briefings-statements/statement-press-secretary -united-kingdoms-decision-expel-russian-diplomats/.

10. Laurie Kellman, "McCain Sees Russia Hacking as Threat to 'Destroy Democracy,'" *Star*, December 19, 2016, https://www.thestar.com/news/world /2016/12/19/mccain-sees-russian-hacking-as-threat-to-destroy-democracy.html.

11. George Will, "Vladimir Putin Is Bringing Back the 1930s," *National Review*, October 9, 2016, https://www.nationalreview.com/2016/10/vladimir-putin-1930s-strategy-russia/.

12. Paul Waldman, "The Russians Are Coming," *Week*, February 14, 2018, http://theweek.com/articles/754987/russians-are-coming.

13. Tim Hains, "Sen. Ben Cardin: Russia Is Trying to 'Bring Down Our Way of Government . . . They Want Corruption to Reign,'" RealClearPolitics, January 11, 2018, https://www.realclearpolitics.com/video/2018/01/11/sen_ben_cardin_russia_is_trying_to_bring_down_our_way_of_government_they_want_corruption_to_reign.html.

14. Timothy Snyder, *The Road to Unfreedom* (New York: Penguin Random House, 2018), p. 225.

15. Dina Smeltz, Lily Wojtowicz, and Stepan Goncharov, "Despite Last Year's Expectations, Publics Sense Strains in US-Russia Relations," Chicago Council on Global Affairs, February 7, 2018, https://www.thechicagocouncil.org/publication/despite-last-years-expectations-publics-sense-strains-us-russia-relations; Dina Smeltz and Lily Wojtowicz, "American Opinion on US-Russia Relations: From Bad to Worse," Chicago Council on Global Affairs, August 2, 2017, https://www.thechicagocouncil.org/publication/american-opinion-us-russia-relations-bad-worse.

16. *American Public Opinion and US Foreign Policy* (Chicago: Chicago Council on Global Affairs, 1995).

17. Zbigniew Brzezinski, "The Premature Partnership," *Foreign Affairs*, March/April 1994, https://www.foreignaffairs.com/articles/russian-federation/1994-03-01/premature-partnership.

18. Strobe Talbott, "The End of the Beginning: The Emergence of a New Russia," US Department of State, https://1997-2001.state.gov/regions/nis/970919talbott.html.

19. James M. Goldgeier and Michael McFaul, *Power and Purpose: US Policy Toward Russia After the Cold War* (Washington, D.C.: Brookings Institution Press, 2003), p. 247.

20. Goldgeier and McFaul, p. 254.

21. Goldgeier and McFaul, p. 265.

22. Strobe Talbott, "The Crooked Timber: A Carpenter's Perspective," US Department of State, https://1997-2001.state.gov/policy_remarks/2000/000121_talbott_oxford.html.

23. "Strobe Talbott: Deputy Secretary of State, 1994–2001," PBS, https://www.pbs.org/wgbh/frontline/interview/strobe-talbott/.

24. Angela Stent, *The Limits of Partnership* (Princeton, NJ: Princeton University Press, 2014), p. 64.

25. *Putin, Russia, and the West, Part 1*, BBC documentary television series, 2012.

26. Peter Baker and Susan Glasser, *Kremlin Rising: Vladimir Putin's Russia and the End of Revolution* (Washington, D.C.: Potomac Books, 2007) p. 138.

27. Goldgeier and McFaul, *Power and Purpose*, p. 89.

28. Thomas E. Graham Jr., *Russia's Decline and Uncertain Recovery* (Washington, D.C.: Carnegie Endowment for International Peace, 2002), p. 83.

29. "Daniel Fried: National Security Council, 2001–05," PBS, https://www.pbs.org/wgbh/frontline/interview/daniel-fried/.

30. "Steven Pifer: US Ambassador to Ukraine, 1998–2000," PBS, https://www.pbs.org/wgbh/frontline/interview/steven-pifer/.

31. "Daniel Fried," PBS.

32. "Thomas Graham: National Security Council, 2002–07," PBS, https://www.pbs.org/wgbh/frontline/interview/thomas-graham/.

33. George W. Bush press conference, White House, Washington, D.C., October 17, 2007.

34. "Victoria Nuland: US Ambassador to NATO, 2005–08," PBS, https://www.pbs.org/wgbh/frontline/interview/victoria-nuland/.

35. "Georgia 'Started Unjustified War,'" BBC, September 30, 2009, http://news.bbc.co.uk/2/hi/europe/8281990.stm.

36. Ronald Asmus, *A Little War That Shook the World* (New York: Macmillan, 2010), p. 30.

37. "John Beyrle: US Ambassador to Russia, 2008–12," PBS, https://www.pbs.org/wgbh/frontline/interview/john-beyrle/.

38. Michael McFaul, *From Cold War to Hot Peace: An American Ambassador in Putin's Russia* (New York: Houghton Mifflin Harcourt, 2018), p. 240.

39. "Susan Glasser: Co-author, 'Kremlin Rising,'" PBS, https://www.pbs.org/wgbh/frontline/interview/susan-glasser/.

40. "Evelyn Farkas: Defense Department, 2009–15," PBS, https://www.pbs.org/wgbh/frontline/interview/evelyn-farkas/.

41. Anne Gearan and Phillip Rucker, "Obama Cancels Summit Meeting with Putin," *Washington Post*, August 8, 2013, https://www.washingtonpost.com/politics/obama-cancels-upcoming-meeting-with-putin/2013/08/07/0e04f686-ff64-11e2-9711-3708310f6f4d_story.html?utm_term=.a8774c375223.

42. "William Burns: US Ambassador to Russia, 2005–08," PBS, https://www.pbs.org/wgbh/frontline/interview/william-burns/.

43. "Daniel Fried," PBS.

44. "John Beyrle," PBS.

45. Scott Wilson, "Obama Dismisses Russia as 'Regional Power' Acting Out of Weakness," *Washington Post*, March 25, 2014, https://www.washingtonpost.com/world/national-security/obama-dismisses-russia-as-regional-power-acting-out-of-weakness/2014/03/25/1e5a678e-b439-11e3-b899-20667de76985_story.html?utm_term=.82bec4af0f7e.

46. "Michael McFaul: US Ambassador to Russia, 2012–14," PBS, https://www.pbs.org/wgbh/frontline/interview/michael-mcfaul/.

47. *Assessing Russian Activities and Intentions in Recent US Elections* (Washington, D.C.: Office of the Director of National Intelligence, 2017), https://www.dni.gov/files/documents/ICA_2017_01.pdf.

48. Wanda Carruthers, "Hayden: Russia Meddling 'Most Successful Covert Operation in History,'" *Newsmax*, July 21, 2017, https://www.newsmax.com/politics/michael-hayden-russia-election-meddling/2017/07/21/id/803152/.

49. "Daniel Fried," PBS.

50. "James Clapper: Director of National Intelligence, 2010–17," PBS, https://www.pbs.org/wgbh/frontline/interview/james-clapper/.

51. "Antony Blinken: Obama Adviser, 2009–15," PBS, https://www.pbs.org/wgbh/frontline/interview/antony-blinken/.

52. McFaul's thesis in *From Cold War to Hot Peace* is a typical example of this belief.

53. "Text: Bush and Putin's Joint Declaration," *Guardian*, May 24, 2002, https://www.theguardian.com/world/2002/may/24/usa.russia.

54. Leonid Bershidsky, "What Scares Russians the Most? Russians," Bloomberg Opinion, March 4, 2019, https://www.bloomberg.com/opinion/articles/2019-03-04/it-s-not-the-pentagon-russia-s-military-fears-it-s-russians.

55. Paul Sonne, "US Is Trying to Dismember Russia, Says Putin Adviser," *Wall Street Journal*, February 11, 2015, https://www.wsj.com/articles/u-s-is-trying-to-dismember-russia-says-putin-adviser-1423667319.

56. Remarks by Foreign Minister Sergey Lavrov at the XXII Assembly of the Council on Foreign and Defense Policy, Moscow, November 22, 2014.

57. Sergei Glazyev, *Genocide: Russia and the New World Order* (Leesburg, VA: Executive Intelligence Review, 1999).

58. "West Is Waging 'Economic War' on Russia to Topple Kremlin—Bank CEO," *Moscow Times*, January 24, 2018, https://themoscowtimes.com/news/west-is-waging-economic-war-russia-regime-change-bank-ceo-60266.

59. "Vyacheslav Nikonov: Russia and America Are Very Close to Nuclear War," *Russkiy Mir*, February 5, 2015, https://russkiymir.ru/en/news/184576/.

60. William Taubman, "Why Gorbachev Likes Putin More Than You Might Expect," *Washington Post*, September 12, 2017, https://www.washingtonpost.com/news/made-by-history/wp/2017/09/12/why-gorbachev-likes-putin-more-than-you-might-expect/?utm_term=.49033f9232a3.

61. "Irina Borogan: Co-author, 'The Red Web,'" PBS, https://www.pbs.org/wgbh/frontline/interview/irina-borogan/.

62. Goldgeier and McFaul, *Power and Purpose*, p. 184.

63. Norman Kempster and Dean E. Murphy, "Broader NATO May Bring 'Cold Peace,' Yeltsin Warns: Europe: Russian President Accuses US of Being Power Hungry. Speech Comes as Nations Finalize Nuclear Treaty," *Los Angeles Times*, September 6, 1994, http://articles.latimes.com/1994-12-06/news/mn-5629_1_cold-war.

64. Goldgeier and McFaul, *Power and Purpose*, p. 247.

65. Foundation for Public Opinion, April 3–4, 1999, http://www.fom.ru.

66. Fiona Hill and Clifford G. Gaddy, *Mr. Putin: Operative in the Kremlin* (Washington, D.C.: Brookings Institution Press, 2013) pp. 298–299.

67. "Vice-Speaker of the State Duma Apologized for the Fact That the Russian Federation Could Not Help Serbia," *Regnum*, March 24, 2017, https://regnum.ru/news/2254405.html.

68. Madeleine Albright, "Clear on Chechnya," *Washington Post*, March 8, 2000.

69. Nikolai Paklin, "Chechnya ne Kosovo, NATO ne Pomozhet," *Rossiskaya Gazeta*, October 13, 1999.

70. Stent, *The Limits of Partnership*, p. 46.

71. Vladimir Putin, "Why We Must Act," *New York Times*, November 14, 1999, https://www.nytimes.com/1999/11/14/opinion/why-we-must-act.html.

72. Dmitry Suslov, "The Russian Perception of the Post–Cold War Era and Relations with the West," talk given at the Harriman Institute, Columbia University, November 9, 2016.

73. Suslov, "The Russian Perception of the Post–Cold War Era."

74. Stent, *The Limits of Partnership*, p. 65.

75. "Mikhail Zygar: Author, 'All the Kremlin's Men,'" PBS, https://www.pbs.org/wgbh/frontline/interview/mikhail-zygar/.

76. For example, a group of retired Russian generals and admirals published an open letter to Putin rejecting his support for America, objecting to the closure of bases in Cuba and Vietnam, and warning about the arrival of

American troops in Central Asia. "Sluzhit Rodinye," *Sovietskaya Rossiya*, November 10, 2001.

77. Stent, *The Limits of Partnership*, p. 69.

78. Pavel Felgenhauer, "Washington Is Putting Russia in Its Place," *Moscow News*, December 18, 2001.

79. Bilyana Lilly, *Russian Foreign Policy Toward Missile Defense* (London: Lexington Books, 2014).

80. Aleksey Pushkov, "Rossiya I SShA: Predely Sblizhenia," *Nezavisimaya Gazeta*, December 27, 2001.

81. Igor S. Ivanov, "Organizing the World to Fight Terror," *New York Times*, January 27, 2002, https://www.nytimes.com/2002/01/27/opinion /organizing-the-world-to-fight-terror.html.

82. "John Beyrle," PBS.

83. "Assistant Secretary for European and Eurasian Affairs Beth Jones on US Relations with Central Asia; February 11, 2002," Yale Law School, http:// avalon.law.yale.edu/sept11/jones_004.asp.

84. Sergei Ptichkin and Aleksei Chichkin, "Otkuda Rossiya Vidna Kak Na Ladoni," *Rossiskaya Gazeta*, January 22, 2002.

85. Suslov, "The Russian Perception of the Post–Cold War Era."

86. Hill and Gaddy, *Mr. Putin*, p. 304.

87. "President Bush's Second Inaugural Address," NPR, January 20, 2005, https://www.npr.org/templates/story/story.php?storyId=4460172.

88. The CSCE became the OSCE (Organization for Security and Cooperation in Europe) in 1995.

89. Eugen Tomiuc, "Moldova: Caught Between a Hammer and a Sickle as Anti-Communist Protests Continue," Radio Free Europe / Radio Liberty, November 28, 2003, https://www.rferl.org/a/1105158.html.

90. Aleksey K. Pushkov, "Russia's Foreign Policy and Its National Interests," in *Enduring Rivalry: American and Russian Perspectives on the Post-Soviet Space*, ed. Paul Saunders (Washington, D.C.: Center for the National Interest, 2011).

91. "Putin Tells the Russians: 'We Shall Be Stronger,'" *New York Times*, September 5, 2004, https://www.nytimes.com/2004/09/05/world/europe/putin -tells-the-russians-we-shall-be-stronger.html.

92. "Thomas Graham," PBS.

93. "Gleb Pavlovsky: Former Adviser to Vladimir Putin," PBS, https:// www.pbs.org/wgbh/frontline/interview/gleb-pavlovsky/.

94. William Schneider, "Ukraine's 'Orange Revolution,'" *Atlantic*, December

2004, https://www.theatlantic.com/magazine/archive/2004/12/ukraines-orange
-revolution/305157/.

95. Stent, *The Limits of Partnership*, p. 111.

96. Vladimir Frolov, "Democracy by Remote Control," *Russian in Global Affairs*, November 21, 2005, http://eng.globalaffairs.ru/number/n_5855.

97. "Andrei Soldatov," PBS, https://www.pbs.org/wgbh/frontline/interview
/andrei-soldatov/.

98. Vladimir Putin, "Speech and the Following Discussion at the Munich Conference on Security Policy," February 10, 2007, http://en.kremlin.ru
/events/president/transcripts/24034.

99. Stephen F. Cohen, Vladimir Pozner, Anne Applebaum, and Garry Kasparov, *Should the West Engage Putin's Russia?: The Munk Debates* (Toronto, ON: House of Anansi Press, 2015).

100. James Kirchick, "The Roots of Russian Aggression," *National Review*, May 24, 2018, https://www.nationalreview.com/magazine/2018/06/11/russian
-aggression-ukraine-not-america-fault/.

101. Michael Morell, *The Great War of Our Time* (New York: Twelve, 2015), p. 324.

102. "Steven Pifer," PBS.

103. "Daniel Fried," PBS.

104. "Michael McFaul," PBS.

105. McFaul, *From Cold War to Hot Peace*, p. 421.

106. Paul Pillar, *Why America Misunderstands the World: National Experience and Roots of Misperception* (New York: Columbia University Press, 2016), p. 29.

107. "Lavrov Says Western 'Russophobia' Worse Than During Cold War," Radio Free Europe / Radio Liberty, January 22, 2018, https://www.rferl
.org/a/russia-lavrov-russophobia/28989014.html.

108. Oleg Kashin, "Independent Journalists in Russia Will Have to Live Without Their Western Role Models (Op-ed)," *Moscow Times*, November 15, 2017, https://themoscowtimes.com/articles/independent-journalists-in-russia
-will-have-to-live-without-their-western-role-models-oped-59579.

109. Maxim Trudolyubov, "Russian Meddling Is a Meme," *Russia File*, January 24, 2018, http://www.kennan-russiafile.org/2018/01/24/russian-meddling
-is-a-meme/.

110. Andranik Migranyan, "The US in a Time of Change: Internal Transformations and Relations with Russia," *Russia in Global Affairs*, April 15, 2013, http://eng.globalaffairs.ru/number/The-US-in-a-Time-of-Change-Internal
-Transformations-and-Relations-with-Russia-15927.

111. Dmitry Suslov, interview with the author, June 2018.

112. Dmitri Trenin, *Should We Fear Russia?* (Cambridge, UK: Polity Press, 2017), p. 38.

113. Suslov interview.

114. Vladimir Frolov, "One Hack Too Far," *Moscow Times*, October 13, 2016, p. 5.

115. Sergey Lavrov, "Sergey Lavrov: The Interview," *National Interest*, March 29, 2017, http://nationalinterest.org/feature/sergey-lavrov-the-interview-19940.

116. Susan B. Glasser, "'The Russians Have Succeeded Beyond Their Wildest Expectations,'" *Politico*, October 30, 2017, https://www.politico.com/magazine/story/2017/10/30/james-clapper-russia-global-politico-trump-215761.

117. Vladimir Frolov, "The 'Russian Trail' Saga," Republic.ru, October 29, 2017.

118. Vladimir Frolov, "Worse Than Under Obama," Republic.ru, July 28, 2017.

119. Suslov interview.

120. Kirill Martynov, "Four Years for White Men," *Novaya Gazeta*, November 11, 2016, p. 5.

121. "Armenia: Why Has Vladimir Putin Not Intervened So Far and Will He?," *Russia Matters*, https://www.russiamatters.org/blog/armenia-why-has-vladimir-putin-not-intervened-so-far-and-will-he.

122. Samuel Charap, Jeremy Shapiro, and Alyssa Demus, *Rethinking the Regional Order for Post-Soviet Europe and Eurasia* (Santa Monica, CA: RAND Corporation, 2018), p. 15

3. BRAKE FAILURE

1. Steve Coll, *Ghost Wars: The Secret History of the CIA, Afghanistan, and Bin Laden, from the Soviet Invasion to September 10, 2001* (New York: Penguin Books, 2004), p. 128.

2. Odd Arne Westad, *The Cold War: A World History* (New York, Basic Books, 2017), p. 365.

3. Jeffrey Goldberg, "Netanyahu to Obama: Stop Iran or I Will," *Atlantic*, March 2009, https://www.theatlantic.com/magazine/archive/2009/03/netanyahu-to-obama-stop-iran-or-i-will/307390/.

4. Evgeny Buzhinskiy, *(Un)realistic Threats: DPRK's and Iran's Missile Programs* (Moscow: PIR Center, 2016), http://www.pircenter.org/media/content/files/13/14605468310.pdf.

5. "Putin Compares US Shield to Cuba," BBC News, October 26, 2007, http://news.bbc.co.uk/2/hi/7064428.stm.

6. *Voice of Russia*, May 11, 2011.

7. Theodore Postal, "A Ring Around Iran," *New York Times*, July 7, 2001, https://www.nytimes.com/2007/07/11/opinion/11postol.html.

8. Caroline Wyatt, "Russia Abandons START II Arms Treaty," BBC News World Edition, June 14, 2002, http://news.bbc.co.uk/2/hi/europe/2044941.stm.

9. Vladimir Isachenkov, "Putin: New Nuclear Weapons to Enter Duty in Next Few Years," Associated Press, May 18, 2018, https://apnews.com/88c351c 63b8d4ed8930e5670895880f0.

10. Phillip Bleeke, "Moscow Reportedly Moves Tactical Nuclear Arms to Baltics," Arms Control Association, January/February 2001.

11. Russia later reintroduced military bases to Georgia's breakaway region after the Russo-Georgia war of 2008 and Moscow's recognition of the independence of Abkhazia and South Ossetia.

12. Michael Gettler, "Pershing II: Why It Alarms Soviets," *Washington Post*, March 17, 1982, https://www.washingtonpost.com/archive/politics/1982 /03/17/pershing-ii-missile-why-it-alarms-soviets/20eca6f0-3a64-4bdf-9957 -ae54261b6ca6/?utm_term=.64d765beadae.

13. Robert M. Gates, *Duty: Memoirs of a Secretary at War* (New York: Alfred A. Knopf, 2014), p. 154.

14. Science and Security Board, "It Is Two Minutes to Midnight: 2018 Doomsday Clock Statement," *Bulletin of the Atomic Scientists*, January 25, 2018, https://thebulletin.org/doomsday-clock/current-time/.

15. Elbridge Colby, "If You Want Peace, Prepare for Nuclear War," *Foreign Affairs*, November/December 2018, p. 28.

16. "Putin Claims Russia Has Nuclear-Tipped Underwater Drones and New Supersonic Weapon," *Haaretz*, March 1, 2018, https://www.haaretz.com /world-news/europe/putin-claims-russia-has-nuclear-tipped-underwater -drones-1.5866092.

17. Hans Kristensen, Matthew McKinzie, and Theodore Postol, "How US Nuclear Force Modernization Is Undermining Strategic Stability: The Burst-Height Compensating Super-Fuze," *Bulletin of the Atomic Scientists*, March 1, 2017.

18. David Halberstam, "The Vantage Point Perspectives of the Presidency 1963–1969," *New York Times*, October 31, 1971.

19. This desire dated back at least to 1954, when Soviet foreign minister Vyacheslav Molotov called for a European security conference.

20. William Hill, *No Place for Russia: European Security Institutions Since 1989* (New York: Columbia University Press, 2018), p. 22.

21. Hill, p. 22.

22. Hill, pp. 291–292.

23. Milt Bearden and James Risen, *The Main Enemy: The Inside Story of the CIA's Final Showdown with the KGB* (New York: Ballantine Books, 2003), pp. 396–397.

24. Milt Bearden, interview with the author, November 15, 2018.

25. Damir Marusic, "Why Russia Published Footage of an FSB Agent Beating an American in Moscow," *American Interest*, July 8, 2016, https://www.the-american-interest.com/2016/07/08/why-russia-published-footage-of-an-fsb-agent-beating-an-american-in-moscow/.

26. Litvinenko Inquiry hearings, testimony of Alex Goldfarb, February 4, 2015, pp. 128–129.

27. Bearden interview.

4. TRIGGERS

1. Dean Acheson, *Present at the Creation: My Years in the State Department* (New York: W. W. Norton, 1969), p. 36.

2. See David E. Bell, Howard Raiffa, and Amos Tversky, *Decision Making: Descriptive, Normative, and Prescriptive Interactions*, "Marginal Value and Intrinsic Risk Aversion," United Kingdom: Cambridge University Press, 1988.

3. "The 1983 War Scare Declassified and For Real," National Security Archive, https://nsarchive2.gwu.edu/nukevault/ebb533-The-Able-Archer-War-Scare-Declassified-PFIAB-Report-Released/.

4. "Russian Military Incident Tracker," American Security Project, https://www.americansecurityproject.org/us-russia-relationship/russian-military-incident-tracker/.

5. Thomas Gibbons-Neff, "How a 4-Hour Battle Between Russian Mercenaries and US Commandos Unfolded in Syria," *New York Times*, May 24, 2018, https://www.nytimes.com/2018/05/24/world/middleeast/american-commandos-russian-mercenaries-syria.html.

6. Neil Hauer, "Russia's Mercenary Debacle in Syria: Is the Kremlin Losing Control?," *Foreign Affairs*, February 26, 2018.

7. Natalia Vasilyeva, "Thousands of Russian Private Contractors Fighting in Syria," Associated Press, December 12, 2017, https://apnews.com/7f9e63cb14a54dfa9148b6430d89e873.

8. Ellen Nakashima, Karen DeYoung, and Liz Sly, "Putin Ally Said to

Be in Touch with Kremlin Before His Mercenaries Attacked US Troops," *Washington Post*, February 22, 2018, https://www.washingtonpost.com/world /national-security/putin-ally-said-to-be-in-touch-with-kremlin-assad-before -his-mercenaries-attacked-us-troops/2018/02/22/f4ef050c-1781-11e8-8b08 -027a6ccb38eb_story.html?utm_term=.033a4cd8fba2.

9. John Lewis Gaddis, *The Long Peace: Inquiries into the History of the Cold War* (New York: Oxford University Press, 1989).

10. James M. Acton, "Escalation Through Entanglement: How the Vulnerability of Command-and-Control Systems Raises the Risks of an Inadvertent Nuclear War," *International Security* 43, no. 1 (2018): pp. 56–99.

11. Acton, p. 62.

12. US Department of Defense, *Nuclear Posture Review* (Washington, D.C.: US Department of Defense, 2018), p. 21, https://media.defense.gov /2018/Feb/02/2001872886/-1/-1/1/2018-NUCLEAR-POSTURE-REVIEW -FINAL-REPORT.PDF.

13. Acton, "Escalation Through Entanglement," p. 56.

14. Alexey Arbatov, Vladimir Dvorkin, and Petr Topychkanov, "Entanglement as a New Security Threat: A Russian Perspective," in *Entanglement: Russian and Chinese Perspectives on Non-Nuclear Weapons and Nuclear Risks*, ed. James M. Acton (Washington, D.C.: Carnegie Endowment for International Peace, 2017), p. 13.

15. Polit Navigator, "Kalashnikov Called for Supporting Donbass with Weapons," October 13, 2008, https://www.politnavigator.net/kalashnikov -prizyval-podderzhat-donbass-postavkami-oruzhiya.html.

16. Andy Greenberg, "The Untold Story of NotPetya, the Most Devastating Cyberattack in History," *Wired*, August 22, 2018, https://www.wired.com /story/notpetya-cyberattack-ukraine-russia-code-crashed-the-world/.

17. Dan Glass, "What Happens If GPS Fails?," *Atlantic*, June 13, 2016, https://www.theatlantic.com/technology/archive/2016/06/what-happens-if -gps-fails/486824/.

5. ESCAPING THE SIMPLICITY TRAP

1. For more on the origins of the concept of *wicked problems*, see Horst W. J. Rittel and Melvin M. Webber, "Dilemmas in a General Theory of Planning," *Policy Sciences* 4 (1973), https://web.archive.org/web/20070930021510/http://www.uctc .net/mwebber/Rittel+Webber+Dilemmas+General_Theory_of_Planning.pdf.

2. Paul Schullery, *Searching for Yellowstone: Ecology and Wonder in the Last Wilderness* (New York: Houghton Mifflin, 1997), p. 119.

3. Alston Chase, *Playing God in Yellowstone: The Destruction of America's First National Park* (Boston: Atlantic Monthly Press, 1986), p. 6.

4. Jim Robbins, "Historians Revisit Slaughter on the Plains," *New York Times*, November 16, 1999, https://www.nytimes.com/1999/11/16/science/historians -revisit-slaughter-on-the-plains.html.

5. Andrew Isenberg, *The Destruction of the Bison* (New York: Cambridge University Press, 2000), pp. 179–186.

6. Isenberg, pp. 179–186.

7. Schullery, *Searching for Yellowstone*, p. 126.

8. Chase, *Playing God in Yellowstone*, p. 12.

9. Chase, p. 21.

10. Chase, p. 22.

11. Robert Jervis, *System Effects: Complexity in Political and Social Life* (Princeton, NJ: Princeton University Press, 1997), p. 10.

12. Strobe Talbott, "The End of the Beginning: The Emergence of a New Russia," address delivered at Stanford University, September 19, 1997.

13. David Hoffman, *The Oligarchs: Wealth and Power in the New Russia* (New York: Public Affairs, 2002), p. 184.

14. Dimitri K. Simes, *After the Collapse: Russia Seeks Its Place as a Great Power* (New York: Simon & Schuster, 1999), p. 102.

15. Boris Yeltsin, *The Struggle for Russia* (New York: Random House, 1994), p. 126.

16. Some notable exceptions included fuel, energy, transport, and some staple foods.

17. Hoffman, *The Oligarchs*, p. 212.

18. In the early 1990s, many experts working in the field known broadly as "political economy" made these points about the dangers of shock therapy and the importance of recognizing the links between economic, political, and social factors as Russia attempted to cope with its crisis. Joseph Stiglitz, a Nobel Prize–winning Columbia University economist, was among the most notable critics.

19. P. J. O'Rourke, cited by Chrystia Freeland in *Sale of the Century* (New York: Crown Publishers, 2000), p. 35.

20. Hoffman, *The Oligarchs*, pp. 50–53.

21. Thomas E. Graham Jr., *Russia's Decline and Uncertain Recovery* (Washington, D.C.: Carnegie Endowment for International Peace, 2002), p. 31.

22. Hoffman, *The Oligarchs*, p. 234.

23. Goldgeier and McFaul, *Power and Purpose*, p. 92.

24. Simes, *After the Collapse*, p. 103.

25. "DA. DA. NYET. DA.: Giving Boris a Hand," *Adweek*, May 17, 1993, https://www.adweek.com/brand-marketing/da-da-nyet-da-giving-boris-hand -38240/.

26. Sergey Rogov, interview with the author, May 30, 2017.

27. Grigory Yavlinsky, "Shortsighted," *New York Times Magazine*, June 8, 1997, p. 66.

28. Some diplomats in US embassy Moscow's political section were notable exceptions. Wayne Merry, head of the embassy's political/internal section, warned in a special cable that the elections were likely to prove disastrous for Yeltsin's reformers.

29. Russia's crown jewel industries in the energy and extractive sectors remained at that time exempt from privatization.

30. Thomas Graham's monograph, *Russia's Decline and Uncertain Recovery*, is one of the best explorations of this school of thought.

31. "Masha Lipman: Russian Journalist," PBS, https://www.pbs.org/wgbh /frontline/interview/masha-lipman/.

32. For an excellent history of our repetitive cycle of optimistic partnership initiatives and dashed expectations, see Angela Stent's *The Limits of Partnership: US-Russian Relations in the Twenty-First Century* (Princeton, NJ: Princeton University Press, 2014).

33. Jervis, *System Effects*, p. 291.

34. This has been dubbed the *Lijphart effect*, named after an American scholar who observed such a phenomenon in the Netherlands aimed at avoiding civil war. See Arend Lijphart, *The Politics of Accommodation: Pluralism and Democracy in the Netherlands* (Berkeley: University of California Press, 1968).

35. George F. Kennan, "America and the Russian Future," *Foreign Affairs*, April 1951.

36. J. Y. Smith, "Outsider Forged Cold War Strategy," *Washington Post*, March 18, 2005, http://www.washingtonpost.com/wp-dyn/content/article/2005 /03/26/AR2005032602369_2.html.

37. John Mearsheimer, *The Great Delusion: Liberal Dreams and International Realities* (New Haven, CT: Yale University Press, 2018), p. 224.

6. ABSORBING SHOCKS

1. Henry Kissinger, *World Order* (New York: Penguin, 2014), pp. 78–82.

2. For more on the difference between stability and resilience strategies, see Aaron Wildavsky, *Searching for Safety* (New York: Routledge, 1988).

3. Barbara Tuchman, *The Guns of August* (New York: Random House, 1962), pp. 117-123.

4. Graham T. Allison, *Essence of Decision: Explaining the Cuban Missile Crisis* (Boston: Little, Brown, 1971), pp. 229–230.

5. Anatoly Dobrynin, *In Confidence* (New York: Times Books, 1995), p. 97.

6. Angela Stent, *The Limits of Partnership* (Princeton, NJ: Princeton University Press, 2014), p. 175.

7. Nahal Toosi, "D.C. Snubs Russian Ambassador," *Politico*, March 7, 2018, https://www.politico.com/story/2018/03/07/russian-envoy-congress-election-meddling-443014.

8. Maggie Haberman, Mark Mazzetti, and Matt Apuzzo, "Kushner Is Said to Have Discussed a Secret Channel to Talk to Russia," *New York Times*, May 26, 2017, https://www.nytimes.com/2017/05/26/us/politics/kushner-talked-to-russian-envoy-about-creating-secret-channel-with-kremlin.html.

9. For a discussion of the potential downsides for American interests of criminally prosecuting unregistered agents of the Russian government, see Sarah Lindemann-Komarova, "Maria Butina and the Criminalization of Citizen Diplomacy," *Nation*, December 26, 2018.

10. See Section 312 of the Frank LoBiondo Coast Guard Authorization Act of 2018, https://www.congress.gov/bill/115th-congress/senate-bill/140/text#toc-id89e563a8d5524c5a84cacf66865f7ba1.

11. See, for example, the report by the Department of Transportation on GPS disruption vulnerabilities and the need for backup systems, *Vulnerability Assessment of the Transportation Infrastructure Relying on the Global Positioning System* (Washington, D.C.: US Department of Transportation, 2001), https://www.navcen.uscg.gov/pdf/vulnerability_assess_2001.pdf.

12. Matt Blaze, Jake Braun, Harri Hursti, David Jefferson, Margaret MacAlpine, and Jeff Moss, *DEF CON 26 Voting Village: Report on Cyber Vulnerabilities in US Election Equipment, Databases, and Infrastructure* (n.p.: DEF CON, 2018), https://defcon.org/images/defcon-26/DEF%20CON%2026%20voting%20village%20report.pdf.

13. Margaret Newkirk, "Advocates Say Paper Ballots ARE Safest," *Bloomberg Businessweek*, August 10, 2018, https://www.bloomberg.com/news/articles/2018-08-10/advocates-say-paper-ballots-are-safest.

14. Kim Zetter, "Inside the Cunning, Unprecedented Hack of Ukraine's Power Grid," *Wired*, August 9, 2016, https://www.wired.com/2016/03/inside-cunningunprecedented-hack-ukraines-power-grid/.

15. James Scott and Drew Spaniek, *The Energy Sector Hacker Report* (Washington, D.C.: Institute for Critical Infrastructure Technology, 2016), https://icitech.org/wp-content/uploads/2016/08/ICIT-Brief-The-Energy-Sector-Hacker-Report.pdf.

16. Elbridge Colby, *From Sanctuary to Battlefield: A Framework for a US Defense and Deterrence Strategy for Space* (Washington, D.C.: Center for a

New American Security, 2016), p. 6, https://s3.amazonaws.com/files.cnas.org /documents/CNAS-Space-Report_16107.pdf.

17. James Acton, "Escalation Through Entanglement," pp. 82–92.

18. Colby, *From Sanctuary to Battlefield*, p. 22.

19. Andrew Krepinevich, "The Eroding Balance of Terror," *Foreign Affairs*, January/February 2019, p. 65.

20. Joseph Nye, "Rules of the Cyber Road for America and Russia," *Project Syndicate*, March 5, 2019, https://www.project-syndicate.org/commentary /cyber-rules-for-america-and-russia-by-joseph-s--nye-2019-03.

21. Russian Ministry of Foreign Affairs Statement, "On the History of US Violations and Terminations of Key International Treaties, January 11, 2018, http://www.mid.ru/web/guest/foreign_policy/news/-/asset_publisher /cKNonkJE02Bw/content/id/3394727#13.

7. WORKING THE SYSTEM

1. Alexis de Tocqueville, *Democracy in America*, vol. 2 (New York: Appleton, 1899), p. 432.

2. Jervis, *System Effects*, p. 287.

3. Matthias Walden, "Der finnische Zauerberg," *Die Welt*, August 2–3, 1975; Axel Springer, "Von Jalta bis Helsinki—immer gibt der Western nach," *Die Welt*, August 7, 1975.

4. Thomas Graham Jr., "Time for a Helsinki Communique," *National Interest*, July 7, 2018, https://nationalinterest.org/print/feature/time-helsinki -communique-25192.

5. Russell Ackoff, "The Development of Operations Research as a Science," *Operations Research 4*, no. 3 (June 1956): pp. 265–295.

6. Henry Kissinger, *A World Restored: Metternich, Castlereagh, and the Problems of Peace, 1812–22* (Brattleboro, VT: Echo Point Books and Media, 2013), p. 1.

7. Dmitri Trenin, "If Putin Wanted to Step Up His Fight with America, You'd Know It," *Foreign Policy*, July 31, 2017, http://foreignpolicy.com /2017/07/31/if-putin-wanted-to-step-up-his-fight-with-america-youd-know -it/.

8. Martin Malia, *Russia Under Western Eyes* (Cambridge, MA: Belknap Press of Harvard University Press, 1999), p. 8.

9. Malia, p. 9.

CONCLUSION

1. Thomas Kuhn, *The Structure of Scientific Revolutions* (Cambridge, MA: MIT Press, 1962).

2. Albert Hirschman, *A Bias for Hope: Essays on Development in Latin America* (New Haven, CT: Yale University Press, 1971), pp. 284, 350–353.

INDEX

Able Archer incident (1983), 104–6
ACFE. *See* Adapted Treaty on Conventional Armed Forces in Europe (1999)
active measures (aktivniye meropriyatiya), 17
Adapted Treaty on Conventional Armed Forces in Europe (1999) (ACFE), 79–80
advanced persistent threat, 11–12
Afghanistan, xviii, 34–35, 49, 51–52, 69, 173
aggression, by Russia, xiii–xvi, xv–xvi, xix, 9–10, 15, 25, 33, 39, 93
Air Force, Russian, 104
Air Force, US, 10, 104
Alliance for Youth Movements, 19
ambiguity, for communications resilience, 152–53, 155
American Security Project, 106
Anti-Ballistic Missile Treaty (ABM) (1972), 50–53, 74–75, 77
anti-satellite weapons (ASAT), 111–12, 159
anti-terrorism, 50, 56
anti-terrorist international coalition, 50–51
antivirus software, 9
Arab Spring, 27, 90–91, 150

Armenia, color revolution in (2018), 69–70
arms control, 72–73, 77, 81–85, 161–62, 167
artificial intelligence, 13, 22, 153, 171, 176
ASAT. *See* anti-satellite weapons
al-Assad, Basher, Russia military support for, 27, 39–40
Austria, xii, xvi

backup systems, 157–58, 163
Balkans, xii, 33, 46, 90
ballistic missile defense (BMD), 75–78, 83
Baltic states, xiii, 31–32, 52, 80, 91, 122, 174
banks, in Russia, 137–38
Belarus, xiii
Berlin Wall, fall of, ix
Beslan, North Caucasus, Russia, 56–58
birth rate, Russian, xvii–xviii
black hat hackers, 158
black swan events, 150
blogs, 17, 19–20, 24
BMD. *See* ballistic missile defense
"bolt from the blue" attacks, 102
British Empire, xi–xii

Bush, George H. W., 31
Bush, George W., 34–37, 43, 49–52, 57,
    77, 88, 156

Caribbean crisis, 98, 120. *See also*
    Cuban missile crisis (1962)
Carnegie Endowment for International
    Peace, 110
cell phone tracking, 15–16
Central Asia, United States bases in, 35,
    51, 61, 172–73
Central Intelligence Agency, US (CIA),
    6–7, 41, 63, 72, 94–96, 100–101,
    121
CFE. *See* Treaty on Conventional
    Armed Forces in Europe
Charter of Paris for a New Europe
    (1990), 85–86, 89, 94, 175
Chechnya, 34, 46–49, 55–58, 79, 97, 138
China, 146, 156–57, 161–62, 170–72
    conventional weapons of, 112
    cyberactivities of, 14
    deterrence and, 75
    as great power, xvii, xxi, 60
    Japan and, 101
    Korean War and, 103
    multipolar world and, 82, 84
    Russia cooperation with, xx
    surprise attack from, 102
Chubais, Anatoly, 134–35, 140–41,
    143–44
CIS, 32, 60
civil society, in Russia, 134
Clinton, Bill, 45, 59
Clinton, Hillary
    emails from, 24, 41
    presidential campaign of, xiii, 68
Coast Guard, US, 157
Cold War, 161–62, 165, 170–71, 177,
    180, 183
    animosity of, 95
    arms control and, 84–86
    Austria during, xvi
    blogs and, 21
    "bolt from the blue" attacks and, 102
    confidential channel of
        communication and, 154
    containment strategy of, xiv–xv
    cyberconflict and, 6

cybertechnologies and, 9–10, 13
    decades of, xi
    defectors and, 98
    end of, 27, 31, 34, 41–42, 44, 89, 93,
        145, 147, 159–60
    Europe's security strategy after, xviii
    Helsinki Process and, 99
    information war compared to, 21
    KGB and, 96
    mentality of, 39
    NATO and, 45, 90
    networks of illegal agents and, 7
    nuclear weapons and, 77, 110–11
    Obama on, 39
    rules of, xix, 72–73
    Russia and, 52, 67
    Russian casualties since, 110
    shadow war compared to, 1, 3, 14
    United States and Russia as
        competitors after, xxii
color revolutions, ix, 18–19, 55–56,
    59–61, 63, 68–70, 90–91
communications resilience, 152–57
Communist Party, of Russia, 17, 87, 95,
    116, 132, 140–42, 167, 177
complex adaptive systems, xviii, 127–32,
    146–47
Conference on Security and
    Cooperation in Europe (CSCE),
    39, 45, 54, 86, 88–89
confidential channels, for
    communications resilience, 154–55
Conoco plant, Deir al-Zour, Syria,
    107–10
consolidation of power, by Yeltsin,
    139
conventional weapons, 110–13, 118,
    120–21, 153, 159–61
    Able Archer and, 105
    capped the levels of, 73
    CFE treaty on, 78
    long range missiles as, 75, 85
    military attack by, 70
    Russian aggression and, 93
cooperation, with Russia, 50–51
Countering America's Adversaries
    Through Sanctions Act (2017), 30
counterterrorism, 55, 94, 96, 167
Courses for State Bloggers, 20

Crimea, ix, xiv, 32, 39, 58, 92, 100, 156, 164
cruise missiles, 81–82, 111–12
CSCE. *See* Conference on Security and Cooperation in Europe
Cuban missile crisis (1962), 3–4, 83, 98–99, 104, 120, 152, 154, 162, 183
Cyber Command, US, 6, 119
Cyber War Will Not Take Place (Rid), 24
cyber warfare, by Russia, 30
cyberactivities, 14, 71
cyberattacks, by Russia, xv, 8–9, 112, 120, 152, 158, 163
cyberconflict, 6
cyberdefense, 9
cyberespionage, xxi, 10–16, 21, 24
cyberinfluence, 18–25
    active measures (aktivniye meropriyatiya) as, 17
    PSYOP as, 16–17
    rules for, 163
cyberoperations, of Russia, xiii, 5–6, 12
    cyberintrusions of, 6, 10, 16, 146, 163
    cybermeddling by, 71, 175
cyberpolicy, of United States, 6
cybersabotage, 21, 24
    cybertechnologies for, 9–10
    defense against, 8–9
    strategic, 7
    United States power grid, xiv, 4–6
cybersecurity, 4, 9, 11–12, 14–16, 119, 146, 158
cybersphere, xiv, 26
cybertechnologies, xix, 8–10, 13, 15, 85
cyberwar, fog of, 118–23

decline and destruction, of Russian state, 143
deconfliction channel, in Syria, 108, 152
deep fakes, 22
defectors, 95, 98
Defense Science Board, 7–8
defensive Russia, xiv–xvi, xix–xx
democracy, 26–27, 28–30, 41–42, 65–66
Democratic National Committee, 41
democratization programs, 52–53, 60, 63, 67, 71
demonetization, in Russia, 138

détente, 68, 84, 87–88, 99, 164
deterrence, 75, 107, 110, 122–23, 162, 181
disinformation, 22–23, 177–78
disruption of gas flows, in Russia, 119
Donbass region, 117–18
Donetsk People's Republic (DPR), 116–18
Doomsday Clock, 84
DPR. *See* Donetsk People's Republic
dysfunctional government, of Russia, 133–34

economic stabilization, of Russia, 135
economy, Russian, xvii–xviii
Egypt, protest movement in (2011), 69
electoral systems, 158
emails, from Clinton presidential campaign, 24, 41
encirclement, of Russia, 26, 51, 59, 62, 91–92
Enhanced Long-Range Aids to Navigation (eLORAN), 157–58
Equation Group, 14
escalate to de-escalate doctrines, 84, 120, 122, 184
escalation dominance, 80–81
ethical hackers, 158
ethnic-cleansing, 33, 116
Euphrates River, Deir al-Zour, Syria, 108
Europe
    security of, xviii, 85–94, 145–46
    United States disengagement from, 173–74
European Union (EU), xvi, 56, 58, 90, 146
"evil empire," 104
Evro Polis (Wagner group), 109

facial recognition software, 15
false flag operation, 9
fascist regimes, 180
Federal Bureau of Investigation, US (FBI), 11, 119
Federalnaya Sluzhba Bezopasnosti (FSB), 96–97
Ford, Gerald, 87–88
France, xii, 35–36

Freedom Agenda, 52–53
free-market democracy, in Russia,
    132–33
FSB. *See* Federalnaya Sluzhba
    Bezopasnosti
fundamental attribution error, 29

Gaidar, Yegor, 134–36, 140, 143–44
Gavrilov communication channel,
    94–95
Georgia, xiv–xvi, 31–33, 36–37, 54–56,
    65, 69, 79, 156
Germany, xi, xii, 35–36
glasnost and perestroika, 44, 95
Glasnost Defense Foundation, 19–20
global positioning system (GPS), 5,
    120–21, 157–58
GLONASS, 121
Gorbachev, Mikhail, ix, 19, 28, 44–45,
    76, 78, 94, 134
gosudarstvenniki (statists), 143
Great War. *See* World War I
Green Revolution, Iran, 18–19
The Guns of August (Tuchman), 184

hackers, 4–6, 14, 16, 24, 41, 119, 158
Helsinki Final Act (1975), 72, 87–89,
    168, 175
Helsinki Process, 92–93, 99
Helsinki Rules, 39, 161
Hitler, Adolph, xi, xiii, xv, 103
Holocaust, xi
honey pot, 11
hotline, United States and Russian
    leaders linked by, 98–99, 152
human assets, 16
hyperinflation, in Russia, 135–36

illegal agents, 7
imperial impulse, of Russia, 32–33
India, 65, 75, 82, 84, 170
information technology, 13, 18, 23
information war, US-Russian, 17–19, 21
infrastructure, 158–59
intentions, of adversaries, 102–4
Intermediate-Range Nuclear Forces
    (INF) Treaty (1987), 80–83, 162,
    167–68
International Monetary Fund, 46, 137–38

Internet Research Agency, Saint
    Petersburg, Russia, 120
Iran, nuclear weapons of, 50, 75–77
Iraq, ix, 27, 35–36, 52–53, 63–65
Islamic radicals, 28
Islamic State of Iraq and Syria (ISIS),
    107–8

Japan, 100–102, 110

Kalibr cruise missile, 112
Kaspersky Labs, 9, 14
Kennan, George F., xiv–xv, 147, 177
KGB, 34, 44, 72, 94–96, 134
Kissinger, Henry, xii, xvii, 27, 176
Korean Air Lines flight 007, 105
Korean War, 103–4
Kosovo War, 27, 33–34, 46–48, 50, 61,
    163
Kozak Memorandum, 54, 80
Kremlin, ix, xiii, 18, 21. *See also* Russia
Kremlin School for Bloggers, 17, 20
Kuban Cossack Host, 117–18

Libya, 27, 61, 65
life expectancy, Russian, xviii, 40, 133
Lincoln, Abraham, 26–27
linear problem, Russian threat as,
    144–48, 150–51, 181
Litvinenko, Alexander, 96–97
long range missile, 75, 85
Luhansk People's Republic (LPR),
    116–18

Maidan uprising (Ukraine), ix, 63, 71,
    100
malware, 4, 7, 9, 118–20
Marshall Plan, 177
military capability, 171
military power, Russian, xviii
military self-assertion, of Russia, 32
Moldova, 17–19, 31–33, 53–54, 79–80
monopolies, of Soviet economy, 136–37
Moonlight Maze, 11–12
Moscow, xiii–xvii, xix–xxii, 3–4, 11, 17
multiple independently targetable
    reentry vehicles (MIRV), 77, 83
multipolar world, 60, 82, 84, 161–62,
    170

Munich Security Conference (2007), 36–37
Muslim Brotherhood, 69

National Cyber Strategy (2018), 6
National Intelligence Council, 163
national referendum, for Russia (1993), 139
National Security Agency, US (NSA), 14, 18
NATO, 105, 146
  conventional weaponry and, 73
  expansion of, xv–xvi, 37, 51–54, 56, 58, 61–63, 69, 76, 78, 93, 174
  Kosovo war and, 34
  Moldova and, 80
  Putin and, 28–29
  Russia fearful of, 91
  Russia membership in, xvii, 43, 49
  sabotage of, 7
  security and, 90
  United States decoupled from, 81, 173
  Yugoslavia bombed by, 33, 45–48
  Zapad military exercise and, xiii
NATO-Russia Permanent Joint Council, 45, 92, 156
Naval Academy, US, 16
neoconservatives, 88
New START Treaty (2011), 83
NGO. See nongovernmental organizations
Nixon, Richard, 86–87
nongovernmental organizations (NGO), 19, 55, 59–60
nontraditional sexual relationships, in Russia, 39
North Korea, nuclear weapons of, 50, 75–77, 84
NotPetya malware attacks
  on Russia, 119
  on Ukraine, 118–19
nuclear catastrophe, US-Russian, 104, 183
nuclear deterrence, 50, 75, 107, 110, 122–23, 162, 181
nuclear entanglement, 110–11
Nuclear Posture Review (2018), 84, 112

nuclear weapons, xv–xvii, xx, 7–10, 31, 50, 73–74, 84–85, 110, 160
  Anti-Ballistic Missile Treaty and, 77
  cybersabotage compared to, 7–8
  development of, xi
  Iranian, 50, 75–77
  North Korean, 50
  Obama on, 40
  Presidential Nuclear Initiatives and, 78
  realistic danger of, 31
  tactical, 73
  Upper Volta with, xvii

Obama, Barack, 6, 14, 37–41, 64, 67, 77, 80, 82–83, 155
Office of Strategic Services, US (OSS), 6–7
off-the-record discussions, for communications resilience, 153–54
one-hundred-year political events, 164–65
Operation Barbarossa, 103. See also Hitler, Adolph
Orange Revolution. of Ukraine, 59–60
Organization for Security and Cooperation in Europe (OSCE), 89–92, 106, 163–64
Ottoman Empire, xi, xvii

Pakistan, 82
Palmetto Fusion, 5
paranoia, of Russia, 62, 64
path to progress, 168–69
patriotic hackers, 5
Pax Americana, 172
peace dividend, 31
Pearl Harbor attack, 100–103, 181
perception, of Russia, 26, 28–31, 34–37, 39–40, 64–70
Pershing II missiles, 73, 81, 105, 162, 167
The Plot Against America, 26
Poland, xiii, 46, 63, 75–76, 82, 105, 116–17, 174
political doomsday machine, xii
post-Soviet transition, to capitalism, 135
predators, 129–33, 143

Presidential Nuclear Initiatives (PNI) (1991), 78
President's Foreign Intelligence Advisory Board (PFIAB), 105–6
psychological operations (PSYOP), 16–17
Putin, Vladimir, xiii–xv, xviii, 41–45, 47–48, 54, 167, 172–73
 anti-terrorism and, 56–58
 as authoritarian, 36
 as master of geo-politics, 28–29
 misperceptions of, 64–65
 on nuclear weapons, 84–85
 Obama summit with, 39
 as Presidential candidate, 37–38
 as successor to Yeltsin, 34
 Ukraine religious violence and, 116
 Ukraine visit by, 58–59
 United States criticized by, 27–28

al-Qaeda, 34, 40, 49, 51, 57, 102

railway technology, World War I and, xii
Reagan, Ronald, 44, 104–5, 143, 176
red directors, 141
reforms, in Russia, 132–49
regime change, for Russia, 19, 42–44, 59, 62
reign of the seven bankers (semibankirshchina), 142
repression, by Russia, 29, 66
resilience strategies, 151–52
resilient rules, 160–65
Rid, Thomas, 24
ROC. *See* Russian Orthodox Church
Roosevelt, Teddy, 128
Rose Revolution, in Georgia, 55–56, 59
RT. *See* Russia Today
Russia. *See also specific topics*
 Academy of Science, Moscow, 11
 collapse (1990s) of, xvii, 27, 34, 42, 44, 49, 90–91
 Congress of People's Deputies, 134
 Federation of, 43, 133
Russia Today (RT), 23
Russian legislative building, shelled by tanks, 47, 139

Russian Orthodox Church (ROC), 113–17
Russia's Choice party, 140
Russophobia, 64

Saakashvili, Mikheil, 55–56
sabotage, 6–7
satellites, 5, 111–12, 120–21, 153, 159–60, 163
September 11, 2001, ix, 34–35, 49
Serbia, xii
shadow war, with Russia, xxi, 1, 3–4, 14, 16, 25, 73, 149, 169, 180
Shevardnadze, Eduard, 55–56
"shining city on the hill," 148
shock therapy, for Russian economy, 134–35, 139–40, 143–45
Simple Sabotage Field Manual, 7
single point of failure, 157
Skripal, Sergei, 97–98
Snowden, Edward, 38–39
social media, xiv, 15, 17–22, 41
Soviet Union, ix, xvii, 3, 7, 13, 28, 101. *See also* Russia
 disintegration of, 150
 economic collapse of, 133
 as "evil empire," 104
space-based assets, 159–60
spear-phishing operations, 14
special operations, 18
Special Tasks (Sudoplatov), 7
spies, rules of conduct for, 94–99
"spiral model," 123
SS-20 missiles, 73, 80–81, 105
stability strategies, 151
Stalin, Joseph, 84
Star Wars strategic defense initiative, 105
START II treaty, 77
State Department, US, 18–19
State Duma, of Russia, 20–21, 33, 44, 46, 139–40
state run economic system, of Russia, 134
statists (*gosudarstvenniki*), 143
status quo power, Russia as, 28
Strategic Offensive Reductions Treaty (2002) (SORT), 83
strategic weapons, xix, 73, 77–78, 85, 162

Stuxnet worm, 7
Subvert the Dominant Paradigm,
    180–81
Sudoplatov, Pavel, 7
surprise attacks, 102
Symantec, 4
Syria, xiv, xviii, 27, 39, 96, 104, 107–10,
    112–13, 122, 152, 156–57

Taliban, 51, 172
technological resilience, 157–65
terrorist attacks
    in Beslan, North Caucasus, Russia,
        56–58
    on September 11, 2001, ix, 34–35, 49
Thirty Years' War, 164–65
time, for communications resilience,
    152–53
de Tocqueville, Alexis, 166
Transnistria, 53–54
treaties, withdrawal from, 73–85.
    See also specific treaties
Treaty of Versailles, 86, 176
Treaty on Conventional Armed Forces
    in Europe (CFE), 78, 80, 93
Treaty-Limited Equipment,
    destruction of, 93
Trojan Horse, 43
Trump administration, xiv, 6, 27, 29,
    156–57
tsar, xii, xvii, 38
Tuchman, Barbara, 184
Twitter revolutions, 17–18
2016 presidential election, Russian
    interference in, xvi, 24, 30–31,
    40–41, 66–68, 71, 156, 158

Ukraine, ix, xiv, xvi, 58, 61, 69, 104
    American troops in, 117
    blackouts for, 4–5
    ethnic-cleansing campaign of, 116
    gas pipeline control systems shut
        down in, 118–19
    hackers in, 119
    Maidan uprising in, ix, 63, 71, 100
    NotPetya malware attacks on,
        118–19
    Orange Revolution of, 59–60
    religious violence in, 113–18

Russia war with, 39–41, 71, 80, 92,
    100, 156, 164
    Wagner group in, 109
Ukrainian Orthodox Church
    under Kiev Patriarchate (UOC-KP),
        114
    under Moscow Patriarchate
        (UOC-MP), 114–15
UN Security Council, 46
United States (US), xv–xvii, xxii
    Anti-Ballistic Missile Treaty (ABM)
        (1972) withdrawal from, 50–53,
        74–75, 77
    Central Asia bases in, 35, 51, 61,
        172–73
    cooperation with Russia, 50–51
    cyberpolicy of, 6
    cybersabotage on, xiv, 4–6
    democratization programs of, 52–53,
        60, 63, 67, 71
    disengagement from Europe, 173–74
    as enemy of Russia, 38
    Europe disengagement by, 173–74
    as exceptional nation, 26
    freedom defended by, 180
    GLONASS retaliatory attack by,
        121
    influence of, 171
    infrastructure of, 158–59
    Islamic radicals and, 28
    Japan embargo by, 101
    NATO decoupled from, 81, 173
    NotPetya malware attacks response
        by, 118
    as perceived by Russia, 26–29, 42, 44,
        62–64
    Putin criticism of, 27
    Russia as ally of, 35
    Russia nuclear exchanges with, 84
    Russia regime change and, 19, 42–44,
        59
    Russian forces clash with, 107–10,
        113
    shadow war with Russia and, xxi,
        3–4, 14, 16, 25, 73, 149, 169, 180
    space based assets of, 159–60
    Wall Street malware attacks response
        by, 120
    Yeltsin help by, 138

UOC-KP. *See* Ukrainian Orthodox
    Church under Kiev Patriarchate
UOC-MP. *See* Ukrainian Orthodox
    Church under Moscow
    Patriarchate
US National Security Strategy (2018),
    102

video surveillance systems, 15
violence, against American personnel,
    96
Voice of America, 23
Volyn Oblast, Ukraine, 115

Wagner group (Evro Polis), 109
Wall Street, malware attacks on,
    119–20
Warsaw Pact, 73, 78, 86, 88–89, 91,
    105
weapons of mass destruction (WMD),
    in Iraq, ix
Western airspace, Russian aircraft in,
    106–7
Western democracies, undermined by
    Russia, xiv, xvi, 24
wicked problem, xxi, 127, 166
WikiLeaks, 38–39
World Bank, 137–38
World War I (Great War), xi–xii, xvii,
    xx–xxi, 103, 151, 153, 165, 181,
    184
World War I problem, for Russia, xi
World War II, xi, xiv, 3, 6–7, 33, 86–87,
    165, 180

World War II problem, for Russia,
    xii–xiii
Wright-Patterson Air Force Base,
    Dayton, Ohio, 10–11

Yanukovych, Viktor, 58–59
Yellowstone National Park, 127, 143–45
    cougars and wolves in, 130–32
    elk herds in, 129–31
    predators in, 129–33
    as wildlife refuge, 128
Yeltsin, Boris, 140–43
    Cold War ended by, 31
    consolidation of power and, 139
    economic stabilization by, 135
    election of, 12
    Gaidar and, 136
    as indifferent to popular suffering,
        137
    NATO expansion and, 45
    resignation of, 34
    Russia liberal reforms and, ix
    Russia self-image and, 28
    Russian legislature building shelled
        by, 47
    United States help and, 138
Yugoslavia, bombed by NATO, 33,
    45–48
Yushchenko, Viktor, 58–59

Zapad (West) military exercises, by
    Russia, xiii
zero-day vulnerabilities, 8–9
Zyuganov, Gennady, 141–42